KV-013-451

Feminism and the politics of working women

Women's History

General Editor
June Purvis
Professor of Sociology, University of Portsmouth

Published

Lynn Abrams and Elizabeth Harvey
*Gender relations in German history: power, agency and experience
from the sixteenth to the twentieth century*

Jay Dixon
The romantic fiction of Mills & Boon, 1909–1990s

Carol Dyhouse
No distinction of sex? Women in British universities, 1870–1939

Bridget Hill
Women, work and sexual politics in eighteenth-century England

Linda Mahood
Policing gender, class and family: Britain, 1850–1940

June Purvis (editor)
Women's history: Britain, 1850–1945

Gillian Scott
*Feminism and the politics of working women: the Women's
Co-operative Guild, 1880s to the Second World War*

Barbara Winslow
Sylvania Pankhurst: sexual politics and political activism

Forthcoming titles include:

Shani d'Cruze
Sex, violence and working women in Victorian England

Jane McDermid and Anna Hillyar
*Midwives of the revolution: female Bosheviks and women workers in
1917*

Wendy Webster
Imagining home: gender, 'race' and national identity, 1945–64

WITHDRAWN

LIVERPOOL JMU LIBRARY

3 1111 00853 0741

Feminism and the politics of working women
The Women's Co-operative Guild, 1880s to the Second World War

Gillian Scott
University of Brighton

UCL
PRESS

© Gillian Scott 1998

This book is copyright under the Berne Convention.
No reproduction without permission.
All rights reserved.

First published in 1998 by UCL Press

UCL Press Limited
1 Gunpowder Square
London
EC4A 3DE
UK

and

1900 Frost Road, Suite 101
Bristol
Pennsylvania 19007-1598
USA

The name of University College London (UCL) is a registered
trade mark used by UCL Press with the consent of the owner.

British Library Cataloguing-in-Publication Data
A catalogue record for this book is available from the British Library.

Library of Congress Cataloging-in-Publication Data are available.

ISBNs: 1-85728-798-3

Cover design by Jim Wilkie
Printed and bound in Great Britain by Arrowhead Books Ltd,
Reading, UK.

In Memory of Nick Robin
(1955–1997)

Acknowledgements

Feminism and the politics of working women is a project whose realization in its present form would not have been possible without the advice and assistance of the following colleagues and associates. Jean Gaffin and Chrys Salt both in different ways shared with me their knowledge and insights about the WCG. Mervyn Wilson, Co-operative Education Services Manager at the Co-operative College, has been a rich source of information about the Guild and the Co-operative movement. Stephen Yeo was simultaneously inspiring and patient as my doctoral supervisor; Alan Tuckett provided rigorous intellectual support in the completion of my thesis; Pete Gurney was a kindred spirit as a fellow researcher of the Co-operative movement. Gregory Elliott, Tom Hickey and Eileen Yeo have each made an invaluable contribution to the process of revising my thesis for publication through their intelligent comments and criticisms on various drafts. To all of these, and to other friends and to my family, a big thank you.

Contents

Abbreviations

AUCE: Amalgamated Union of Co-operative Employees
CC: Central Committee (of the WCG)
CP: Communist Party
CU: Co-operative Union
CWS: Co-operative Wholesale Society
ILP: Independent Labour Party
LPWS: Labour Party Women's Sections
NEC: Labour Party National Executive Committee
NFWW: National Federation of Women Workers
NUWSS: National Union of Women's Suffrage Societies
NUSEC: National Union of Societies for Equal Citizenship (formerly NUWSS)
ODC: Open Door Council
PSF: People's Suffrage Federation
SJC: Standing Joint Committee of Industrial Women's Organizations (later the Standing Joint Committee of Working Women's Organizations)
TG: Townswomen's Guilds
TGWU: Transport and General Workers' Union
TUC: Trades Unions Congress
WCG: Women's Co-operative Guild (also referred to as the Guild)
WFL: Women's Freedom League
WI: Women's Institute
WIC: Women's Industrial Council
WLL: Women's Labour League (forerunner of the LPWS)
WLM: Women's Liberation Movement
WSPU: Women's Social and Political Union
WTUA: Women's Trade Union Association
WTUL: Women's Trade Union League

Information about the WCG

Year	Membership	Branches
1885	376	10
1890	1,640	54
1900	12,809	273
1910	25,897	520
1914	32,182	600
1917	27,060	580
1921	50,600	905
1925	53,664	1,139
1930	66,566	1,395
1935	77,807	1,615
1939	87,246	1,819
1940	65,174	1,805
1941	49,222	1,529
1945	51,392	1,671
1950	59,666	1,729
1953	58,785	1,692

Source: WCG *Annual Reports*

General Secretaries 1883–1953

1883–1884	Mrs Acland
1884–1885	Miss Allen
1885–1889	Mrs Lawrenson
1889–1921	Margaret Llewelyn Davies
1921–1925	Honora Enfield
1925–1937	Eleanor Barton
1937–1940	Rose Simpson
1940–1953	Cecily Cook

Introduction

In 1913, Alexandra Kollontai, speaking at the Women's Co-operative Guild Southern Sectional Conference in London, told the delegates that England was not the same place that she had found on her last visit, five years earlier; there was now ' "a great rebel spirit moving the people." It was an atmosphere she liked to breathe'.[1] She was especially struck by what she had learnt of the WCG: 'it was always said that factory women could be politicised but housewives, never – they could never get outside their homes' – now they were proving this wrong, and she longed for the Guild to be represented at the International Socialist Congress 'to show what women had done'.[2]

That Kollontai should have been surprised by such an organization is not in itself remarkable. Social Democrat and feminist, she was well-versed in the theoretical and practical issues relating to the organization of women; indeed, her speech included a description of 'some of the movements going forward amongst women in other countries'.[3] She was therefore well placed to appreciate the Guild's distinctiveness. The continental women's movements of the early 1900s with which Kollontai was most familiar fell into two broad categories.[4] The first was that of middle-class women seeking equality of opportunity with men of their class – to vote, to own property, to be educated, to enter the professions, and so forth – but with little to offer women of the working-class. Accordingly, these liberal groupings were strongly opposed by socialist women whose energies were channelled into the second of the two categories, the organization of working-class women within the social democratic parties affiliated to the

Socialist International. These had been most successful in relation to industrial women, the factory women to whom Kollontai made reference in her Guild speech.

The WCG stood in sharp distinction from both. Here was an organization with a completely different base, the British consumers' Co-operative movement, through which it had drawn into its orbit a completely different constituency – working-class housewives. In contrast to the parties of the Socialist International, the WCG had no explicit political ambitions; it adhered to the Co-operative movement's formal neutrality towards party politics, and recruited broadly from the trading membership of the Societies. Yet the WCG, unlike the liberal organizations of middle-class feminists, was explicitly committed to working-class advancement. 'Women of leisure', explained one of its members, were welcome to join, but they 'must identify themselves with working-class interests, and come as interpreters of the needs and wishes of the workers.'[5]

Kollontai was impressed not simply by the organizational achievement represented by 30,000 women in 600 branches, but by the political significance of 400 working-class housewives delegated to the Conference, adopting what amounted to radical socialist positions on the pressing class issues of the day. A resolution was moved, for example, protesting about the imprisonment of James Larkin, the Dublin union leader, and the way in which the law discriminated against workers and benefited the employers. 'The response was dramatic', it was reported. 'Without the slightest hesitation, the hand of every woman in the room was thrown up in assent. There was no need for speech.' Discussing 'Guild Education' at the same event, the General Secretary, Margaret Llewelyn Davies, outlined the two sides of the Guild's work – 'namely, work for women, and work for labour' – and drew attention to the importance of 'the great upheaval now going on in the country'.[6] Responding to questions she reported on the Guild Citizenship Sub-Committee (formed to represent married women's interests in Parliament) which had that summer successfully won an amendment to the National Insurance Act to make maternity benefit the legal property of the wife.[7]

It was clear from these Conference proceedings that as well as pressing for social reforms in the interests of its members and the wider constituency they represented, the WCG was also in broad solidarity with the most militant sections of the working-class. And yet the Guild was not a socialist party, nor was it affiliated to such a party, and it had no programme or doctrine. Its aims committed it only to the study of Co-operation, and work to secure reforms in the interests of working women. It appeared, then, as a *social* movement whose policies aspired to be the expression of the objective interests of its members, and whose ideology and social composition were seamlessly related. As Davies liked to put it: being 'composed of married women who are co-operators it has naturally become a sort of trade union for married women'.[8] Thus, while there was no sense in which the WCG constituted an ideal vehicle for Kollontai's ultimate project of revolutionary socialist transformation, it clearly possessed a great capacity for mobilizing working-class women to play an active role in such a process. To find this kind of an organization in England, of all places, in 1913, must have been a surprise indeed, and it is no wonder that Kollontai's response was to propose that the Guild be represented at the Socialist International.

What Kollontai witnessed was part of the upsurge of activity among British working-class women before the First World War to which Ellen DuBois has drawn attention in her comparative study of national suffrage movements and the Left.[9] Stressing the exceptional character of the British case, where instead of being split by differences between bourgeois feminists and socialist groupings, the suffrage movement was radicalized by 'the organization of working-class women and the dedication of activists inspired by but independent of socialism', DuBois asks: 'Why were British working women so political?' In answer she makes two observations: firstly, that in contrast to their continental sisters, British women in the labour movement had their own organizations, the WTUL,[10] the predominantly female textile unions, and the WCG; secondly, that these organizations attracted the energies of middle-class suffragists with socialist sympathies. Pursuing this line of inquiry further, I would argue that of these organizations, the WCG stands out in this period as the one best placed to generate an autonomous politics of working women, and the one most successful in that project, but also one whose development is only intelligible if full account is taken of the inspired contribution of its socialist-feminist, middle-class leader, Margaret Llewelyn Davies.

The WCG was founded in 1883 for women associated with the English consumers' Co-operative movement. With a base in the communities served by the Co-op stores, and access to the expanding membership and resources of the movement, the Guild grew steadily for almost 60 years, to a membership peak of 88,000, in 1,800 branches in 1938. In the intervening decades, under the leadership of Davies (General Secretary from 1889 to 1921), it established a reputation unique in British politics as a self-governing organization of working-class housewives. Commensurate with this role, but transcending the normal limits of sectional trade-union politics during Davies' years in office, the Guild also became the organizational expression of a wide-ranging working-class feminist agenda, pursued single-mindedly and, where necessary, in defiance of Co-operative officials, on the grounds that working women[11] needed their own organizations, autonomous but affiliated to the wider working-class movement. It tackled issues of both class and gender, and promoted a vision of a future ideal democracy, while its internal structure and *modus operandi* were designed to empower the tens of thousands of housewives who became members. By the second decade of the century, although formally non-aligned, its policies kept pace with those of the most advanced socialist and feminist groups.

Yet the conditions which nurtured this progressive movement were fragile. This remarkable success in uniting a working-class female membership with a radical socialist agenda, both informed by and expressive of feminist ambition, was to prove shortlived. In the 1920s changes in the leadership, combined with structural change in the working-class movement, and in organized feminism, turned the Guild towards a different kind of political project which terminated its former independent outlook and radical policies. The foundation of the Co-operative Party in 1917, operating local electoral alliances with the Labour Party, brought to the fore a new generation of Guild leaders whose priorities were to dedicate the WCG to the cause of Labour and Co-operative parliamentarism, while simultaneously taking advantage of the new opportunities for women to pursue political careers, through the Co-operative and Labour parties. As a consequence of these drives, the political anchor that Davies' vision had provided in the earlier period was progressively eroded, and the ambitions for the Guild to which that vision had given rise gradually abandoned. Working-class feminist policies of the kind that had formerly provided organizational cohesion were dropped in deference to official Labour Party and trade-union opinion, and superseded by increasingly pragmatic equal rights aspirations, constrained by parliamentarism. The politically heterogeneous membership that was the inevitable outcome of the Guild's location in the trading movement now appeared an electoral liability; rank-and-file democracy was curbed, and authoritarian internal structures introduced in an attempt to silence alternative political positions of the right and the left.

Although continued numerical expansion between the wars partly disguised its political decay, the WCG did become the site of bitter internal conflicts as an autocratic leadership sought to control dissenting members. Major struggles were fought over the relationship between the Guild and party politics, the status of Communist members, and the leadership's attempt to abolish branch autonomy. Ultimately, it was the leadership's determination to pursue its own agenda, whatever the potential cost to the organization, that ensured its downfall. In the 1930s a number of influential guildswomen cast aside their loyalty to Labour to put absolute pacifism ahead of all other considerations, refusing any official involvement with war work; while women's organizations generally mushroomed in the Second World War, the Guild lost about 40 per cent of its members between 1939 and 1941, and never recovered its former size and influence. Despite the retention of a core of loyal but ageing members in the post-war period,[12] the steady decline in recruitment and in overall size was not reversed.

It is the argument of *Feminism and the politics of working women* that the demise of the WCG – which became visible through the loss of members from 1939 but was already indicated by the earlier internal conflicts – was a consequence of the close association with the Labour and Co-operative parties into which it had been drawn by an ambitious group of leading guildswomen, chief amongst them Eleanor Barton. In order to fit the electoralist

5

requirements of Labourism, the Guild not only abandoned its working-class feminist aspirations but also the democratic practices that had sustained its vitality as a broad-based movement.

Alongside its general historical interest, the course of the Guild's development from the 1880s to the Second World War prompts a number of important social and political questions. What kinds of resources, what style of leadership, what organizational form, and what educational methods, did the Guild develop to 'bring into active life'[13] unwaged women with only limited schooling and uneven political experience, otherwise isolated in the home? How in theory and in practice were the unitary categories of 'the working class' and 'women' interrogated and redefined to generate a working-class women's perspective? How was the binary division between public and private spheres breached in order to place married women's domestic circumstances on a political agenda? How were relationships and alliances with feminist groupings and the labour movement negotiated so as to maximize effective interventions, without compromising the all-important condition of self-government? Conversely, how did the changed circumstances of the 1920s cause that commitment to working women's autonomy to dissolve so rapidly? How did the dominant interests of the Labour Party effect an erasure of the Guild's former consciousness of gender-conflict within the working class? How did the second generation of Guild leaders attempt to deal with the organizational problems produced by this new and subservient relationship to the Labour Party, and how precisely did their responses corrode not only the distinctive working-class feminism the Guild had pioneered, but also the very fabric of its organizational viability? These are the matters with which this text is engaged.

Its thematic analysis of the history of the WCG from the 1880s to the Second World War begins with an account of the organization's genesis and early development in the Co-operative movement, and an overview of its strengths before 1920, and its qualitative decline thereafter. Chapter 2 establishes the pivotal nature of Margaret Llewelyn Davies' contribution as General Secretary, tracing the evolution of her socialism from her privileged English radical background through her involvement in the Guild. The following three chapters explore the ideological and political significance of the Guild's work, as Davies spearheaded a move to bring a feminist analysis to bear on the situation of working-class women. Chapter 3 analyses the Guild's reconstruction of working-class femininity, which challenged the constraining orthodoxies of respectable domesticity to assert the capacities and strengths of working women as actors in the public sphere, while simultaneously contesting their sexual oppression in the private sphere. Chapter 4 considers the campaigning work which the Guild initiated, from activity in support of trade unionism and the suffrage movement to its pioneering work on behalf of married women to secure statutory provision of maternity care. The subject of Chapter 5 is the Guild's conflict with officials of the Co-operative movement over its support for divorce law reform, the most radical episode in its history.

Chapters 6, 7 and 8 chart the steady unravelling of the WCG's progressive qualities during the 1920s and 1930s. In the changed circumstances of women's enfranchisement, the ascendancy of the Labour Party, and the foundation of the Co-operative Party, the politics of the Guild leadership moved from a non-aligned socialism to a right-wing Labourism. Mapping the Guild's faltering involvement with the campaigns for birth control and family allowances, and the political ambitions of Eleanor Barton (General Secretary from 1925 to 1937), the Guild's most forceful inter-war leader, Chapter 6 examines its abandonment of working-class feminism in the face of Labour Party hostility towards divisive 'sex issues'. Continuing the theme of the impact of Labour politics on the WCG, Chapter 7 turns to the constitutional changes which centralized power within the organization in an attempt to impose a party-political discipline on the ideologically diverse trading membership. These authoritarian methods generated considerable internal conflict, and eventually fatally damaged the organization's capacity to respond effectively to wider social and political change. Chapter 8 considers the Guild's relationship with feminism and feminine identity during these years of gradual decay. In retreat from the rank-and-file issues of birth control and family allowances, the Guild fell back on an equal rights feminism that had little resonance for the bulk of the membership. In any case, its new political priorities required not active involvement, but the passive loyalty of the membership, as voters and shoppers, and in the resulting vacuum Guild work became porous to an emergent, modernized ideology of working-class femininity that firmly positioned women in the home and at the heart of the family.

What is offered here, then, is a critical analysis of the Guild's history from its formation to the Second World War. The central concern is not simply to chronicle the development of the organization but to assess and evaluate its political significance during the decades of its greatest influence, and in considering the circumstances and causes of its demise, to advance a thesis about the effects of social context and political leadership in the fortunes of working-class women's organizations.

A number of different kinds of secondary literature have been helpful to this undertaking. Firstly, there is the Guild's own historiography. Until the 1920s the WCG produced a steady output of publications about its history and work, and following a gap of almost six decades, an official centenary history, and a collection of reminiscences, appeared in 1983 to mark the centenary of the Co-operative Women's Guild, as it had been re-named in 1963.[14] Yet the object of all the official publications was to record and to promote the organization rather than to engage in critical historical analysis of it. Apart from other work by myself,[15] however, there are few non-official studies which focus exclusively on the WCG. Two pieces of writing, articles on the Guild's early achievements, and on its peace work, appeared in 1977 and 1984 respectively, and played an important part in rescuing the organization from obscurity;[16] and in the late 1980s Tamae Mizuta compiled and published a full Guild bibliography.[17]

Secondly, the growth of feminist history and gender studies since the 1970s has generated a quantity of scholarly work which illuminates specific aspects of the Guild's activities and the context in which it developed. Studies by Jill Liddington and Jill Norris, and by Sandra Holton, on the suffrage agitation, and by Jill Liddington on the peace movement, are particularly valuable in the first respect,[18] while Gerry Holloway's research on the industrial women's movement from 1888 to 1918, Pamela Graves' study of Labour women from 1918 to 1938, and Martin Pugh's history of women's organizations from 1914 to 1959 all offer wider perspectives on these various phases of the Guild's existence.

Finally, however, the Guild's history needs also to be understood in relation to the working-class movement. While I have not attempted to provide a contextual account of socialist, trade union and Co-operative developments during these decades, I have drawn upon perspectives offered in a number of key texts: the work of James Hinton, and Ralph Miliband on socialism and labour,[19] G.D.H. Cole's 1944 history of the Co-operative movement, especially his intelligent and laudatory chapter on the WCG,[20] and the work by Pete Gurney and Stephen Yeo on the progressive character of consumers' Co-operation.[21]

In the absence of any monograph-length political analysis of the Guild, and given the shortage of secondary commentary, the unearthing of the twists, turns and nuances of policy, especially evidence of internal conflict, has involved an all-but-complete reliance on primary sources. For the greater part, the evidence used in this study has been drawn from the printed, typed and manuscript records and publications of the WCG, and of the Co-operative movement. Most of this material is held in the British Library of Political and Economic Science, although the WCG Central Committee Minutes and other papers from the Guild Head Office are housed in Hull University Library; the Co-operative Union Archive in Manchester, and the Co-operative College Library near Loughborough, have also been useful. Of this seemingly inexhaustible body of material, the 'Women's Pages' feature in Co-operative News has proved to be the most valuable source; consistent adherence to liberal editorial principles ensured the publication of letters and reports, especially in the 1920s and 1930s, which enable the researcher to get beneath the surface of an increasingly sterile official record to learn of internal criticism and dissent. Among a number of other miscellaneous sources, the Co-operative Archive in Bishopsgate Library, the Gertrude Tuckwell Collection, the Fawcett Library, the Woolf Archive in the University of Sussex, and an unpublished history of the Llewelyn Davies family, in private possession, have all yielded particularly useful information. The single most important insight I gained in my research – about the Guild's contentious 'political rule' – was the gift of Mabel Cumins whom I interviewed in Brighton in 1982, when she was 83, and still an active member of the Guild.

Notes

1. *Co-operative News*, 22 November 1913, p. 1552. Alexandra Kollontai (1872–1952), in political exile, and based in Germany. 'She has written books, but all in Russian. She is now doing one on all the maternity schemes in Europe.' (*Obshchestvo i materinstvo* (Society and Maternity), St Petersburg, 1916.) M. Llewelyn Davies to L. Woolf, Tuesday n.d. (?November 1913), Monks House Papers (MHP), University of Sussex. After the Boshevik Revolution, Kollontai was appointed Commissar for Public Welfare, the only female member of Lenin's government, see C. Porter, *Alexandra Kollontai: a Biography* (London: Virago, 1980). Both Kollontai and Porter are confused about dates: Kollontai was last in England not five years earlier but in the spring of 1909. Porter, following Kollontai's 1921 autobiographical essay, has Kollontai next in England in autumn 1912 but given her appearance at the Guild conference in November 1913, this must be a year out, Porter, op. cit., pp. 188–9.

2. MLD to L. Woolf, Tuesday n.d. (?November 1913), MHP. Founded in 1889, the Second International (after the 'First' International Working-men's Association, founded in 1864) was a loose federation of national socialist and labour parties; it disintegrated with the outbreak of war in 1914. Its most prominent British figure was Keir Hardie. See J. Joll, *The Second International, 1889–1914* (London: Routledge & Kegan Paul, revised edition 1974).

3. *Co-operative News*, 22 November 1913, p. 1552.

4. W. Thonnessen, *The Emancipation of Women: the Rise and Decline of the Women's Movement in German Social Democracy 1863–1933* trans. Joris de Bres (London: Pluto Press, 1973); Porter, op. cit., chapters 7 and 8.

5. Priscilla E. Moulder, 'What the WCG is doing for working women', *The Englishwoman*, April 1914.

6. The great wave of strikes between 1910 and 1914, see J. Hinton, *A History of the British Labour Movement 1867–1974* (Brighton: Wheatsheaf, 1983, chapter 5).

7. *Co-operative News*, 22 November 1913, p. 1552.

8. MLD, 'Co-operation at the Fountainhead', *Life and Labour*, Chicago, K, no. 7 (September 1920), pp. 199–202, typed MS, 'Material illustrating the work of the guild and kindred interests,

manuscript, typed and printed papers, photographs, erstwhile property of Margaret Llewelyn Davies (1890–?1944)', 11 vols., British Library of Political and Economic Science, 1, item 25. This idea was first expressed in a paper delivered at the 1907 Guild Congress, Rosalind Nash, *The Position of Married Women* (Manchester: CWS Printing Works, 1907) (see Chapter 1).

9. E. DuBois, 'Woman Suffrage and the Left: An International Socialist-Feminist Perspective', *New Left Review*, 186, March/April, 1991, p. 35.

10. To which should be added the National Federation of Women Workers, a general union set up from the WTUL in 1906.

11. 'Working women' was commonly used to distinguish working-class housewives from 'industrial women' – paid workers.

12. See J. Gaffin & D. Thoms, *Caring and Sharing The Centenary History of the Co-operative Women's Guild* (Manchester: Co-operative Union, 1983).

13. Miss Reddish, *Women's Guilds With Special Reference to their Claims on the Attention and Support of Educational Committees*, Co-operative Educational Committees' Association Annual Meeting (Bolton: Henry Smith, 1890, p. 4).

14. M. Llewelyn Davies, *The Women's Co-operative Guild* (Kirkby Lonsdale: WCG, 1904); M. Llewelyn Davies (ed.), *Maternity Letters from Working Women* (1915) (London: Virago, 1978); C. Webb, *The Woman with the Basket: the History of the WCG, 1883–1927*, (Manchester, The Guild, 1927); M. Llewelyn Davies (ed.), *Life As We Have Known It by Co-operative Working Women with an Introductory Letter by Virginia Woolf* (1931) (London: Virago, 1977); E. Sharp, *Buyers and Builders: A Jubilee Sketch of the WCG 1883–1933*, (Manchester: CWS, 1933; Gaffin & Thoms, op. cit.; C. Salt, P. Schweitzer, M. Wilson, *Of Whole Heart Cometh Hope: Centenary Memories of the Co-operative Women's Guild* (London: Co-operative Retail Services/Age Exchange Theatre Company, 1983).

15. G. Scott, 'The Politics of the Women's Co-operative Guild: Working Women and Feminism during the First World War', Sussex University MA Dissertation, 1981; G. Scott, ' "The working-class women's most active and democratic movement": the WCG, 1883–1950', Sussex University D.Phil. thesis, 1988; G. Scott, 'Women's Autonomy and Divorce Law Reform in the Co-operative Movement, 1910–1920', in S. Yeo (ed.), *New Views of Co-operation* (London: Routledge & Kegan Paul, 1988); G. Scott, ' "A Trade Union for Working Women": the WCG 1914–45', in S. Oldfield (ed.), *This Working Day World: Women's Lives and Culture(s) in Britain, 1914–45* (London: Taylor & Francis, 1994); G. Scott, 'Basket Power

and Market Forces: the WCG 1883–1920', in B. Einhorn & E. Yeo, *Women and Market Societies* (Aldershot: Edward Elgar, 1995).

16. J. Gaffin, 'Women and Co-operation', in L. Middleton (ed.), *Women in the Labour Movement* (London: Croom Helm, 1977); N. Black, 'The Mother's International: the WCG and Feminist Pacifism', *Women's Studies International Forum*, 7, no. 6, 1984, pp. 467–76.

17. Mizuta's study also embraced the Scottish, Irish and International Women's Guilds, see T. Mizuta, 'A Bibliography of the Co-operative Women's Guild', *The Journal of Social Sciences*, Nagoya Economics University, Ichimuragakuen Junior College, no. 46, November 1988; no. 47, March 1989.

18. J. Liddington and J. Norris, *One Hand Tied Behind Us* (London: Virago, 1978); S. Holton, *Feminism and Democracy: Women's Suffrage and Reform Politics in Britain 1900–1918* (Cambridge University Press, 1987); J. Liddington, *The Long Road to Greenham: Feminism and Anti-Militarism in Britain since 1820* (London: Virago, 1989); G. Holloway, 'A Common Cause? Class Dynamics in the Industrial Women's Movement, 1888–1918', Sussex University D.Phil. thesis, 1995; P. Graves, *Labour Women in British Working-Class Politics 1918–1939* (Cambridge University Press, 1994); M. Pugh, *Women and the Women's Movement in Britain 1914–1959* (London: Macmillan, 1993).

19. Hinton, op. cit.; R. Miliband, *Parliamentary Socialism: a Study in the Politics of Labour* (London: Merlin Press, 1973).

20. G.D.H. Cole, *A Century of Co-operation* (George Allen & Unwin for the Co-operative Union, 1944).

21. P. Gurney, *Co-operative Culture and the Politics of Consumption in England 1870–1930* (Manchester University Press, 1996); S. Yeo, 'Notes on Three Socialisms – Collectivism, Statism and Associationism', in C. Levy (ed.), *Socialism and the Intelligentsia 1880–1914* (London: Routledge & Kegan Paul, 1987); S. Yeo (ed.), *New Views of Co-operation* (London: Routledge, 1988). For the vision, and impeccable probity of one of the movement's most dedicated employees, see S. Yeo, *Who was J.T.W. Mitchell?* (Manchester: CWS Membership Services, Co-operative Press, 1995).

Chapter One

Beginnings

The Women's Co-operative Guild grew out of the English consumers' Co-operative movement. As Margaret Llewelyn Davies wrote, 'it is through Co-operation that the married woman living at home finds her work and place in the Labour world.'[1] On the face of it the late 19th century Co-operative movement might seem an unlikely location for a radical women's organization. Generally regarded as a leading institution of working-class self help, its success and dynamism as a trading enterprise was accompanied by a reputation for political moderation and social conservatism. To understand why it should have spawned the Guild project it is necessary to appreciate both the size and scope of the movement, and the unusual opportunities that it afforded its female membership.

The Co-operative movement originated in the aspiration of the 'Rochdale Pioneers'[2] in the 1840s to contest the ways in which private retailing exploited working people. Half a century later it consisted of hundreds of self-governing Societies (retail shops), grouped into two federations – the Co-operative Wholesale Society (CWS), for supplies, and the Co-operative Union (CU), with its structure of sections and districts, for education and propaganda purposes[3] – and was set on a course of continued expansion that would not peak until the Second World War. In 1880, it had 600,000 members and share capital of £2,246,000; in 1900, 1,780,000 members and £23,256,000.[4] By 1920 the Co-operative Societies 'accounted for 18 per cent to 20 per cent of the total national sales of groceries and provisions', and from 1914 to 1938 membership doubled to 6.5 million,[5] with total capital at

£229,605,509 in 1935.[6] Although growth in its share of retail trade slowed between the wars,[7] wartime registration for rationing further strengthened the movement, and by 1944 about one in five of the British population belonged to a Co-operative Society.[8]

While Co-operation thus became 'an intrinsic part of working-class life', and the movement's vision of a Co-operative Commonwealth clearly implied some kind of socialism,[9] labour historians have formed rather different judgements about the movement's commitment to, and capacity for, socialist transformation. On the one hand, its typical relationship with capitalism has been seen as one of peaceful co-existence rather than mutual antagonism, with active Co-operators defining themselves as social reformers by trade rather than as class warriors. According to this line of argument, increasing prosperity brought to the fore 'men who were chiefly preoccupied with the practical details of successful commercial trading ... the belief that the movement would peacefully put an end to the competitive system,' and create the Co-operative Commonwealth, while 'never formally abandoned, became more and more a pious hope', divorced from routine business.[10] Alongside its formal position of political neutrality ran strong Liberal sympathies, while the retail and wholesale Societies had their own tricky labour relations to manage, and a far from shining record in regard to the Co-operative trade unions.[11] In times of adversity, such writers concede, the Societies functioned as a 'line of defence'[12] for working people, providing credit during strikes, for example, but at least until the First World War the movement was detached from working-class politics, and 'almost wholly neglected by Socialist propagandists and theorists.'[13]

Yet there have also been moves to reinterpret the significance of Co-operation, emphasizing the movement's achievements as a unique form of working-class association[14] whose strength lay in its capacity to combine sound business practice with an ethos of mutuality and social justice. From the outset, as well as supplying wholesome food, Co-operative Societies were run on democratic lines, allocating one vote to each member regardless of the number of shares they owned, and distributing their trading surplus as a dividend (the 'divi') proportional to purchases not investment.[15] With its huge trading operations, and large undertakings for combined services that spanned banking, insurance, social, educational and propaganda activity, Co-operation was conceived by many as 'a new economic system in embryo',[16] that would in time supersede the old competitive system because it was more rational, more efficient, and more democratic. Far from being 'a pious hope', this argument runs, the Co-operative Commonwealth was a real ambition for many active members.

Certainly, and whatever its status as a blueprint for a future good society, actually existing Co-operation held out possibilities for women that were not to be found elsewhere in the working-class movement. The sexual division of labour which relegated women to a peripheral place as direct producers, and, therefore, as trade unionists, necessarily ensured that they would be active in an association of consumers: the stores were dependent upon the trading loyalty of the working-class housewife for their survival and growth. Buttressing this reality was the movement's historic commitment to sexual equality, a legacy of its Owenite past.[17] Women had never been excluded from the terms of its constitution and, in theory, enjoyed membership, including voting rights and access to educational provision, on the same terms as men.

The practice did not always match these egalitarian principles. In line with the mores of the respectable working class, Co-operative managers and officials generally agreed that women should be in their proper place – at home – and that the feminine virtues did not include a capacity to deal with facts, figures, and policy-making. Very few women actually attended Co-operative meetings, even fewer spoke at them, and in many working-class families, although it was the wife who shopped at the store and collected the 'divi', it was the husband who held the membership of the society.

Yet the movement was a sufficiently broad church for some active female Co-operators to feel entitled to challenge the gap between rhetoric and reality, and to press for their own organization. 'What are men always urged to do when there is a meeting held at any place to encourage or start Co-operative institutions?' asked Mrs Acland,[18] the Guild founder. 'Come! Help! Vote! Criticize! Act! What are women urged to do? Come and Buy! That is the limit of the special work pointed out to us women. We can be independent members of our Store, but we are only asked to come and buy...'. In the same breath, however, Mrs Acland made it plain that she was not proposing a major assault on the sexual hierarchy. Why 'should not we women do more than we do?', she reasoned.

> Surely, without departing from our own sphere, and without trying to undertake work which can be better done by men, there is more for us women to do than to spend money. Spend money at our own Store we must, that is a matter of course; but our duty does not end here, nor our duty to our fellow creatures. To come and 'buy' is all we can be asked to do; but cannot we go further ourselves? Why should not we have our meetings, our readings, our discussions?[19]

In response to this appeal, at a special meeting at the 1883 Co-operative Congress, the Women's League for the Spread of Co-operation was launched (changing its name the following year to the Women's Co-operative Guild), with a membership of 50.[20] In the first instance its aim was relatively modest – to foster Co-operative principles among women – and sufficient male associates were convinced of the value of the project to guarantee its success. For progressives like Samuel Bamford, the editor of *Co-operative News*, who from 1883 included a regular 'Women's Pages' in the paper, greater opportunities for women was an inherently good thing. More pragmatically, for those whose first concern was trade, there was the possibility that the women might recruit more customers, and in 1886 the Co-operative Union awarded a grant of £10, in recognition of the Guild's educational and propaganda value to the movement.

Despite an encouraging start, the Guild remained a delicate plant in the 1880s, uncertain about its purpose, and the extent and propriety of its claims on the Co-operative movement. Signs of organizational vigour began only with the arrival of a leader who had the vision and the confidence to exploit what the movement had to offer. 'Members have not yet half realised', Margaret Llewelyn Davies wrote in the 1892 Report:

> all they may get and give by means of the Guild. Self governed, free from outside patronage, with money at its back, it ought to become a very powerful instrument for bringing all kinds of help to women in their different capacities, and for forwarding the cause of labour generally. There is a good deal yet in the

lives of women that is not exactly rose-coloured, and changes are not very likely to occur without determined action on the part of women themselves.[21]

Davies' first priority as General Secretary was to place the Guild on a sound organizational and financial basis. Until 1890 it consisted only of a Central Committee and free-standing branches. Consequently, the centre was overloaded, there was no stimulus to growth, branches were isolated and often collapsed, while lack of funding was a major constraint on new initiatives. In the early 1890s Davies and her assistant Lilian Harris tackled these problems through a major restructuring. The constitution which they devised, modelled on that of the CU, established the Guild as a federal organization to which branches affiliated on the conditions that members belonged to a Co-operative Society and subscribed to the Guild Central Fund. Following the CU model of sections and districts, and maximizing the points of contact between the Guild and the wider movement, branches were clustered into districts, and districts into sections, each tier with its own elected officers, and federated, by means of subscription, to the national office which carried out educational and propaganda work. This structure facilitated steady growth, efficient administration, and an effective exchange of ideas and information. In 1892 a national WCG Festival was held, and from 1893 an annual delegate Congress, to agree policy which was then implemented by an elected Central Committee (CC), with the General Secretary and office staff undertaking routine tasks.

Painstaking work, and the employment of a full-time paid organizer, soon yielded results. Between 1890 and 1894, membership went up from 1,640 to 7,511, and branches from 54 to 170. But this growth was not without cost. In the same period expenditure jumped from £19 to £245,[22] exposing the central difficulty in building an organization of mainly unwaged housewives. As the Annual Report noted, 'the addition to our income from new branches can never equal the increasing outlay necessary upon the growth of the whole work of the guild.'[23]

To make up the shortfall, forceful arguments were mobilized to unlock funds from the wider movement. The Guild was working to the 'aims and policies of the Co-operative Union', the 1894 Annual Report pointed out, and was convinced that there were 'unutilised forces' which they could put at the disposal of the Union 'but for lack of funds'. Was it fair that while the Guild struggled with debts, many Societies' education budgets were underspent? Surely, it was 'a little hard that women should not only give their services, but should have to pay for the privilege of working by subscribing to our funds, while men have money thrust upon them.'[24] In May, the CU Central Board received a Guild deputation on finances. When asked to indicate the amount required, Davies replied that 'they did not want to make an undue claim upon Union, but last year the Board was good enough to vote the sum of £50. This year she hoped the Board might see its way to double that amount. [Laughter]'.[25] The grant was duly increased to £100, and through subsequent increments took account of expanding membership, more than doubling the income from subscriptions, and making possible national initiatives that would otherwise have been out of the question.

Locally, too, there were valuable resources to be tapped. Ideally, but subject to negotiation, a Guild branch could expect from the Society an annual grant, free use of a meeting room, some or all of the cost of printing programmes, and assistance with sectional and district conferences.[26] Where such facilities were not forthcoming Guild officers were ready with their objections. 'I should very much like to know', wrote Mrs Carr, the Northern Sectional Secretary, in 1896:

> out of the 11,357 members there, how many are women; or, if any: and if there are not among them any women members, to ask the men this question, "Who makes the dividend – is it the men?" I am inclined to think the £94 spent for educational purposes is not a fair proportion of the £84,884 net profits made during the year. Do not the women deserve a small share of this?[27]

Persistent reminders of the movement's reliance upon its female membership steadily unlocked the funding necessary for sturdy growth. By 1897 the Guild had 223 branches, 10,555 members, an extremely busy head office,[28] and was well on the way to becoming a standard feature wherever the movement was active. As Davies shrewdly put it in 1904: 'It has been the aim of the Guild, to arouse women to a sense of the basket power which they specially possessed.'[29] While the Guild was never lavishly resourced, women's role as consumers had none the less been used effectively to acquire the means by which to build an organization whose basic constituency was housewives without money of their own.

As well as gaining material security from the trading movement, the WCG also benefited significantly from the highly developed democratic and broad church culture of Co-operation. The movement's organic unity was defined by membership of the trading societies, by a commitment to democratic procedures, and by a common concern with the spread of 'Co-operation', which itself conveyed a range of meanings from ethical retailing through to Owenite socialism. As an auxiliary body of what was arguably the most democratic institution in Britain, the Guild was, from the outset, in control of its own affairs. No formal mechanisms bound the Guild to any particular method of working or policy. Guild subjects were introduced by the Central Committee, educational literature distributed, discussions instigated and positions adopted at conferences, branches, and the annual Congress. Guild policy could thus express the views of its members as distinct from majority opinion in the wider movement. Of course, there were constraints. The movement's political neutrality, let alone women's disenfranchised status, meant that there was no question of the Guild being formally involved in party politics. But by the same token it was not to be rigidly bound by a 'Co-operative line', and was free to arrive democratically at its own interpretation of the nature and purpose of the movement, and of the interests of Co-operative women.

Davies was shrewd enough to appreciate the advantages to the Guild of being 'self governed', and 'free from outside patronage'. Determined that the WCG would be far more than a mechanism for increasing Co-operative sales, she and her allies fostered initiatives that would make the Guild a progressive force within the movement and in national life. A key step in this direction was to divide Guild activity under two headings: while Co-operative work focused on the trading movement, Citizenship work enabled the Guild to pursue reforms in the interests of working women.

In both areas of work, the Guild took up positions that were more radical than the Co-operative mainstream. It advocated a broad alliance between Co-operation and Trade Unionism, worked to strengthen the position of the Amalgamated Union of

Co-operative Employees, and aimed to bring into active life within the movement those groups conventionally excluded from working-class organization: women and the poor. From 1899 to 1904 it was preoccupied with a scheme to set up Co-operative Societies in deprived neighbourhoods – combating poverty by organizing the poor – and then fought a long battle to secure a minimum wage for Co-operative female employees. The Guild's radical vision of Co-operation – a movement encompassing an assertive women's auxiliary, and Societies capable of drawing in casual and unemployed urban workers – soon gained it a reputation as 'the left wing of the movement'.[30]

Yet it was through its pre-war Citizenship campaigns that the WCG most thoroughly exploited its autonomy, transmitting 'the message of the movement for the emancipation of women'[31] to working-class housewives, and asserting an identity that was as much feminist as Co-operative. Certainly, a great variety of feminist influences converged in the Guild. Even Mrs Acland's cautious request – that women should have more to do than just come and buy – signalled a discontent with the sexual status quo. If the Guild's feminists had a key text on the 'woman question' it was John Stuart Mill's *The Subjection of Women* (1869), but Davies and the women she drew around her were also variously inspired by the sexual egalitarianism of Owenite socialism; by the reformist interventions of middle-class campaigners since the 1850s for the vote, property rights, education and employment opportunities; by the more recent attempts of middle-class reformers and socialists to unionize women workers; and by the growth of a working-class women's suffrage movement among the organized textile workers of Lancashire and Cheshire. 'Working-women are now beginning to find out,' began an 1896 Guild pamphlet, *How to Start and Work a Branch*, 'as men have done, that the means for improving their conditions and redressing their wrongs lie largely in their own hands.' 'Some privileges', it continued, 'have belonged too exclusively to one sex; other privileges too exclusively to one class. It is high time that, as far as possible, all that makes a life most happy and fruitful should be brought within the reach of *all*.'[32]

The Guild's first steps in this direction emulated the existing currents of women's organization. During the 1890s guildswomen began to lend support to suffrage campaigns, and to groups concerned with the position of industrial women;[33] by the 1900s, these efforts had solidified into a general Guild consensus on the importance of female trade unions, protective legislation for women workers, and equal political rights for women. But the most significant development of these years was the way in which an increasing awareness of the circumstances of its members generated a more precise inflexion of the Guild's feminist aspirations.

Guild branches recruited from the women who shopped at the Co-op stores. The typical guildswoman was married, of the skilled or semi-skilled working-class, and in her middle age; very few were in paid employment. The 1893 Annual Report included some unusual details about the marital and employment status of the 6,412 members. The majority were wives and mothers, with only about 100 of the married guildswomen employed in trades (including dressmaking). Most of those who were mill and factory workers came from the minority younger age group, the nearly 700 members who were under 25.[34] Early efforts to recruit from the female labour force had only limited success: in 1894 it was reported that some of the Luton members were employed in straw hat manufacturing, working long hours at the height of the season, and the 'guild meetings consequently suffer'; in Failsworth, near Manchester, it was reported, '(m)any women work in the mills, and have not time for meetings.'[35] This pattern became more pronounced as the Guild grew in size. In 1910 Davies characterized the 25,897 members as 'married women', who came not from 'the lowest class of all', but were 'the wives of every kind of artisan, miners, weavers, railway men, all the ordinary trades that belong to the locality where the branch is.'[36]

The educational and political background of Guild members was enormously diverse. In the 1890s, while a handful of middle-class women like Davies had attended high school and even university, there were branches which found a demand for literacy classes.[37] Guildswomen were equally varied with regard to party politics. Co-operation was a social movement and not a political party; membership of a Co-operative Society did not imply a belief in anything but the value of the dividend, and Co-operative women ranged across the spectrum of working-class political allegiances to socialism and the Independent Labour Party, Lib–Lab Radicalism, and even Conservatism; many, probably the majority, regarded politics as being outside their domain.

Accordingly, despite a comparative social homogeneity, the Guild leaders could make no assumptions about the values and commitments that new members brought with them. Every position had to be won through debate and persuasion within the organization. This set in train a growing focus on the everyday lives of guildswomen. Thus it became clear that few of its members were trade unionists, and that the most effective way for them to support trade unionism was through the Co-operative movement. Equally, the demand for the vote needed to be related to the situation of married women. Increasingly this process exposed the problems working women experienced as wives and mothers, a reality more or less invisible in public life and one which immediately suggested a role for the Guild.

The idea that the WCG might act as a kind of 'trade union for married women' was first articulated by Rosalind Nash, a close friend of Davies. Her paper, *The Position of Married Women*, presented at Guild Congress in 1907,[38] used Mill's incisive critique of marriage, extended to take account of small changes in the intervening four decades, but also the concerns of propertyless women. One of the most important insights Nash offered was that the 'sacred privacy' of the home concealed abusive relationships, a view that was strikingly confirmed by the evidence the Guild collected as part of its submission to the Royal Commission on Divorce in 1910, and in its work for statutory maternity provision from 1911, campaigns which crystallized the Guild's self-identity as an organization of and for working-class wives, and as such its distinctive contribution to the women's movement.

Yet this assertion of working-class women's rights provoked opposition from the leaders of the working-class movement. In 1913 Labour MPs tried to block the Guild's efforts to make maternity benefit the legal property of the wife, and the Guild's Citizenship work in general caused unease among Co-operative officials for being overtly political and hence un-Cooperative. For the Co-operative Union to interfere directly in the business of any part of the movement was alien to its democratic traditions and for many years the Guild was left to its own devices. But the limits of bureaucratic tolerance were reached in 1913 when a Catholic association's objections to the Guild's support for divorce law reform provided the CU Central Board with the opportunity to use its funding powers to try to curb its female auxiliary body. This outside interference prompted a stock-taking within the Guild of its strengths and achievements. Surprising even Davies with their militancy, members showed themselves determined to fight for self government. The 1914 Guild Congress voted almost unanimously to forego its £400 grant in the interest of self-government, prepared if necessary to look elsewhere for funding rather than sacrifice its organizational freedom.

The stand on divorce law reform constitutes the high point of the commitment to an autonomous politics of working women that was the driving force behind this period of the Guild's development. 'From my general experience', Davies wrote, 'I have found that, so long as there is class and sex inequality, it is necessary that working women should have their own separate and affiliated organisations.'[39] It is this determination to hold class and gender relations in equilibrium that distinguishes the WCG from the range of groups with an interest in the organization and representation of working-class women in this period.

In the decade prior to the First World War, the Guild was an integral part of a network that spanned labour and suffrage organizations, and whose nodal points included such women as Margaret McMillan of the ILP, Gertrude Tuckwell of the WTUL, Mary Macarthur of the NFWW, Margaret Bondfield of the WLL, and Helena Swanwick of the NUWSS.[40] While there was scope for cross fertilization and mutual support in each of these organizational relationships, the Guild's closest ally during these years was the WLL, formed in 1906 by women associated with the infant Labour Party.[41] In 1911, for example, there was a remarkable piece of joint action when WCG and WLL members invaded a meeting of the London County Council in protest at a refusal to meet their deputation on school medical service proposals.[42]

Such interventions notwithstanding, it is the WCG that stands out as the organization best placed to give a direct voice to working women, and to foster policies that addressed sexual oppression in the working-class family. There are a number of reasons for this. Firstly, no other organization had the Guild's ready access both to unwaged, married women and the resources that would compensate for low subscription levels without introducing the problem of patronage. The women's trade unions, like the working-class strongholds of the suffrage movement, were work-place based, with a low proportion of married women among their membership; domestic issues generally remained in the background. Secondly, the Guild's democratic practices discouraged the tendency for overbearing middle-class women to take control of proceedings and policy that was apparent both in suffrage societies, and industrial women's organizations. Finally, the Guild belonged to a working-class institution in which women could hope to gain some leverage by virtue of their structural importance as consumers; in contrast, the marginal position women occupied in the labour movement is reflected in the WLL's willingness to accommodate the views of the male leadership and hold back from supporting either the wife's claim to maternity benefit or divorce law reform.

The picture that emerges of the Guild by 1914 then is of an organization receptive to the influences of both a strong women's movement and rising industrial militancy, fully exploiting its autonomous position within the Co-operative movement to support radical and progressive causes, and striving as far as possible to involve its own members in those struggles. The broad definition of its members' interests enabled the Guild to draw on a range of opinion from Liberals through the ILP, and to span the labour-socialist divide, as with its 1913 support for Jim Larkin and the Dublin strikers. Members of the radical intelligentsia among Davies' acquaintanceship were persuaded to produce educational material for the Guild,[43] and its supporters included socialists such as George Lansbury, who, for example, presented the women's case to the LCC in 1911. Significantly, Davies maintained a critical distance from the Labour Party: the 'lack of power to unite & concentrate & see the main things is very marked',[44] she wrote of it to Leonard Woolf just before the war.

The Guild's general situation was dramatically transformed by events which took place during, and in the immediate aftermath of, the First World War. Most obviously, the organization lost Margaret Llewelyn Davies, who retired in 1921. But even by then the Guild's structural position in the Co-operative movement and, by extension, the Labour movement, had already shifted in ways that significantly reduced its independence, and undermined its connections with radical politics.

The Guild's strength prior to 1914 lay in its bold leadership, and the fact that, insulated from party politics by its position in the Co-operative movement, it was not subject to strict policy guidelines. The enfranchisement of women signalled the end of the Guild's ability to intervene in parliamentary proceedings from a non-aligned position, but otherwise to ignore party politics. After 1918, the major parties sought to incorporate women and women's issues, albeit on their own terms; for their part, many women activists, especially those involved in local or national politics, were anxious to prove their worth to qualify for office.

As the WLL was wound up and the Labour Party Women's Sections formed, the Labour Party received a layer of zealous female officials who were fully alert to the potentially divisive impact of 'sex issues'. During the 1920s the party became the site of major policy battles between the rank and file and the bureaucracy over such questions as birth control and family allowances. Labour successfully resisted the more radical agenda, adopting instead a family-centred social policy that subsequently found expression in post-1945 welfare legislation. That Labour *women* played an important role in committing the party to such reforms,[45] which were, in turn, of benefit to working *women*, should not detract from the significance of the 'gender struggles'[46] of the 1920s as a moment of defeat for working-class feminism, not only in the Labour Party, but in the other organizations, most notably the WCG, that were now pulled into its orbit.

After the war, with its autonomy intact, and an influx of 20,000 new members from 1919 to 1921, the Guild might have seemed well-placed to escape the disciplining weight of the Labour leadership and resume its distinctive campaigning role. Its formal entry into party politics was through the newly formed Co-operative Party, which despite much common ground remained organizationally distinct from the Labour Party. The WCG was not affiliated to the Labour Party,[47] had no official role in its policy-making, and was not bound by its decisions. The Guild's gradual subordination to Labour Party politics was the outcome of its leadership's involvement in two separate developments: the process by which senior Labour women asssumed control of the whole working-class women's movement; and the drive within the Guild to secure its support for a formal alliance between the Labour Party and the Co-operative Party.

In the 1920s, the Labour-dominated Standing Joint Committee of Industrial Women's Organizations (SJC) assumed effective control of the women's labour movement. Originally formed in 1916 to coordinate representation on national and local government bodies in wartime, the SJC was reborn in 1918 as the Labour Women's Advisory Committee. Under the skilful management of Marion Phillips,[48] SJC secretary and Labour Party chief woman officer, and with the loss of independent-minded women like Davies, and Mary Macarthur of the NFWW, it soon began to exercise considerable power over its member bodies. The Labour line, as presented by Phillips and her colleagues at meetings of the SJC, became the sole determinant of the policies to be pursued by the working-class women's organizations. Yet the SJC did not become a site of conflict between Guild leaders and the Labour women because, by the mid-1920s, the Guild leaders themselves shared the same political position as their Labour counterparts.

The majority of leading and active guildswomen were committed to the Co-operative Party, and, as a matter of course, the Labour Party;[49] they believed that social reform should be secured through the legislature, and accepted the need to maintain a distance from the militant, extra-parliamentary strategies advocated by, among others, the Communist Party.[50] Many were also pursuing political careers in local government or seeking nomination as prospective Co-operative–Labour candidates. Officially, their position was Guild policy: in 1918 the Guild Congress voted in support of the Co-operative Party and the Co-operative–Labour alliance, and thereafter remained formally committed to the Co-operative Party.[51] Yet there were many guildswomen who did not share this view. While its leadership undoubtedly wished otherwise, the Guild's relationship with the Co-operative Party did not replicate that of the LPWS with the Labour Party.[52] Whereas the LPWS consisted of women who had joined a political party, the Guild consisted of women who had joined a trading movement with a long tradition of political neutrality behind it.

It is a measure of the Co-operative movement's detachment from working-class politics that serious attempts by Labour and Co-operative leaders to establish a formal relationship during the upsurge of industrial action from 1910 to 1914 were defeated by Co-operative Congress in 1913 and again in 1914.[53] The situation was partially transformed by the government's rough treatment of the movement in wartime, especially the imposition of an excess profits tax, and the 1917 Congress voted 'to seek direct Co-operative representation in both national and local government.'[54] This did not signal a willingness to work with the Labour Party, however, despite considerable overlap of programmes and constituencies, and the concomitant necessity for local agreements to prevent the vote from being split. Proposals for a formal alliance drawn up by Co-operative and Labour Party leaders had to be approved on the Co-operative side not by the Co-operative Party Conference, but by the full Co-operative Congress, where there was hostility to Labour, not to mention residual ambivalence over Co-operative politics. 'The rank and file of Co-operative members,' Cole notes, 'even more than the rank and file of the Trade Unions, is politically divided; and the impetus towards political activity comes from quite a small fraction of the total membership.'[55] Carr Saunders made a similar observation: 'The vast majority of co-operators are members of their societies as trading concerns, and have no interest in their political affiliations; a great many are attached to other political parties.'[56] An attempt to institutionalize relations between the two parties was defeated by Congress in 1921, with the result that electoral questions had to be settled locally and informally.[57] In practice, 'the Labour–Co-operative alliance was complete inside the House of Commons, though it had no counterpart in the relations between the two parties outside Parliament.'[58]

In the inter-war period, the WCG, divided in ways that reflected the wider Co-operative movement, thus presented major difficulties for its dominant Labour Party supporting faction. Unable to require support for the Co-operative–Labour Parties as a condition of membership of the Guild, the leadership settled instead for imposing that requirement as a qualification for Guild officers. This required stronger and more centralized forms of internal discipline, which in turn generated hostility from those wedded to traditional forms of rank-and-file democracy. Throughout the 1920s and 1930s, there were internal conflicts as the leadership sought to prevent guildswomen from rival groupings, particularly the Communist Party, from gaining positions of influence within the organization.

These changes in the Guild's internal dynamics were accompanied by a loss of clarity and momentum in its campaigning work. Despite the internal conflicts, it retained its position as a leading women's organization. Its size – membership grew from 50,600 in 905 branches in 1921, to 87,246 in 1,819 branches in 1939 – and its position in the mighty Co-operative movement combined to give it an authoritative voice in a variety of local and national public forums. Yet it no longer possessed the progressive and dynamic characteristics that had been evident prior to 1920.

As the autonomy that had underpinned pre-war interventions on behalf of working women was sacrificed in the interests of Labour–Co-operative solidarity, the old area of Citizenship lost its radical edge. The demands for birth control and family allowances proved to be incompatible with the dominant concerns of the Labour Party; in response, the Guild leadership abandoned both in favour of more anodyne social policies. In the 1920s the Guild resumed its work to extend maternity provision, defended the right of married women to paid employment, and pressed for more women on public bodies, but did not produce an equivalent of the big single-issue campaigns of the pre-war period. Co-operative work to 'Push the Sales' and promote loyal buying accounted for an increasing proportion of the routine work of the organization, and brought with it a more traditional set of norms about women's role. Imperceptibly, the Guild absorbed norms and values that underlined women's primary responsibilities as wives and mothers.

Aside from parliamentarism, and joint work within the movement, the most distinctive subject to emerge in the inter-war Guild was peace work. Attempts to win an anti-war position at Guild Congress during the war of 1914–18 were defeated, but in the 1920s growing numbers of branches affiliated to such organizations as the No More War Movement, and lent support to a range of initiatives to secure international disarmament and a permanent peace. In the 1930s, however, this mutated into an absolutist pacifist position heavily sponsored by Eleanor Barton and other committed pacifists among the leadership, which in the late 1930s became their one major departure from Labour Party policy, and simultaneously the cause of serious division within the Guild. By this stage, however, the leadership lacked the ability to respond effectively to internal or external change. Pacifism was rigorously adhered to, and the WCG refused any formal involvement in organizing women for war-work. Consequently, in the early years of the war, about 40 per cent of the membership left, and the Guild never regained its former size or influence.

Yet for several decades the WCG had been justified in its claim to represent 'the largest class of women in the country'.[59] Firstly, the average guildswomen belonged to the majority occupational group in Britain, the working class, whose circumstances kept her above the level of destitution or severe want;[60] secondly, her marital status was typical of adult females;[61] thirdly, as a full-time housewife, she was representative of the general trend for women to cease paid employment at marriage unless great need dictated otherwise.[62] Equally valid was the Guild's observation that, 'voteless and voiceless', this group's 'isolation in married life' had previously prevented 'any common expression of their needs'.[63] Politically and economically, married working-class women were not so much marginal as invisible,[64] subject to a consensus shared by both philanthropists and the official trade-union movement that their proper place was in the home.[65] When the Guild came into being, the working-class housewife was completely unrepresented in public life. 'Without money of her own, with no right even to her housekeeping savings, without adequate protection against a husband's possible cruelty, with no legal position as a mother, with the conditions of maternity totally neglected, married women in the home had existed apart, voiceless and unseen.' While the Guild did not single-handedly win the vote, advocate maternity benefit and other allowances for married women, or highlight the issue of sexual abuse and domestic violence, and while it certainly did not follow through on all these questions between the wars, by the 1920s, and with some justification, Davies could claim that the outstanding fact about the Guild movement 'is the emergence of the married working woman from national obscurity into a position of national importance.'[66]

Notes

1. MLD, 'Co-operation at the Fountainhead', *Life and Labour*, Chicago, K, no. 7 (September 1920), pp. 199–202, 'Material illustrating the work of the Guild and kindred interests, manuscript, typed and printed papers, photographs, erstwhile property of Margaret Llewelyn Davies (1890–?1944)', 11 vols., British Library of Political and Economic Science, 1, item 25.

2. The Rochester Co-operative Society was formed in 1844 with £28 of pooled capital; its success, in Beatrice Webb's judgement, constituted 'a unique romance in the industrial history of the world'; B. Webb, *My Apprenticeship*, 2, (Harmondsworth: Penguin, 1938, p. 427).

3. The CWS was governed by Quarterly Meetings of delegates representing the Societies, and its business carried on by a Board of Directors; the policy of the Co-operative Union was agreed by an annual delegate Congress, its affairs were managed by a United Board, and its smaller working committee the Central Board.

4. G.D.H. Cole & R. Postgate, *The Common People 1746–1946* (London: Methuen, 1966 edn, p. 437).

5. N. Killingback, 'Limits to Mutuality: Economic and Political Attacks on Co-operation during the 1920s and 1930s', in S. Yeo (ed.), *New Views of Co-operation* (London: Routledge, 1988, pp. 213 and 216). By 1921 membership was over 4.5 million, total capital £66 million; the volume of trade handled by the movement and exempt from tax was an increasing source of concern for the Treasury as well as private traders. See also P. Maguire, 'Co-operation and Crisis, Government, Co-operation and Politics, 1917–1922', in Yeo (ed.), op. cit.

6. A.M. Carr, P. Sargant Florence, R. Peers, *Consumers' Co-operation in Great Britain: An Examination of the British Co-operative Movement* (London: Allen & Unwin Ltd., 1938, p. 138).

7. Killingback, op. cit., p. 216. The 'consumers' cartel' was still well placed to hold its own in an increasingly concentrated market: in the mid-1930s, for example, the CWS was one of the top three millers, with Spillers, just behind Rank, C.L. Mowatt, *Britain between the Wars* (1955) (Cambridge: Methuen University Paperback, 1983, p. 454).

8. G.D.H. Cole, *A Century of Co-operation* (London: Allen & Unwin for the Co-operative Union, 1944, p. 390).

9. R. McKibbin, *The Evolution of the Labour Party 1910–1924* (Oxford: Clarendon Press, 1974, p. 43).

10. Cole & Postgate, op. cit., p. 383.

11. For a survey of Co-operative work conditions and trade unionism, see Carr *et al.*, op. cit., ch. XXI.

12. J. Hinton, *Labour and Socialism A History of the British Labour Movement 1867–1974* (Brighton: Wheatsheaf, 1983, p. 7).

13. Cole & Postgate, op. cit., p. 437.

14. See Introduction, note 21.

15. Cole, op. cit., p. 64.

16. Carr *et al.*, op. cit., p. 38.

17. B. Taylor, *Eve and the New Jerusalem* (London: Virago, 1983).

18. Alice Acland (1849–1935), founder and first secretary of the WCG, wife of Sir Arthur Acland, Liberal MP, Oxford don, and an active Co-operator, see J.M. Bellamy & J. Saville (eds.), *Dictionary of Labour Biography (DLB)*, vol. I (London: Macmillan, 1972).

19. Cole, op. cit., p. 216; italics in original. Significantly, Davies cut the undertaking not to transgress sexual boundaries when she quoted the passage 20 years later, M. Llewelyn Davies, *The Women's Co-operative Guild* (Kirkby Lonsdale: WCG, 1904, p. 10).

20. In addition to middle-class women like Mrs Acland, many of these founder members were related to prominent working-class Co-operative men, notably, Miss Greenwood, daughter of a Rochdale pioneer; Miss Holyoake, daughter of veteran Co-operator, G.J. Holyoake; MLD, *The WCG*, pp. 12 and 19.

21. 'Report of Women's Guild', *Co-operative Congress Report (CCR)*, 1892, p. 56.

22. Sarah Reddish speaking at a joint meeting of the Co-operative Union Educational Committee and the WCG at the 1894 Co-operative Congress, 'Education and the Women's Guild', *CCR*, 1894, p. 139.

23. 'Report of Women's Guild', *CCR*, 1894, p. 56.

24. Ibid.

25. WCG deputation to the Central Board, *CCR*, 1894, p. 3.

26. Usually as part of the Society's education budget. As Sarah Reddish argued: 'By means of the Women's Guild, we are endeavouring to bring into active life the great body of women in the Co-operative movement. ... Having such an object in view, each local branch of the Guild has, I hold, a claim on the attention and support of the Educational Committee of its own Society.' Miss Reddish, *Women's Guilds With Special Reference to their Claims on the Attention and Support of Educational Committees*, Co-operative Educational Committees' Association Annual Meeting, Bolton, Henry Smith, 1890, p. 4.

27. 'Northern Section Guild Report,' *CCR*, 1896, p. 61.

28. By 1914, there were 32,182 members and 600 branches; apart from levelling out during the 1914–18 war, this upward curve continued until the end of the 1930s, *Annual Reports of the WCG*.

29. MLD, *The WCG*, p. 65.

30. MLD, 'Co-operation at the Fountainhead', 'Material ...' (see note 1).

31. Cole, op. cit., p. 217.
32. WCG, *How to Start and Work a Branch* (Kirkby Lonsdale: WCG, 1896, p. 3).
33. In particular, the Women's Trade Union League, and the Women's Trade Union Association (both formed in 1889 from the earlier Women's Protective and Provident League), and the Women's Industrial Council (founded in 1894). For a full account of the development of these groups and their links with organized feminism, see Gerry Holloway, 'A Common Cause? Class Dynamics in the Industrial Women's Movement 1888–1918', Sussex University D.Phil. Thesis, 1995, chapters 1 and 2.
34. WCG, *Annual Report*, 1892–93, p. 4.
35. 'Report of Women's Guild', *CCR*, 1894, pp. 111 and 93.
36. 'Miss M. Llewelyn Davies', *Minutes of Evidence taken before the Royal Commission on Divorce and Matrimonial Causes, Minutes of Evidence* (1912), 3 (Cd. 6481) PP 1912–13, XX, p. 149.
37. For example: 'Two branches have had writing classes,' 'Report of Women's Guild', *CCR*, 1891, p. 42.
38. R. Nash, *The Position of Married Women* (Manchester: CWS Printing Works, 1907).
39. MLD, MS article for *Norges Kvinder* (Norwegian women's paper), 1931, 'Material ...'. (see note 1), 1, item 39.
40. Margaret McMillan (1860–1931) socialist and educational reformer, see C. Steedman, *Childhood, Culture and Class in Britain: Margaret McMillan 1860–1931* (London: Virago, 1990); Gertrude Tuckwell (1861–1951) president of the WTUL following the death of her aunt, its benefactor, Lady Dilke in 1904, *DLB*, VI, 1982; the NFWW was a general labour union for women workers, Mary Macarthur (1880–1921), its most dynamic leader, *DLB*, II, 1974; Helena Swanwick (1864–1939), prominent figure in the NUWSS, and editor of its journal, *The Common Cause*, from its foundation in 1909 to 1912, *DLB*, IV, 1977.
41. C. Collette, *For Labour and For Women: The Women's Labour League, 1906–1918* (Manchester University Press, 1989).
42. MLD & Dr Ethel Bentham (WLL) took seats on the dais while Cllr. Lansbury put questions on their behalf, 'Women Invade LCC', *Co-operative News*, 4 February 1911, p. 144.
43. L.T. Hobhouse & Leonard Woolf, for example, *Co-operative News*, 20 September 1913, p. 1282 (see Chapter 2).
44. MLD to L. Woolf, n.d. (?1914), Monks House Papers, University of Sussex.
45. P. Thane, 'Visions of gender in the making of the British welfare state: the case of women in the British Labour Party and social policy, 1906–1945', in G. Bock & P. Thane (eds.), *Maternity and*

Gender Policies: Women and the Rise of the European Welfare States, 1880–1950s (London: Routledge, 1991); P. Thane, 'Women in the British Labour Party and the Construction of State Welfare', in S. Koven & S. Michel (eds.), *Mothers of a New World: Maternalist Politics and the Origins of Welfare States* (London: Routledge, 1993).

46. P. Graves, *Labour Women in British Working-Class Politics 1918–39* (Cambridge University Press, 1994, chapter 3).

47. Contrary to the claim that the Guild was affiliated to the Labour Party from 1918, see M. Pugh, *Women and the Women's Movement in Britain 1914–1959* (London: Macmillan, 1993, p. 168).

48. Marion Phillips (1881–1932), *DLB*, V, 1979 (see Chapter 6).

49. Cole, op. cit., p. 324.

50. Formed in August 1920, with about 10,000 members. See L.J. Macfarlane, *The British Communist Party: Its Origin and Development until 1929* (London: MacGibbon & Kee, 1966); H. Dewar, *Communist Politics in Britain: the CPGB from its Origins to the Second World War* (London: Pluto, 1976).

51. McKibbin, op. cit., pp. 178–91.

52. Graves notes the Guild's tradition of independence under Davies (while overlooking her retirement in 1922) but her remarks about the Guild's relationship with the movement are based on the mistaken assumption that the Co-operative Union and the Co-operative Party were one and the same thing. Graves, op. cit., chapter 1.

53. A working relationship of this kind could have provided the labour movement with such facilities as investment, banking, and the distribution of food and benefits to strikers, McKibbin, op. cit., pp. 43–7. It should not be assumed from these initiatives, however, that the Labour and Co-operative leadership, any more than their trade-union counterparts, were sanguine about the rank-and-file militancy of these years. See Hinton, op. cit., chapter 5.

54. Tax exemption had been granted through the Industrial and Provident Societies Act, passed in 1862 and refined in 1892. For an analysis of this shift from political neutrality, see Cole, op. cit., p. 315; S. Pollard, 'The Foundation of the Co-operative Party,' in A. Briggs & J. Saville (eds.), *Essays in Labour History*, 2, 1886–1923 (London: Macmillan, 1971); T. Adams, 'The Formation of the Co-operative Party Re-considered', *International Review of Social History*, XXXII, 1987–81, pp. 48–68; McKibbin, op. cit., pp. 178–80.

55. In 1918, 563 Societies affiliated to the Co-operative Party but this figure dropped to 393 in 1924 before slowly increasing again; Cole, op. cit., pp. 320 and 331.

56. Carr Saunders *et al.*, op. cit., p. 212.

57. McKibbin, op. cit., pp. 181–3.

58. Cole, op. cit., p. 321.

59. 'Miss M. Llewelyn Davies', *Royal Commission on Divorce*, p. 149.
60. H. Perkin, *The Rise of Professional Society: England since 1880* (London: Routledge, 1989, p. 35).
61. J. Lewis, *Women in England 1870–1950: Sexual Divisions and Social Change* (Brighton: Wheatsheaf, 1984, p. 3).
62. Ibid., chapter 4.
63. MLD, 'Introduction', in M. Llewelyn Davies (ed.), *Maternity: Letters from Working Women* (1915), (London: Virago, 1978, pp. 1 and 8).
64. From 1881 the census returns began to classify women not in paid employment as 'unoccupied', an innovation which sharply reduced the apparent economic activity rates for women, Lewis, op. cit., p. 146.
65. And not 'dragged into competition for livelihood against the great and strong men of the world.' Henry Broadhurst speaking to the TUC in 1875, quoted in S. Boston, *Women Workers and the Trade Unions* (London: Lawrence & Wishart, 1987, p. 16).
66. MLD, 'Preface', in C. Webb, *The Woman with the Basket: the History of the Women's Co-operative Guild* (Manchester: The Guild, 1927).

Chapter Two

Vision

It is evident from even a cursory review of the history of the WCG that Margaret Llewelyn Davies (1861–1944) was the dynamic force behind its most progressive achievements. During her years as General Secretary, from 1889 to 1921, it grew from the relatively modest role envisaged by its founders to gain a national reputation as an autonomous women's section of the working-class movement. Those who took her work seriously, and attempted to give an account of it, found themselves reaching for superlatives that would do justice to her. 'In personal quality and in disinterested idealism', wrote G.D.H. Cole in 1944, 'Margaret Llewelyn Davies is, to my thinking, by far the greatest woman who has been actively identified with the British Co-operative Movement. From the moment when she assumed control of the affairs of the Women's Guild it began to become a really progressive force.'[1] Leonard Woolf considered her 'one of the most eminent women I have known', who had 'created something of great value – and at the same time unique – in the Guild.'[2]

So who was Margaret Llewelyn Davies, and what was her political project? Despite her achievements in the Guild, and her membership of a circle that included such luminaries as the Coles, the Woolfs, the Webbs, Bertrand Russell, Keir Hardie and Ramsay MacDonald, Davies is a relatively obscure historical figure. Woolf attributed this to her sex. 'Had she been a man', he wrote, 'her achievements would have filled probably half a page in *Who's Who*; though she lived to be over 70, you will not find the name of Margaret Llewelyn Davies in any edition of it.'[3] Yet the lives of such female contemporaries as Beatrice Webb, the Pankhursts, and

Eleanor Rathbone have been well-documented in biographical and autobiographical studies (if not *Who's Who*). Davies, however, was a woman with an aversion to publicity: moulded by a Victorian ethos of disinterested public service, she left little in the way of private papers or memoirs for would-be biographers.[4] In addition, her political career unfolded in the Co-operative movement which, although not actually concealed from the historian, has tended to occupy a marginal position in both labour and feminist research.

The most substantial source for Davies are the records of the WCG, and even there it is necessary to read against the grain of her instinctive self-effacement. She consistently emphasized the contribution of the membership, either ignoring her own role, or treating it as that of a mere functionary. Her modesty was well known. 'Considering the authorship', noted a reviewer of Davies' 1904 Guild history,[5] 'the reader is not surprised to find a conspicuous blank as to the part played by the present General Secretary.' A range of important innovations, it seemed, 'happened of themselves', or were 'started and carried on by nobody in particular'. The story unfolded so smoothly, and with so few interventions, that 'one would almost conclude it was an easy matter to organize a body of nearly 19,000 working women, were it not for the fact that such an organization is rare, or we think it may be said, unique.'[6]

An obvious initial question about Margaret Llewelyn Davies is what made this upper-middle-class-Victorian woman able and willing to invest 30 years of her life in a working-class women's organization? Davies' birthright was a combination of privilege and enlightenment which bestowed upon her numerous advantages. Leonard Woolf found her family 'remarkable'; all 'extremely intelligent, finely built, beautiful', they had 'great personal charm, immense energy' and were 'unlike so many serious and good people, amusing and interesting, companionable and lovable.'[7] Margaret was well endowed with these family traits. 'Tall, gracious, with a deep, pleasant voice and a personality which commanded respect and admiration',[8] she possessed 'immense energy and enthusiasm', 'a deep contralto spontaneous laugh', a 'fresh English beauty of hair and eyes and skin', and 'chiselled classical features'.[9] She had 'an extraordinarily vivid personality', 'immense vitality and gaiety in all that she did' and was 'much loved by all who knew her'.[10]

Critically, from the point of view of the WCG, Davies' upbringing gave her a highly developed social conscience, and a degree of independence unimaginable for the majority of women of her time. The Llewelyn Davies family was firmly embedded in the 19th-century radical intelligentsia, and she grew up in 'a fine grand atmosphere',[11] of 'advanced social and religious thought'.[12] The paterfamilias, the Reverend John Llewelyn Davies (1826–1916), was a scholar,[13] theologian, fellow of Trinity College, Cambridge, and a Christian Socialist. A broad church Anglican, he was one of the growing number of clerics in the mid-century who condemned poverty and inequality, and sought to use the church as an instrument for combating the ills of industrial society.[14] With other Christian Socialists he was involved in efforts to stimulate working-class association – early producers' and consumers' co-operatives – and in the foundation of the London Working Men's College in 1854;[15] he was also an earnest supporter of trade unionism. A 'strong but independent Liberal', his friends and correspondents included Robert Browning, F.D. Maurice, John Ruskin, Tom Hughes, Charles Kingsley, Thomas Carlyle, Matthew Arnold, and J.S. Mill, who paid tribute to his 'intellectual and moral fairness' in controversy.[16]

Mary Crompton, who married J.L.Davies in 1859, was 'a woman with a remarkable brain ... remarkably independent in thought',[17] the daughter of Sir Charles Crompton, Judge of the Queen's Bench. The Cromptons were a prominent Unitarian family, long associated with progressive social attitudes and like the Davies family, supporters of women's emancipation. Mary's brother-in-law George Croom Robertson was an ally of J.S. Mill in the early attempts to secure the female suffrage; J.L.Davies, Principal of Queen's College, London, from 1873–4 and 1878–86, actively pioneered higher education for women and, like the rest of the family, was an ardent supporter of women's suffrage.[18]

Emily Davies (1830–1921), his younger sister, was a leading equal rights campaigner, and the founder of Girton College, Cambidge.[19] Margaret Llewelyn Davies respected her aunt's role as 'an opener-of-doors and a breaker-down of barriers', but commented drily that she wanted the vote 'more because she thought it infra dig for an employing lady not to have a Vote when her gardener did, than because the Vote was a protection from injustice and a weapon for reform'.[20]

Nevertheless, the family's commitment to women's rights gave Margaret opportunities denied as a matter of course even to the daughters of lettered men with otherwise impeccable liberal credentials.[21] The Llewelyn Davies family possessed the means to provide their six sons and one daughter with the best education available, which for Margaret meant Queen's College and Girton. Instead of assuming her destiny to be marriage and motherhood, both parents supported her determination to find a meaningful occupation outside the home, and given the family's financial resources the accent was on useful rather than gainful employment. Margaret's earliest acquisition of capital seems to have been a legacy of £3,000 from Charles Crompton in 1892, and the net worth of her will at her death in 1944 was £20,725. There was never any need for her to earn a living.[22]

After Cambridge, Margaret returned to Marylebone, where her father was rector of Christ Church. Drawn, like other middle-class women in the 1880s,[23] to the expanding area of social work, she was occupied for a time as a volunteer sanitary inspector.[24] With college friends she became involved in trying to start 'profit-sharing workshops' (producers' co-operatives), but these were unsuccessful and increasingly she was impressed by the social value of consumers' co-operation.[25]

By her own account, it was reading a book by the English Radical William Thornton, *On Labour*, that persuaded her in 1886 'to set her hand to active progressive work' by joining the Marylebone Co-operative Society.[26] Presumably, she was inspired by Thornton's account of Co-operation as the 'child of Socialism ... destined to beget, at however remote a date, a healthy Socialism as superior to itself in all its best attributes as itself is to its parent'.[27] She rapidly gravitated towards the Guild, serving as secretary of the newly formed Marylebone branch before her election as General Secretary in 1889. This soon became, she wrote, 'the pivot of my work',[28] and so it was to remain for more than three decades.

Davies was well placed to take on this minor appendage of the Co-operative movement and transform it into an effective organization. Not the least of her assets was her freedom to ensure that her time, 'that commodity much needed by working women', could be placed at the disposal of the Guild.[29] In the year she became General Secretary, the family moved out of London. J.L. Davies, said to have sacrificed a promising ecclesiastical career when he delivered 'a blistering attack on imperialism' in a sermon he gave before Queen Victoria, left Marylebone not for a Bishop's See, as had been expected, but for the remote parish of Kirkby Lonsdale in Westmorland, a Trinity College living secured for him by his Cambridge friends.[30] There, Guild duties were integrated into the Llewelyn Davies household. Her father provided Margaret with a room on the ground floor of the vicarage in which to set up the Guild's first permanent office.[31] Not many clerks, so she confided in an article in Co-operative News, enjoyed such a pleasant environment: long, whitewashed, as befitted a 'factory', the walls lined with desks, cupboards, books, pictures and three windows looking out along an avenue of limes towards the village, from which on one memorable occasion the post was conveyed in a wheelbarrow, such was its volume![32]

Mary Davies also found ways of aiding the new General Secretary. Dutiful wife, mother of seven, and mistress of the vicarage, she was outwardly a conventional woman whose talents were known only to intimates, but towards her daughter she displayed feminist sympathies which widened Margaret's scope for self-development. While the bourgeois norm was for young women to remain glued to their mother's sides until separated by marriage, Mary was 'advanced' and 'unselfish' enough to relinquish the company of her only daughter. Thus relieved of time-consuming family obligations, Margaret 'would attend meetings and Co-op parties nearly every evening', while her office at the vicarage 'was swamped with pamphlets on various progressive questions of the day'.[33] Mary also made an annual subscription to the Guild,[34] and in 1893 a major donation. 'I saw an envelope on my chest of drawers', Margaret later recalled, 'looking inside I found a cheque for £100, with a note from my mother. She knew that what we needed at the time was a Guild organiser, and thus made it possible to offer this post to Miss Reddish, who held it for two years, and gave great stimulus to the work of the Guild.'[35]

In 1895 when her mother died, however, Margaret was claimed by familial obligations, and for the next two decades her father's welfare became her first concern:[36] his illness prevented her from attending the 1904 Guild Congress, for example.[37] They resided together in Kirkby Lonsdale until he retired in 1910, and then in Hampstead where he died in 1916.[38] As a single woman and the only sister, she was also claimed by other members of the family in times of need. In 1907 her brother Arthur died of cancer, almost a year after a tumour was found in his jaw. This was a great personal bereavement for Margaret: 'the memory of what Arthur was', she wrote 30 years later, 'is one of my most precious possessions'.[39] During the long months of his dying she was constantly in attendance, caring for the children, supporting his wife, and sitting at his bedside. Arthur's son, Peter,[40] later praised her 'unselfish and warm-hearted support',[41] recalling that other relatives were not much in evidence and all 'the dirty work was nobly shouldered by Margaret'.[42]

Family crises apart, Margaret continued Guild work on what was effectively a full-time basis. In Kirkby Lonsdale, moreover, she recruited an important ally and lifelong companion,[43] Lilian Harris, the daughter of a wealthy Bradford banker who had settled there in 1850.[44] 'I found her', Margaret told Guild Congress delegates in 1922, 'sitting at home in the lovely country of Westmorland, trying to occupy herself with carving and embroidery'.[45] Lilian Harris soon proved to be a formidable organizer, officially as Cashier from 1893, and Assistant Secretary from 1901.[46] It was Lilian Harris who, after considerable research on 'trade union and women's organizations', was largely responsible for the Guild constitution,[47] and who drew large coloured maps which were used in visits to new branches to explain the layout of districts and sections.[48] At their joint retirement in 1922 Davies paid tribute to her: 'Whether it has been economic problems, co-operative and democratic ideals, "Bradshaw" conundrums[49] – (laughter) – Congress organisation, branch dilemmas, mysteries of accounts, one and all have turned to Miss Harris and relied on her for guidance and help.'[50] Virginia Woolf thought her 'extremely sensible and unselfish, and independent';[51] Lilian Harris was to Congress, Woolf recalled, having seen her in action at Newcastle in 1913, 'what the heart is to the remoter veins'.[52]

The pattern of life Davies thus settled into – care for an ageing parent combined with running the Guild from home, and a close friendship with a woman whose life and interests straddled both worlds – facilitated an equilibrium between private and public commitments that often proved elusive for her contemporaries. Many of the women who put their energy into the working-class movement in the 1890s sooner or later faced an unhappy choice between marriage and career.[53] The life of an activist was often relentlessly lacking in nurture and comfort, with 'constant open-air speaking, constant journeying, poor food, uncomfortable quarters',[54] and the sacrifice of close bonds with other individuals, all taking a toll. Alternatively, marriage, even to the most progressive young man, usually carried expectations of domesticity and motherhood which almost invariably ruled out political activity.[55] Only an exceptional partnership, such as that crafted by the Webbs,[56] would have provided Davies with the combination of freedom and security she enjoyed, and of which the WCG was the obvious beneficiary.

Nurture as well as nature furnished Davies with personal qualities which made her an outstanding leader. She was a skilful communicator: lucid, fluent and persuasive in writing and in speech in ways that bore the imprint of her parents' influence as well as her formal education. The Rev. Davies' preaching 'was not rhetorical and made no parade of learning', but was remarkable for its 'depth of conviction, independence of thought, and an unfailing clearness of exposition',[57] qualities that are evident in Margaret's work, and in the advice she gave to Leonard Woolf, as a novice journalist, about an article he was offering to Co-operative News. 'It might be as well to leave out the Latin quotation?' she asked, adding of another sentence, 'I think it isn't quite clear enough.'[58] Within the family circle, her mother, a great reader of literature and poetry, was admired for her ability to transform 'dry and difficult' passages into 'things of interest and excitement and beauty, reading aloud so well and so naturally, explaining any difficult parts or words so simply'[59] – talents which her daughter also manifested 'with her clear ringing tones', her 'beautiful voice', and her fondness for incorporating illustrative lines of poetry into her texts.[60]

For Woolf, Davies embodied 'that strange and usually inexplicable phenomenon, "a born leader"', in her ability 'to inspire thousands of uneducated women with her own passion ... for liberty, equality, and fraternity.'[61] Many guildswomen, like the members of Lincoln Central Branch, looked back on a visit from the General Secretary as a landmark in their history: 'The eloquence of Miss Llewelyn Davies that evening', wrote the author of the branch's 'coming of age' history in 1913, 'inspired some of the women to strive to attain the ideals set before them, to which end they have worked untiringly.'[62] The letters written by guildswomen when she retired also signal their appreciation of her warmth, her humour, and her unusual facility for relating without condescension or patronage to women from different backgrounds. A member from Aintree recalled a particularly resonant moment in one of her early talks: 'I remember you saying that our husbands would be willing to stay in one night a week to let us go out to the Guild and if there happened to be one who could not be persuaded to give up an evening to his wife, you quoted a verse which I cannot now remember except that it ended with "well then give him the rolling pin"'. Sarah McArd of Liverpool wrote to her: 'You are in my opinion, although only a humble rank & filer, *A Nobleminded Woman.*' 'I feel', wrote Mrs Beresford, 'I have lost a friend for I always felt able to speak so naturally to you no matter what the subject and I am sorry to say it is not always so with officials.'[63]

Davies' charm and eloquence were conditioned by the ethical values that Woolf, not himself a frivolous person, characterized as the Llewelyn Davies' almost 'fanatical ... integrity and high principles', J.L. Davies' 'austere sense of social responsibility', and the 'terribly serious' and 'austere' side of Margaret's nature.[64] The family had little time for self-centred sentiment. Any notion of the egotistical pursuit of happiness, or self-aggrandizement seems to have been alien, and personal fulfillment meaningful only in the context of public duty. 'I am sure', observed a family friend, of Mary Davies' compliance with Margaret's long round of meetings, 'she hardly breathed it to herself that she would have liked the feminine companionship of a daughter and her help.'[65] Margaret's own emotional self-discipline was revealed to her sister-in-law during Arthur's cancer. Sylvia, apparently made of less stern stuff herself, confided to a friend that Margaret's '"luxury of woe" attitude nearly killed her and her intenseness about everything'.[66]

Yet Davies was by no means lacking in empathy or emotional sensitivity in response to the distress of others. The guildswomen she worked with never doubted her compassion; neither did Leonard Woolf who received vital support from her during one of Virginia's mental breakdowns. 'I should like', he began, in a letter to her in September 1915, 'to tell you what you've done for us both these last months and what we feel about it and to you but it's impossible.'[67] His feelings were echoed by Virginia: 'all through that terrible time I thought of you, and wanted to look at a picture of you, but was afraid to ask! You saved Leonard I think, for which I shall always bless you, by giving him things to do. It seems odd, for I know you so little, but I felt you had a grasp on me, and I could not utterly sink. I write this because I do not want to say it, and yet I think you will like to know it.'[68]

Davies' austerity, her disavowal of what she would have regarded as self-indulgence, reflected not a deficiency of sensibility but a personal philosophy that guided her whole life. 'Altruism', she once wrote, 'is the only finally satisfying course of conduct'.[69] As she preached, so she practiced. Cole highlighted her 'disinterested idealism',[70] and many of her fellow Co-operators were similarly struck by her unselfishness: the Birmingham Society President remembered her as 'a very capable organiser, and a self-sacrificing woman'.[71] Her nephew recalled that she had been 'a most distinguished figure in her day, and would have been more so had she not had her full share of that unwillingness to indulge in the normal vulgarities of ambition for which her family was remarkable'.[72]

The Llewelyn Davieses were not unique. In an age brimful of confidence in progress, many worthy Victorians nurtured sincere and unselfconscious desires to contribute to the social good, either bending their Christian faith towards social service or making a 'secular religion' of it.[73] Sidney Webb's self-proclaimed goal was 'never to act alone or for myself' but 'to feel at every moment that I am acting as a member of a committee and for that committee on behalf of larger human ends.'[74] Given the Victorian celebration of 'womanly self-sacrifice', this doctrine had resonance for those women who sought to escape the confines of the domestic sphere without compromising their feminine respectability.[75] Virginia Woolf discerned a quality 'praised and practised' by Victorian women: 'a negative one ... not to be recognized; not to be egotistical; to do the work for the sake of doing the work.'[76] Josephine Butler, for example, refused 'to have a life of herself written' and wrote of her fellow workers in the campaign against the Contagious Diseases Act that the 'utter absence in them of any desire for recognition, of any vestige of egotism in any form, is worthy of remark. In the purity of their motives they shine out "clear as crystal" '.[77]

While Davies' style of leadership echoed this tradition, its substance firmly refused any impulse towards philanthropic work. Those 'who are concerned with the problem of poverty', she noted, 'are beset with anxious and baffling problems.' There was the persistent drive to separate the deserving from the undeserving poor; there was the disappointing evidence that, however well-intentioned, charity tackled only the symptoms, not the cause of the problem. 'Is it possible', she wrote in 1904, 'that those who seek to help the poor are baffled because they are not ready for a remedy, involving deeper sacrifices than have yet been made, a change in life's conditions, when "the odious words 'rich' and 'poor' will be wiped out of our vocabulary?" Perhaps it is only by embracing and acting on such a belief that difficulties will disappear, and brotherly love be able to become simple, and free, and universal.'[78] Philanthropists, she might have added, looked only to 'improve' the poor; the point was to abolish the causes of poverty, and this conviction led Davies towards socialism.

By comparison with the other exceptional bourgeois women who became socialist converts in the late 19th century through encounters with New Unionism, the ILP and other socialist groups,[79] Davies' point of entry into the working-class movement was eminently moderate. Co-operation was established as an ultra-respectable institution of working-class self-help, closely associated with the Liberal Party, and a long way from the cutting edge of working-class politics. Yet for the young Margaret Llewelyn Davies, searching for an environment in which to develop a public role, it held out enormous potential as a vehicle of future social transformation.

Davies identified with that section of Co-operators who saw the movement as an embryonic industrial democracy.[80] Her convictions about the socialist character of Co-operation are set out in a paper, *The Relations between Co-operation and Socialistic*

Aspirations, which she delivered to the 1890 Co-operative Congress.[81] By socialism she meant the Fabian-statist model; there are no references to continental or English Marxism.[82] She argued that both Co-operation and socialism had a common lineage, citing the work of Robert Owen, 'the father' of both, and Lasalle's advocacy of 'co-operative productive workshops'. In essence, she claimed, the two systems were 'so much in harmony' as to be practically identical. Both were a response to the 'reign of free competition' ushered in by the industrial revolution – in which 'enormous fortunes' co-existed with 'poverty and degradation', capital was 'all triumphant, and labour was crushed under a remorseless tyranny' – and both aimed 'to substitute a system of association for one of competition'.

A system of association, the paper continued, would be superior in two respects. Firstly, it would bring a more rational and equitable economic system, based on collective forms of production and consumption that should eliminate the wastage endemic in the present system, improve the condition of the workers and hence the quality of their work, and ultimately generate more wealth. Secondly, there would be moral and intellectual gains. As 'a brotherhood', instead of 'a collection of warring atoms', society might satisfy basic human needs – 'food, comforts, leisure' – without causing suffering to others, and thus foster 'altruism', characterized by Davies as the 'highest human quality', instead of its antithesis: selfish competition.

Co-operators and socialists shared a common goal but differed in their methods, Co-operators advocating voluntary association and gradual education, socialists compulsory legislation. Davies was wary of state intervention, yet unconvinced that 'the monster of self-interest, with its many heads of competition, capitalism, landlordism, etc.' would be 'slain by the co-operative sword alone'. Co-operators possessed a seemingly limitless capacity to adapt to the competitive system, without ever restraining competition and self-interest. Socialism also faced 'immense practical difficulties', but at least it presented a comprehensive method, and Co-operators should consider its potential gains: 'however much there is to disgust in party politics', she reasoned, 'we should all, I think, be inclined to believe in the good results that might be obtained from Acts passed by an educated labour majority.'[83]

Davies' paper supposed that a socialist or co-operative system would free labour, and provide workers with 'an authoritative voice' as regards their conditions of employment; the agency which she envisaged achieving this goal, however, was not the organized working class but enlightened individuals, connected with the labour movement, in the legislature. Yet she expressed deep reservations about relying on the state for progressive reforms, and was by no means about to join the Fabians.[84] As she confessed to the delegates, some might 'fancy that she was more of a socialist than she could really say she was. She was merely a student of the question and did not see her way clearly at present.'[85] What began to clarify the question for her was not further study but active involvement with working women.

As well as satisfying Davies' appetite for constructive social work, the WCG opened up a space in which her ideals and aspirations continually rubbed up against basic organizational issues. Here was a fledgling organization that brought together the causes with which she had grown up – the advancement of working people, the rights of women – but in a form that for Davies represented a point of departure rather than arrival. Her feminist and socialist leanings were tested out and refined not in the abstract but as part of a concrete project. 'The Guild', she wrote in 1895, was most likely to attract those 'who combine some of the qualities of both worker and thinker ... whose theory is guided and shaped by practice and whose actions are illumined and harmonized by theory.'[86] She thus embarked on a journey from the middle-class sponsored Radical reformism of her family,[87] to a militant, even revolutionary, politics which identified the working class as the agent not the recipient of emancipation.

By the time she retired from the Guild, Davies' experience in the working-class movement, and the developments which she had witnessed both nationally and internationally, had brought her to an uncompromising set of socialist convictions. Gone was the uncertainty in her 1890 paper about how labour might be delivered from the tyranny of capital (by progressive legislation or by enlightened Co-operators), and in its place was complete confidence in the power of labour. '(T)he workers of every country', she wrote in 1920, were determined:

no longer to live at the mercy of a system which enriches the few and exploits the many. Industry, they declare, must be controlled by the People for the People. In one form or another, with varying transitional methods, they demand that the structure of the world which they were encouraged to hope for after the war, should be that of a real Industrial and Social Democracy. Whether this transformation of society will be peacefully accomplished depends on the attitude of the rich more than on the revolutionary desires of some sections of the people.[88]

The precise contours of Davies' political evolution during her years in the Guild must be inferred: at each end of her career as General Secretary she produced explicit political reflections, but in the intervening years virtually all her writing was concerned with specific Guild issues. Running through this output, however, are the themes which finally constituted her politics: the importance of organizational structure and grass-roots democracy; her insistence on the need for women's autonomy within the working-class movement; and her developing appreciation of the potential agency as well as the actual oppression of working-class women.

Davies attached great importance to self-government both in terms of the Guild's relationship with the Co-operative movement and in its internal workings. Her experience in the Guild, notably in the dispute over divorce law reform, convinced her that autonomy, the freedom to decide and implement policy untrammelled by officialdom, was especially important for a women's organization. It was equally necessary that the Guild's own constitution should protect rank-and-file autonomy as a check on autocratic leadership. There should be no compulsion on Guild branches to pursue policies with which they disagreed – a principle which Davies upheld even in matters which contradicted her own beliefs.[89] Conversely there should be democratic controls to ensure that the leadership pursued policies which accurately reflected the views and interests of the membership. 'In every Democracy', she wrote:

> there is a Platform and a Floor. If a Democracy is to flourish, the leaders must lead, and the rank-and-file must be keenly alive and taking an active part in the whole work. A Movement as a whole needs to be educated as well as

individuals, and this can only be brought about by vigorous and open-minded leadership joined with helpful and intelligent mass pressure on authority.[90]

While Davies recognized that there were some members who were 'not at all progressive',[91] she gained a basic confidence in the sound judgement of guildswomen which persuaded her that the appropriate policies – those which reflected the objective interests of working women – would be arrived at through a democratic constitution which facilitated the free expression of rank-and-file opinion.

Despite her commitment to the cause of working women, coming as she did from a protected (albeit enlightened) environment, the young General Secretary knew very little about the circumstances of their lives. Guild work, she later wrote, opened up for her 'a new world practically unknown to the well-to-do classes.'[92] Travelling around the country on speaking tours, and staying in the homes of members gave her access to the inner workings of family life, and convinced her that far from constituting a homogeneous social block, the working-class was riven by sexual divisions. She was 'primarily moved and shocked' by 'the grimness, hardship, narrowness of the lives to which most working-class wives and mothers were condemned.'[93] Often, she witnessed 'hard battles being waged against heavy odds, or the marks which such fights have left behind them … struggles with want, concealed under thick coverings of pride; daily work done under the weight of constant ill-health; unselfish devotion rewarded by lack of consideration.'[94] These impressions, fleshed out over the years by the personal details made public through Guild campaigns, thoroughly convinced Davies of the need for every effort to improve the situation. 'I have 200 letters from guildswomen giving their experiences over childbirth', she wrote to the Woolfs just before the war broke out. 'No one realises what their life is.'[95]

Determination to do something for these women was increasingly tempered by an appreciation of their ability to act for themselves. As 'she got to know them individually and in the mass,' Woolf explained, she was 'exhilarated to find in them great strength and resilience of character, great potentialities, not merely as human beings, but also as political animals.'[96] 'I seldom return from a Co-operative tour', Davies wrote in 1899, 'without feeling impressed ... by the great capacity – the practical wisdom and public spirit – which the guild is bringing out and turning to valuable account.'[97]

In these perceptions Davies was strongly influenced by women in the mill towns of Lancashire and Cheshire, the urban centres closest to her base in Kirkby Lonsdale. This centre of the industrial revolution was the heartland of Co-operation, with prosperous Societies in nearly every town; in addition, the large-scale employment of women in textiles had nourished a strong tradition of female trade unionism.[98] This was fertile soil for Guild organization with women like Mrs Bury, in her early teens a Lancashire mill-worker, later a Guild vice-president and a Poor Law Guardian, and Mrs Ashworth, for 21 years a Burnley cotton-weaver, president of the Doncaster Congress in 1894, playing a prominent role.[99] When Davies moved to the region in 1889, there were only 7 of a total of 50 Guild branches in the north; a decade later, the North Western Section accounted for 100 out of a total of 262 branches, and 6,600 of the 12,537 members.[100]

One of Davies' greatest allies was Sarah Reddish (1850–1928), an unusual woman whose life was shaped by a culture and a politics of working-class education and association that stretched back through her father to the Owenites. In certain respects her biography provides a working-class mirror of Davies' own. Her father was a prominent Co-operator, honorary librarian and secretary to the Bolton Society, who held enlightened views on the intellectual training of girls, and passed on to his daughter a passion for public work. There, however, the resemblances between the two women end, for Reddish began earning aged 11, as what she termed a 'disciple of the apostles' – an out-worker winding silk for her mother and neighbours to weave. She later worked in a cotton-spinning mill, as a 'winder', a 'reeler', and a 'roller-coverer', which included giving first aid to women injured by the machinery, and then as a forewoman in a hosiery factory. She was President of the Bolton Women's Guild from 1886–1901; a member of the Guild Central Committee from 1889–91 and 1895–8, and from 1893–5 its full-time paid organizer, courtesy of Mary Llewelyn Davies.[101] 'On Wednesday, February 27,' she reported in 1893, 'I paid a visit to our General Secretary at Kirkby

Lonsdale, and I was very soon introduced to the guild office, where there are letters, papers, and work almost unlimited in amount.'[102]

Reddish was an inspirational co-worker for the General Secretary, who shared and perhaps extended Davies' vision of what the Guild could achieve and how it could do it. A close bond developed between the two women. In her 1904 Guild history, Davies offered 'a slight tribute of affection and admiration for her character and untiring work';[103] and in 1928 she wrote of the death of 'my old friend Sarah Reddish', one of the most honoured names in the Guild annals, 'whose life was devoted to the causes of women and labour', and recalled sitting over the fire at Kirkby Lonsdale while Sarah Reddish dwelt upon 'the large Socialistic vision of a new life which filled her mind'.[104] Her ideas struck an immediate chord with Davies. For Reddish the 'first and highest duty' was the 'sacred duty of each to labour for and promote the highest good of society, and that of society to promote the highest good of each individual comprising it'; their 'best efforts' should be used to bring about 'universal Co-operation' to ensure 'that poverty and idleness should disappear from the land; that idleness should no longer glitter in the palace and virtue droop in the hovel; that man's inhumanity to man be a thing only of the past.'[105]

Davies' appreciation of working-class women's aptitude for political activity combined with her growing awareness of the suffering that many endured to inform the conviction that they needed their own organization within the working-class movement. Yet the status and influence that the Guild had acquired by 1914 did not come about through the spontaneous action of the membership, but through intelligent campaigning work of which Davies herself was the main author. Under her leadership from about 1900 there were radical initiatives within the Co-operative movement to extend Co-operation to the poorest sections of the working class,[106] and to improve the conditions of female workers in the movement;[107] and then pioneering work to improve the situation of married working women through divorce law reform and maternity benefit. Davies' political and organizational skills were critical during these years. 'Much of her work', read an official appreciation, 'was done unknown to the movement at large. It would be impossible to estimate the number of papers sent out by the general secretary for discussion at Guild conferences, and sufficient energy followed these papers to make them powerful factors in co-operative developments.'[108]

The General Secretary was the key player not only in the choice of subjects, but in the strategic direction and tactical detail of the intense, precisely focused campaigns on which the Guild's reputation was built. These were Davies' speciality, and demonstrate the political agility and sophistication of her leadership. The first step was always to secure an internal consensus through educational work which served to strengthen and unite the organization around a common purpose, while at the same time legitimizing the demand being advanced. Then began the work of persuading others, and in this respect the General Secretary's social capital was a great asset.

Davies was in touch with many of the most progressive figures of the period. You 'seem to see the whole of the rest of London in your various country residences from Hobhouse to Ponsonby', Leonard Woolf once wrote to her.[109] She was a visitor to the home of the McMillan sisters, Margaret and Rachel,[110] and when Woolf started out in journalism, Davies offered him introductions to a range of prominent labour people, including Ramsay Macdonald, Keir Hardie, and the editors of the *Daily Herald* and the *Labour Leader* (presumably George Lansbury and Fenner Brockway, respectively).[111] Such people were well placed to be of assistance, and Davies had no reservations about exploiting influential connections when necessary. The economist J.A. Hobson could be persuaded to write on the Guild's demand for a minimum wage for Co-operative women workers in *Co-operative News*;[112] the Guild's position on maternity benefit could be explained in the correspondence columns of *The Times*,[113] and to Lloyd George at the Webb's dinner table (she considered the Webbs 'wire pullers' whose support was 'amusing' but 'valuable'); and as Virginia Woolf, pressed into service for suffrage work in 1913, confided to Lady Robert Cecil, Davies could 'compel a steam roller to waltz.'[114]

By the 1910s Davies had arrived at a strong sense of the Guild as part of a workers' movement that had international as well as national dimensions. In this, she was evidently inspired and influenced by political activists well to the left of her Fabian and Liberal acquaintances, and of whom she wrote freely to Leonard

Woolf. James Larkin, the Dublin Syndicalist, made a great impact upon her: 'Larkin is most interesting, so impressive. You feel he is somehow "the people marching on" – glorious'.[115] She was equally struck by 'the glorious success of that wonderful fragile Sylvia Pankhurst'; the East London Suffrage Federation (led by Pankhurst and Lansbury), was the 'best one going', Davies wrote to Woolf, 'and I'm going to subscribe'.[116] Also 'glorious' was the speech given by Alexandra Kollontai at the Guild conference she attended in November 1913. 'I am very sorry she had to leave –', Davies wrote afterwards, 'she says her life is not her own and she has to go where Russian friends send her. I wanted to know more of her and her work. She was clever and particularly charming.'[117]

Davies' confidence in political progress was undoubtedly damaged by the war, which left her a confirmed pacifist. 'The only refuge to be found in the appallingness of things', she wrote to Woolf at the outset, 'is in the thought of a new civilisation without armaments and war being built up on the ruin now coming. If this could be I feel we must be ready to sacrifice everything but my horrible fear is that we shall just sink back again.'[118] In 1915, Davies was one of the left-wing feminists involved in setting up the anti-war British Committee of the International Women's Congress;[119] with other guildswomen, she attempted, unsuccessfully, to win anti-militarist positions at Guild Congresses.[120]

Militant affiliations continued on a rising note after 1918. Congress that year passed a resolution 'welcoming the Russian Revolution'.[121] In August 1920 the CC sent telegrams to the Prime Minister, and to the Miners' International Congress in Geneva, and a letter to the press, all protesting the threat of war against Russia over Poland, and some guildswomen participated in local 'Councils of Action'.[122] In September the CC condemned the government's breach of faith over the Sankey Report and its failure to prevent wartime profiteering in the mining industry.[123] At the same meeting a CC resolution on Ireland condemned the government's 'suppression of national aspirations by methods which have reached an intolerable brutality', and demanded military withdrawal, the release of the hunger strikers, and the right of self-determination for the Irish people; a strong resolution of protest was subsequently passed by All Councils (the annual gathering of Sectional Councils), and sent to the Prime Minister, the Chief Secretary for Ireland, and the press.[124] During Leonard Woolf's brief career as a parliamentary candidate, Davies privately took him to task for a draft address in which he denounced murder on either side in Ireland. 'I do hope you wont [sic] get in', she wrote, and then explained, 'I cannot, as an English-woman condemn acts which we have caused. Nor do I think that actions by oppressed and oppressors are on the same plane'.[125]

In 1922, the year after her retirement, Davies was honoured as the first woman president of the Co-operative Congress, and used her address to set out her political stall.[126] It was an emotional occasion. When she stood to give her address, she received a loud standing ovation which clearly moved her. 'However, her lips trembled but a moment, and then she opened clearly and distinctly. She said she interpreted the welcome accorded to her, as one who had never sat in the seats of the mighty – (laughter) – as a recognition of the position which the rank and file held in democracy: it was a tribute to the democratic character of co-operation.'[127] Afterwards, the chairman presented her with an illuminated address, and paid fulsome tribute to her work: her name, he said, would always be remembered among the great. 'Up got Margaret', wrote Virginia Woolf, a member of the audience, 'and said with great spirit, and some gratitude, but she was far from obsequious, "Not my name but the names of Mrs Laurenson, Mrs Reddish etc., etc."' She would accept the volume only 'because it identified her with that host of other women without whom she would have been nothing'.[128]

In her address, Davies discussed the world situation, the revolutionary potential of the Co-operative movement, and the role of self-governing, rank-and-file organizations like the Guild in realizing that potential. She began with a class analysis of the post-war world. The weakness of capitalism was apparent in the weakness of its post-war recovery, but that in turn meant that labour was being squeezed by high unemployment; in Britain the recent defeats had enabled employers to take advantage of the 'temporarily crippled position of the workers' and claim 'autocratic power'.[129] Russia, however, had become 'the first nation where co-operation had been accepted as the dominant industrial system', a gain which had not only to be defended but extended: the world had become 'one large market' and unless international trade was conducted on 'non-profit making and democratic lines, any country socialising its industry', as was Russia, 'might have its supplies cut off by the action of capitalistic countries.' In such confrontational circumstances, there was no middle ground: 'We are working', she insisted, 'for no patchwork modifications, for no "reconciliation of capital and labour," for no "infusion of a better spirit" into old industrial forms.' The rallying cry for the whole Labour world is the replacement of capitalism by an industrial democracy producing for use. Co-operation supplies the means to transfer

> the power of capitalism into the hands of the people organised democratically as consumers; makes capital the servant of labour; allows for a partnership with the workers; abolishes profit, socialises rent, and will ultimately get rid of the present wages system. It opens the great portals of international trade in such a way that all nations may pass through it fraternally together. *It gives real power to our political democracy by the creation of an economic democracy.* Co-operation is surely subversive enough for the violent revolutionary, orderly enough for the pacifist reformer.

Co-operation, she insisted, was not, in essence, a reformist movement. Its two main principles – the abolition of profit and democratic control – marked it out 'as nothing less than a revolution, so fundamental, vital, and transforming is the change it is effecting in the economic structure of society.' Yet this 'revolutionary character' had not been generally grasped. Just as higher wages had blinded trade unionists to the 'larger possibilities of trade unionism' so Co-operators' personal gains from saving-by-spending obscured 'the wider outcome of their action'. Furthermore, the movement was prone to reactionary forms which had to be guarded against: a 'tendency to bureaucracy', and to act as 'autocratic employers' instead of extending to co-operative employees 'a recognised share of control over their own working lives'. The pressing task was therefore the development of democratic forces to promote the movement's revolutionary potential: 'We must secure a rank and file which will act as a rational and courageous critic, and at the same time give loyal support in times of difficulty, and enthusiastic backing to progressive policies.'

These remarks not only constitute a sharp contrast with her views back in 1890, but also disclose the nature of Davies' project as it had evolved during the intervening three decades in the Guild. The creation of active and critical rank-and-file organizations was, for her, fundamental to the 'development of democracy' and should be the priority of the various wings of the working-class movement.[130] Her first premise was that guildswomen or, by extension, working-class women naturally inclined to the policies that would benefit their class and their sex. Married working women, she later wrote, 'belong to the class that, consciously or unconsciously, stands for the re-construction of society.'[131] In their normal circumstances, ignorance and isolation prevented them achieving this consciousness, but like water finding its own level, once opportunities for association and informed reflection were created, they would inevitably tend towards the positions that objectively corresponded to their interests. Being made up of married Co-operative women, she wrote in 1920, the Guild had '*naturally* [my emphasis] become a sort of trade union for married women'.[132] The Guild's advanced position on divorce, for example, derived from the fact that the women were 'dealing with what they know – with questions which concern them'.[133] By implication, guildswomen would gradually become, if not full-blown socialists, then increasingly sympathetic to socialist ideas.

For Davies, the fostering of vigorous and enlightened rank-and-file movements involved two essential elements: the constitutional machinery to guarantee democratic procedures and 'adult mass education'. It is in relation to workers' education that Davies came closest to discussing politics and political education in rank-and-file movements. Education was certainly not conceived of as the transmission of a value-free body of knowledge, but instead as 'frankly based on the sectional point of view': to 'show the common aim of all to be the abolition of capitalism and the building of a world founded on brotherhood and freedom'.[134]

In 1933, Davies set out her ideas on Guild education for a German publication. She rejected as 'entirely unsuitable' the mainstream education provided to schoolchildren and students, 'with its tests of efficiency, its subjects, its methods of State control and financial support'. Education 'for married working women (and of the adult rank and file of workers in general)', she wrote, 'must take into account the capitalist foundation on which present-day society rests.' Education for guildswomen should proceed from what is 'concrete and affecting their everyday life. It is frankly biassed in favour of a social system founded on fellowship, and it should, in the main, be thoroughly practical. Its acknowledged basis must be the co-operative principle of organizing industry and social life by the people for the people, until such time as real industrial and political democracy has been established, till far greater equality of income has been obtained, and class distinction abolished. When such a situation is reached our educational ideas and methods will be transformed.'[135]

Certain of these ideas had been rehearsed in 1913 when the Guild CC launched an initiative to stimulate rank-and-file education. In an introductory paper, Davies counterposed the 'poor kind of polish' of 'an education rooted in social prejudices' to the abundance of common sense and practical experience found among guildswomen. However, she pointed out that guildswomen were also 'seekers', 'greedy for knowledge', and possessed of 'the desire to be able to "express themselves" '. They knew:

what it is to feel mentally as if we were beating in darkness against bars, and we can see the power which knowledge and training give, and the freedom which comes with enlighten- ment. Even a little knowledge is a blessedly dangerous thing. It causes a smouldering discontent which may flame into active rebellion against a low level of life, and produces a demand, however stammering, for more interests and chances. Where we see ferment, there has been some of the yeast of education.

Almost invariably, this ferment was 'accompanied by some form of organized fellowship. Workers' movements and women's movements are the result of the education which has been going on, and are upheavals by which a higher standard of life and thought is being reached.'[136]

The objective, then, was an educated membership. But the education of 30,000 women was no easy matter so the first step would be to hold schools for 'Guides' who would then go back to the branches. Guides, Davies explained in an address, were different from teachers. 'A "guide" opened out the road to be travelled, and showed the vision, the kind of ideal, for which the Guild was out. At the present time there was great unrest going on in the country in what were known as the labour and the women's movement, and through the co-operative movement they (the Guild members) must learn to take their parts in these movements.'[137] These aspirations were evident in the programme of the first 'School for Guides', held at the Guild offices in October 1913: Helena Swanwick[138] on 'The Law and Problems Relating to the Married Working Woman', and Margaret Bondfield on 'Local Government in Relation to Maternity', while forthcoming papers included Leonard Woolf on 'Syndicalism' and L.T. Hobhouse on 'The Labour Movement.'[139]

This was Davies' most explicit attempt to produce a layer of Guild members who would be actively engaged in fostering radical commitments within the organization, notably, to women's equality and to workers' control. Yet the wider political analysis informing this choice of subjects was only spelt out at the general level of 'work for women and labour', and not in terms of the variety of political positions and strategies that could be adopted in relation to those questions. There were good reasons for this avoidance of explicit political debate, indeed, given the Co-operative movement's formal commitment to political neutrality, and the very uneven level of political awareness across the Guild organization, it is difficult to see how such a debate might have been accomplished. But apart from these constraints, it is possible to identify in Davies' method a set of assumptions about the nature of the rank and file and the role of leadership that perhaps made politics less of a pressing issue than might otherwise have been the case. In her work as General Secretary, Davies, it would appear, conceived of her own political positions as synonymous with the interests of the membership. While she recognized that the organization contained political differences, she believed that with sufficient time and conducive circumstances, those interests would ultimately express themselves in a common political position. A democratic culture, underwritten by a carefully crafted constitution, would be sufficient to guarantee the requisite policy and ideological content, and thus the long-term future of the Guild project.

Davies' emphasis upon democratic form rather than political substance was deeply in harmony with her self-effacing style of leadership. Her personal modesty and her confidence in the rank and file led her to behave as though her own importance was as a useful coordinator rather than a pivotal inspiration, historically and politically invisible except as a facilitator of the latent capacities in working women. This perspective flourished in the pre-war years as the mounting industrial unrest, and the associated political radicalism of the moment, impacted on the Guild membership to push it politically closer to Davies' position, a convergence that would have served to strengthen her conviction that, given the appropriate structures, a working-class women's organization would 'naturally' incline towards socialism. It also provided further grounds for erasing her own significance, and, by extension, that of any other leadership. But Davies' unwillingness to acknowledge fully the power of leadership in the Guild blinded her to the possibility that she might be succeeded by leaders who, firstly, might be possessed of different political priorities, and secondly, might prove capable of capturing and transforming both the democratic organizational shell, and the progressive kernel.

Davies' priority was to enable working women to become conscious of their objective situation and to intervene to change it; so long as she was in charge, the Guild's progressive agenda was assured. Once she departed from the organization, however, it became apparent that Davies was mistaken in her belief that structures, carefully designed to facilitate the 'natural' evolution of debate, would be sufficient to secure the Guild's politics. Despite all her efforts to embed in the Guild's constitution a set of core values that would ensure the survival of the project to which she was committed, Davies underestimated the importance of her own contribution as leader. As the subsequent history of the Guild was to demonstrate, on its own a working-class constituency was no guarantee that the women who were drawn into active life and reached positions of influence in the Guild would subscribe to the same progressive and democratic values that Davies had advocated.

Notes

1. G.D.H. Cole, *A Century of Co-operation*, (Manchester: George Allen & Unwin, 1944, p. 218). The high regard was reciprocal. Recommending Cole's *The World of Labour* (1913) to Leonard

Woolf, Davies commented: 'How does a fellow of Magdalen come to be able to write so much to the point? Who is he – we must get to know him.' MLD to L.Woolf, 26 November (?1913), Monks House Papers (MHP), University of Sussex. By contrast, Quentin Bell, who would seem not to have appreciated Davies, or her work, characterized her as 'a battleaxe and a bore', a verdict which could hardly reflect first-hand knowledge (he was born in 1910), see H. Lee, *Virginia Woolf* (London: Chatto & Windus, 1996, p. 328).

2. L.Woolf, *Beginning Again: An Autobiography of the Years 1911–18* (London: The Hogarth Press, 1972, p. 101).

3. Ibid. Woolf added that this was 'the kind of fact which made – and makes – feminism the belief or policy of all sensible men.'

4. 'I have lately been going through (and destroying) ... a large quantity of letters & papers,' MLD to her nephew, Peter Llewelyn Davies, c.1940, 'The Morgue', unpublished family chronicle in private possession, 7 vols. (thanks to Chrys Salt for access), vol.5, 1897–1907, p. 219.

5. M. Llewelyn Davies, *The Women's Co-operative Guild* (Kirkby Lonsdale: WCG, 1904). 1,170 copies were sold in four months; reviews and notices appeared in the *Manchester Guardian*, *Speaker*, *Spectator*, *Queen*, *Daily News*, *Labour Leader*, *Glasgow Herald*, *Women's Trade Union Review*, *The New Age*; copies of the book were sent to Finland, Russia, Poland, Germany and Hungary; *Co-operative News*, 5 November 1904, p. 1367.

6. The first chapter, for instance, described how '1889 showed a considerable advance in the general organisation of the Guild'. The branches were clustered under six District Secretaries, two Sectional Secretaries were appointed, and two Sectional, and three District Conferences held. The first 'Winter Circular', listing lecturers, was published; and the Annual Report, based on a short 'schedule of questions' sent to all branches, appeared in book form for the first time. Yet only a passing reference five pages earlier revealed that in 1889 'the post of General Secretary ... was taken by the present writer'. *Co-operative News*, 28 May 1904, p. 662; MLD, *The WCG*, pp. 32 and 27.

7. L. Woolf, op. cit., p. 101. He met Davies through his wife, Virginia, but was acquainted with Margaret's brothers, Theodore and Crompton, as fellow members of the Cambridge 'Apostles'; J.L.Davies tutored Leslie Stephens at Cambridge.

8. *Co-operative News*, 3 June 1944, p. 1.

9. L. Woolf, op. cit., p. 103.

10. 'Margaret Llewelyn Davies', J.M. Bellamy & J. Saville (eds.), *Dictionary of Labour Biography (DLB)*, 1 (London: Macmillan, 1972).

11. See Georgia Pearce, 'Miss Llewelyn Davies and the People's Suffrage Federation', *The Woman Worker*, 10 November 1909, p. 437.

12. M.LD, article for *Norges Kvinder*, 1931, typed MS, 'Material illustrating the work of the guild and kindred interests, manuscript, typed and printed papers, photographs, erstwhile property of Margaret Llewelyn Davies (1890–?1944)', 11 vols., British Library of Political and Economic Science, 1, item 39.

13. In 1852, before taking Orders, he and David James Vaughan published a translatation of Plato's *Republic*, 'John Llewelyn Davies', *Dictionary of National Biography (DNB)*, 1912–21, (Oxford University Press, 1927).

14. In 1854, *The Spectator* published a letter from him, then a young curate in Whitechapel, about the state of the poor, and expressing criticisms of the Bishop of London, 'The Morgue', 1, 1750–1840, p. 108.

15. For Christian Socialist involvement in the Co-operative movement see Cole, op. cit., ch. VI; on general bridge-building between middle-class enlightened professionals and the respectable working class, see E. M. Janes Yeo, *Contest for Social Science in Britain: Relations and Representations of Gender and Class in the Nineteenth and Twentieth Centuries* (London: Rivers Oram, 1996, chapter 4).

16. 'J.L.Davies', *DNB*.

17. Dolly Ponsonby's reminiscences of MLD, 'The Morgue', 4, 1889–1897, p. 87.

18. Queen's College, the first serious academic institution for girls and women, was founded in 1848 by F.D. Maurice. 'J.L.Davies', *DNB*; 'The Morgue', 1, pp. 124–5.

19. 'The Morgue', 1, p. 172; Barbara Stephens, *Emily Davies and Girton College* (London: Constable, 1927).

20. MLD to Barbara Stephens, n.d., 'The Morgue', 1, p. 145.

21. For a scathing attack on the education provided for the average middle-class girl at the turn of the century, see V. Woolf, *Three Guineas* (London: The Hogarth Press, 1938).

22. 'The Morgue', 4, pp. 115 'M.L.Davies', *DLB*, 1.

23. See E. Janes Yeo, op. cit., chapter 9.

24. 'Account of Margaret Llewelyn Davies' & Lillian Harris' work in the WCG,' typed MS, n.d. (?1944), 'Material ...', (see note 12), 1, item 48.

25. *Co-operative News*, 27 May 1922, p. 1.

26. Georgia Pearce, 'Miss Llewelyn Davies', op. cit.; W. Thornton, *On Labour; its wrongful claims and rightful dues; its actual present and possible future*, (1869); facsimile of second edition (1870), with a supplementary chapter on the Co-operative movement (Dublin:

Irish University Press, 1971).

27. Thornton, op. cit., p. 499.
28. MLD, 'article for *Norges Kvinder*', 'Material ...' (see note 12), 1, item 39.
29. MLD, *The WCG*, p. 150.
30. A. Birkin, *J.M. Barrie and the Lost Boys* (London: Constable, 1979, p. 46).
31. 'Account of MLD' and Harris' work', 'Material ...', (see note 12) 1, item 48.
32. *Co-operative News*, 10 July 1897, p. 766.
33. 'The Morgue', **4**, p. 87.
34. WCG, *Annual Report*, 1893, p. 47.
35. *Co-operative News*, 3 March 1928, p. 13.
36. It seems reasonable to assume that the Llewelyn Davies's employed the usual complement of servants so these responsibilities would have involved keeping J. L. Davies company, and supervising domestic arrangements. See Q. Bell, *Virginia Woolf: an Autobiography*, 2 vols., **1** (London: Triad/Granada, 1976, pp. 55–7, on the servant question).
37. *Co-operative News*, 23 July 1904, p. 902.
38. 'The Morgue', **6**, 1907–10, p. 441; L. Woolf, op. cit., p. 103.
39. MLD to Peter Llewelyn Davies, n.d. (?1939), 'The Morgue', **5**, p. 219.
40. An incongruous postscript to this episode is the information that the sons of Arthur Llewelyn Davies, and his widow Sylvia, born du Maurier, provided inspiration for the Darling children in the story book *Peter Pan*; its author J.M. Barrie was a close friend of the family. See Birkin, op. cit.
41. 'The Morgue', **1**, p. 151.
42. 'The Morgue', **5**, p. 266.
43. She moved with the Llewelyn Davies's to Hampstead, and then in the 1920s the two retired to a cottage in the grounds of Maurice Llewelyn Davies's (Margaret's brother) house in Dorking, 'The Morgue', **5**, p. 218.
44. 'MLD', *DLB*, 1.
45. *Co-operative News*, 1 July 1922, p. 12.
46. MLD, *The WCG*, p. 57.
47. *Co-operative News*, 28 January 1950, p. 13.
48. 'Northern Section Guild Report,' *CCR*, 1893, p. 69; 'Report of Women's Guild', *CCR*, 1894, p. 57.
49. A reference to the train timetables.
50. *Co-operative News*, 1 July 1922, p. 12.
51. 'V. Woolf to Vanessa Bell, 24 Sept. 1916', N. Nicolson & J. Trautmann (eds), *The Letters of Virginia Woolf*, 6 vols. (London:

Hogarth Press, 1975–1980, **2**, 1920–24, 1978, p. 119.

52. V. Woolf, 'Introductory Letter', in M. Llewelyn Davies (ed.), *Life As We Have Known It by Co-operative Working Women* (1931) (London: Virago, 1977, pp. xxvi–xxvii).

53. See S. Yeo, 'A New Life: The Religion of Socialism in Britain, 1883–1896', *History Workshop Journal*, 1977, no. 4.

54. E.S. Pankhurst, *The Suffragette Movement* (London: Virago, 1977, pp. 127–8).

55. Caroline Martyn, socialist lecturer, who died, worn out, aged 29, wrote: 'In general I count my escape from marriage as one of my greatest blessings, but for that I could never have done my work; probably could never have opened my eyes to see that it needed to be done.' Yet she confessed herself to be sometimes 'overwhelmed with a miserable sense of my own loneliness.' Lena Wallis, *Life and Letters of Caroline Martyn* (London: Labour Leader, 1898, pp. 78 and 79). Enid Stacey, one of the most original and provocative socialist propagandists of the time, married Percy Widdrington, a young cleric, when she was in her late twenties with an established political career. She struggled with the conflicting demands of running a home, and then arranging for the care of a son, and her busy travelling schedule, but died of an embolism during her second pregnancy, aged 35, Angela Tuckett, 'The Life and Work of Enid Stacey, 1868–1903', unpublished MS (thanks to Stephen Yeo for access).

56. See B. Webb, *My Apprenticeship*, 2 vols. (Penguin, 1938); also L. Woolf, op. cit., pp. 116–18 for insight into the nature of their marriage; E. Janes Yeo, op. cit., pp. 211 and 288 for other examples of such partnerships.

57. 'J. L.Davies,' *DNB*.

58. MLD to L. Woolf, 25 July (?1913), MHP.

59. Dolly Ponsonby's reminiscences, 'The Morgue', **4**, p. 87.

60. *Co-operative News*, 17 June 1922, p. 12; for example, lines from Walt Whitman quoted in 'Branch work of the Women's Guild', Open Guild Meeting, *CCR*, 1888, p. 107.

61. L. Woolf, op. cit., p. 103.

62. WCG, *Lincoln Central Branch Coming of Age*, Lincoln, 1913, p. 3.

63. Letters of appreciation, Material ...' (see note 12), 8.B.

64. L. Woolf, op. cit., pp. 101, 103 and 104.

65. 'The Morgue', **4**, p. 87.

66. She also described how when Margaret 'says she hates money and rails against it', she would tease her, saying 'I should love to have it. I shd. like to have gold stays and a scented bed and real lace pillows,' whereupon Margaret would be 'shocked and swallows it all'. Lady Ponsonby's reminiscences, 'The Morgue', **5**, p. 284.

67. L. Woolf to MLD, 12 October 1915, MHP.
68. V. Woolf to MLD, 25 February 1915, *Letters*, 2, p.60.
69. Miss Llewelyn Davies, 'The Relations Between Co-operation and Socialistic Aspirations', *CCR*, 1890, p. 12.
70. Cole, op. cit., p. 218.
71. *Co-operative News*, 8 October 1921, p. 13.
72. 'The Morgue', 6, p. 442.
73. See E. Janes Yeo, op. cit., chapter 8.
74. Sidney Webb's personal correspondence, quoted in S. Pierson, *Marxism and the Origins of British Socialism* (Cornell University Press: 1973, p. 119).
75. M. Vicinus, *Independent Women* (London: Virago, 1985, p. 112).
76. V. Woolf, *Three Guineas* (London: Hogarth Press, 1938, p. 88).
77. J. Butler, *Personal Reminiscences of a Great Crusade* (London: Horace Marshall, 1896, p. 189).
78. MLD, *The WCG*, p. 96, drawing on Jane Addams, *Democracy and Social Ethics* (New York, 1902). Addams was the warden of the Chicago Social Settlement. The phrase, 'the odious words rich and poor', appeared again in Davies' address to the Co-operative Congress in 1922, on that occasion attributed to William Morris.
79. See S. Yeo, 'A New Life: The Religion of Socialism in Britain, 1883–1896', *History Workshop Journal*, 1977, no.4; C. Steedman, *Childhood, Culture and Class in Britain: Margaret McMillan 1860–1931* (London: Virago, 1990, chapter 8).
80. P. Gurney, *Co-operative Culture and the Politics of Consumption in England 1870–1930* (Manchester University Press, 1996).
81. MLD, 'The Relations between Co-operation and Socialistic Aspirations', pp. 12–15.
82. The one reference is to a collection of Fabian essays published the previous year, G.B. Shaw *et al.*, *Fabian Essays* (London: Fabian Society, 1889).
83. MLD, 'The Relations between Co-operation and Socialistic Aspirations', pp. 12–13.
84. Who expected to accomplish a great deal through the Liberal Party, and through municipal politics; Pierson, op. cit., pp. 126–7. Sidney Webb was among her audience at the Glasgow Congress.
85. *CCR*, 1890, p. 105.
86. WCG, *Annual Report*, 1895, p. 31.
87. 'The Morgue', 7, 1911–15, p. 586.
88. MLD, 'Co-operation at the Fountainhead', typed MS for *Life and Labour*, Chicago, **K**, no. 7 (September 1920), pp. 199–202, 'Material ...', (see note 12), 1, item 25.
89. In 1913, for example, during a strike of Leeds Society Co-operative workers, a popular senior Guild official, Miss Gration, a

Conservative, served in the Store for three days. Davies was privately appalled by her strike-breaking but upheld the right of local branches to settle the matter; consequently Miss Gration remained Sectional secretary. MLD to L. Woolf, n.d. (?Oct. 1913), MHP; *Co-operative News*, 29 November 1913, p. 1588.

90. 'Peaceful Campaigns by Two Old Campaigners', MS, 1933, 'Material ...' (see note 12), 1, item 41.
91. MLD to L. Woolf, n.d. (?Oct. 1913), MHP.
92. MLD, Article for *Norges Kvinder*, 'Material ...' (see note 12), 1, item 39.
93. L. Woolf, op. cit., p. 102.
94. *Co-operative News*, 4 February 1899, p. 114.
95. MLD to L. Woolf, Sunday, n.d. (?1914), MHP.
96. L. Woolf, op. cit., p. 102.
97. *Co-operative News*, 4 February 1899, p. 114.
98. See J. Liddington and J. Norris, *One Hand Tied Behind Us* (London: Virago, 1978); J. Liddington, *The Life and Times of a Respectable Rebel Selina Cooper 1864–1946* (London: Virago, 1984).
99. MLD, *The WCG*, pp. 61–2.
100. WCG, *Annual Report*, 1898–9, p. 3.
101. She later worked as an organizer for the Women's Trade Union League, and filed monthly returns on women's employment for Clara Collet at the *Labour Gazette*; she was also a prominent figure in the northern suffrage movement; *Co-operative News*, 3 March 1928, p. 13; MLD, *The WCG*, pp. 28–32; Liddington and Norris, op. cit., pp. 93 and 291.
102. WCG, *Annual Report*, 1893, p. 13.
103. MLD, *The WCG*, p. 28.
104. *Co-operative News*, 3 March 1928, p. 13.
105. MLD, *The WCG*, p. 31.
106. Ibid., chapter 4; E. Janes Yeo, op. cit., chapter 9.
107. See Guild Reports, CCR, 1907, p. 154; 1909, p. 397; 1910, pp. 229–30; 1911, pp. 193–4; 1912, pp. 180–1; 1913, p. 238; P. Redfern, *The Story of the CWS: the Jubilee History of the Co-operative Wholesale Society Ltd. 1863–1913* (Manchester, CWS, 1913, pp. 358–64); Cole, op. cit., p. 224.
108. *Co-operative News*, 27 May 1922, p. 1.
109. L. Woolf to MLD, 6 October 1922, MHP. L.T. Hobhouse (1864–1929), social philosopher, Professor of Sociology, London University from 1907. Arthur Ponsonby (1871–1946), Liberal MP (later joined the Labour Party and became prominent in the inter-war peace movement).
110. Steedman, op. cit., p. 30.

111. MLD to L. Woolf, 1 July (?1913); 25 July (?1913), MHP; for more on these labour people, see C. Benn, *Keir Hardie* (London: Hutchinson, 1992, Part II).

112. 'Report of Women's Guild', *CCR*, 1912, p. 180.

113. MLD to L. Woolf, Thursday, n.d. (? summer 1913); 19 May (?1913); *The Times*, 10 July 1913 10d; 4 August 1913 8c – letters from MLD and Margaret Bondfield arguing that maternity benefit should be the property of the mother (although the following year, Bondfield took the opposite view, see Chapter 4).

114. V. Woolf to Lady Robert Cecil, (?)28 May 1913, *Letters*, 2, p. 30.

115. MLD to L. Woolf, 26 November, n.d. (?1913), MHP.

116. Ibid., Sunday, n.d. (?1914). See L. Garner, *Stepping Stones to Women's Liberty Feminist Ideas in the Women's Suffrage Movement 1900–1918* (London: Heinemann Educational Books, 1984, chapter 6, for more on the East London Suffrage Federation).

117. MLD to L. Woolf, Tuesday n.d. (?November 1913), MHP.

118. Ibid., n.d.

119. Liddington, op. cit., p. 263.

120. CC resolution condemning conscription, *The Star*, 14 December 1915; CC anti-war resolution defeated at 1915 Congress, *Liverpool Post*, 17 June 1915; CC resolution for a non-punitive, negotiated peace, defeated 397 to 336, *Yorkshire Observer*, 13 June 1918; file of cuttings, Gertrude Tuckwell Collection. Virginia Woolf noted that the 1918 Congress vote, 'against Peace', seemed to Margaret to be 'of unspeakable importance and horror'. *The Diary of Virginia Woolf*, 1, 1915–19 (Harmondsworth: Penguin, 1977, 24 June 1918, p. 159.

121. 'Report of Women's Guild', *CCR*, 1918, p. 369.

122. WCG Central Committee Minutes, 7 August 1920; 'Report of Women's Guild', *CCR*, 1921, p. 188.

123. CC Minutes, 24–26 September 1920.

124. Ibid.; 'Report of Women's Guild', *CCR*, 1921, p. 189.

125. MLD to L. Woolf, 8 March (?1920), Leonard Woolf Papers (LWP), University of Sussex. Woolf was chosen as the Labour candidate for a Universities seat in 1920; he came third in the 1922 election.

126. In preparing the address she asked Woolf for a copy of 'Marx's *Communist Manifesto* (in English)', MLD to L. Woolf, Monday, n.d, LWP. Woolf replied that he could not find it, L. Woolf to MLD, 9 March 1922, MHP. He thought her draft text admirable, but advised her to leave out such phrases as ' "I venture to think" – you are too modest all through', L. Woolf to MLD, 21 April 1922, MHP.

127. *Co-operative News*, 10 June 1922, pp. 7–8.

128. V. Woolf to Janet Case, 7 June 1922, *Letters*, 2, p. 535. The names should have been Mrs Lawrenson and Miss Reddish.

129. 'Black Friday,' 15 April 1921, when the National Union of Railwaymen and the Transport Workers' Federation pulled out of the Triple Alliance leaving the Miners' Federation to strike alone, and ineffectively, for three months, marked 'the beginning of a major attack on wage levels.' J. Hinton, *Labour and Socialism A History of the British Labour Movement 1867–1974* (Brighton: Wheatsheaf, 1983, p. 114). In the spring of 1922, the Amalgamated Society of Engineers faced a series of lockouts which virtually exhausted its funds, G.D.H. Cole & R. Postgate, *The Common People 1746–1946* (London: Methuen, 1966, p. 563).

130. *Co-operative News*, 10 June 1922, pp. 1–3.

131. MLD, 'Special Education, Divorce and Independence', MS article for German publication (?1933), 'Material . . .' (see note 12), **1**, item 42.

132. MLD, 'Co-operation at the Fountainhead', 'Material . . .' (see note 12), **1**, item 25.

133. MLD to L. Woolf, n.d., MHP.

134. *Co-operative News*, 10 June 1922, pp. 1–3.

135. MLD, 'Special Education, Divorce and Independence', 'Material . . .' (see note 12), **1**, item 42.

136. MLD, *The Education of Guildswomen* (London: WCG, 1913, pp. 1–2). This was the paper that she delivered at the conference attended by Alexandra Kollontai (see Introduction).

137. *Co-operative News*, 13 December 1913, p. 1655.

138. See Chapter 1, note 40.

139. Woolf's paper was later published by the Guild as 'Control of Industry by Co-operators and Trade-unionists', *Co-operative News*, 20 September 1913, p. 1282; 'Report of Women's Guild', *CCR*, 1914, p. 253.

Chapter Three

Identity

The creation, virtually from scratch, of an organization with the kinds of qualities that so impressed Alexandra Kollontai in 1913, required ideological as well as organizational and political innovation. One of the greatest obstacles confronting the early Guild was the widespread belief that by nature and custom 'women'[1] belonged in the domestic sphere. This ideal of femininity – the 'angel in the house', possessed of special nurturing qualities but congenitally unfit for rational activity in the public domain – emerged as part of the ideological formation of the industrial middle class,[2] but then became a yardstick against which the virtue of all classes was measured. By the late 19th century, the middle-class model of a housebound wife, along with a sentimental idealization of homelife, were hallmarks of the respectable working-class, pressing as hard on Co-operative women as on their social superiors.[3]

Not the least effect of this ideology was to provide grounds for women's exclusion from public life, and accordingly it set an agenda for those women who sought to widen their sphere of activity: as part of their bid for equal rights, feminists produced sexually egalitarian definitions of woman's nature and woman's place. A recent study has suggested that middle-class women in the suffrage movement led the way in this reconstruction of gender, while the working-class women's organizations were too preoccupied with practical issues such as wages and working conditions to play a role in this contest of ideas.[4] Yet as the Guild's early history demonstrates, the ideology of separate spheres, with its binary divisions of masculine/feminine and public/private, was so integral to English society that it could not be ignored: any initiative that took women outside their 'proper sphere' required some radical version of their rights and responsibilities, if only as a pre-condition for their further actions, and from the 1890s, under Davies' leadership, the Guild was to the fore in developing a new and emancipatory identity for working women.

The experience of the infant Guild provides plentiful evidence of the extent to which respectable working-class culture was saturated with rigid assumptions about feminine identity. Despite some official recognition of the potential value of a separate women's association, the new venture also attracted scepticism and even hostility from male Co-operators. While shopping at the Co-op store was undoubtedly part of the housewife's responsibilities, going out to meetings, and taking on organizational work, were seen by many as an unacceptable departure from the norm. Attempts to start Guild branches often provoked strong statements about a woman's proper place, especially in the traditional mining communities in the north. One miner proclaimed that his wife should 'stay at home and wash my moleskin trousers';[5] at a Burnley Co-operative meeting, the idea of a Guild aroused 'a stir and a hubbub. "Education for Women!"', men exclaimed. '"Let them stop at Whoam [sic]."' '"Who's to mind the childer?"'[6] In 1894, the North Western Section secretary reported that 'there was still a certain amount of masculine prejudice to overcome. One of the branches in this section meets with a degree of opposition that almost amounts to persecution'.[7] Other branches were simply 'ignored in a very chilling manner',[8] and left to struggle on without any resources. 'Considerable friction' arose in 1896 at Hucknall, Nottingham, 'in consequence of guild members desiring to become members of the society as well as their husbands. The society, however, have [sic] decided not to allow this, and gives no recognition or assistance to the branch which is thrown entirely upon its own resources.'[9]

If the conservative response was simply to close ranks against the women, liberals purporting to offer the women every form of support often succeeded in supplying patronizing forms of endorsement, accompanied by a strict demarcation of a womanly sphere of activity in the movement. Consider, for example, the fulsome remarks of Mr Rae, chairman of Sunderland Society's

Educational Committee, in favour of a greater role for women Co-operators. In cloying language redolent of Ruskin's text on sexual difference, 'Of Queen's Gardens',[10] he told a joint meeting of the CU Education Committee and the WCG, at the 1894 Co-operative Congress, that they should all take a special interest in the influence the movement:

> exerted in the home life, because all that was highest and best in the home life circled round that which was truly womanly. It was not only the right, but the duty of lady members to see that all business connected with the social side of co-operation shall have its place in the front. The charms and graces and winning ways of women must have an influence in directing the attention of men to the social side of the movement.

Yet even this paean to feminine virtue included the suggestion that women were inherently deficient. Not only were they assumed to be incapable of playing a part in the economic side of Co-operation, they also had great difficulty in learning how to behave properly in public. Mr Rae appealed for accommodation on both sides:

> the women should be careful that their enthusiasm does not cause irritation ... Likewise the harsher and harder members of the education committees, who had the misfortune to be men, must have patience. Ladies could not learn in a day the best possible way of conducting meetings; and, if rude men smiled at some of their methods, we must remember that they were new to the arrangements of public meetings.[11]

It was not only men who were troubled by the prospect of women venturing into masculine territory. Many of the Guild's potential recruits, the women who shopped at the Co-operative stores, were themselves convinced that they could not join an organization. Some, like Mrs Layton in London, saw only the practical difficulties: 'I was far too busy. I thought a meeting in the middle of the week was quite impossible. I still had to wash and iron for my living.'[12] Others simply accepted that they belonged at home. The 'painful experience' of a Norwich branch secretary when 'asking mothers to come out for an hour or two to enjoy themselves,' was that 'they nearly all make one answer – "Oh, Thank you! but I never go out, my daughter will come, or my husband and children will come." '[13]

The pervasiveness among Co-operators of separate spheres ideology is also apparent in the attitudes of the first generation of Guild leaders who, in their anxiety not to antagonize respectable opinion or risk any charge of impropriety, added their voices to those affirming the primacy of women's domestic duties. The founder, Mrs Acland, stressed that Guild work should go on without taking up the 'vex'd question of women's rights'.[14] Their duties, she explained in 1885, should include the promotion of loyal buying, educating other women, and training the young in Co-operative values. 'Quiet influence', she maintained, 'in the home, and from home to home, cannot fail to have an effect.'[15]

The tone of Guild culture in the 1880s is captured in the proceedings of the 1885 'fringe meeting', an annual event for guildswomen attending the Co-operative Congress which merited a one-page summary in the massive tome of the Co-operative Union Annual Report.[16] In 1885 the meeting was attended by about '80 ladies'. The General Secretary, Miss Allen, reported a membership of 376, and 10 branches whose activities had included 'three scientific dress-cutting classes, five plain and fancy needlework classes, one choral society, one self-improvement class for young people from 14 to 20, two children's classes, one writing and one dressmaking class'. Mrs Lawrenson (Woolwich) 'gave a most interesting address on the way in which the Guild might be made of the greatest use and help to young people.' Miss Webb (Vice-President) spoke rather despondently of the difficulties in establishing Guild branches: 'some of the most unjust criticism', she remarked, 'comes from co-operators, or so-called co-operators. We are told by some of them that "we should do more good staying at home and educating our children". My answer is, a woman who has no feelings of humanity, or does nothing to help her fellow women, cannot educate her children, for children are educated by your words and deeds. Some of us have no children to educate; we have taken upon ourselves a higher education, that of humanity.' A mildly discordant note came from Mrs Ben Jones who bravely suggested that, when accompanying their husbands to meetings connected with the movement, women might, if invited to do so, speak from the platform; however, no resolution was passed on this subject and subsequent correspondence in the 'Women's

Corner' of *Co-operative News* made it plain that some members did not think that it would be proper for a woman to speak in public on behalf of the Guild.[17]

Despite the aspirations of Miss Webb and Mrs Ben Jones, branches were mainly taken up with the fostering of the domestic arts, and there were frequent enjoinders to women not to neglect their husbands and children. Mrs Ben Jones, who became the Guild president, was particularly anxious not to undermine the primacy of the domestic realm: 'one thing they should guard against above all others', she warned, 'was the neglect of their household duties'.[18] She maintained that members had 'a duty to their husbands and children, and though they should try to help one another, still they had to remember in the first place home duties.'[19] That she herself succeeded in this respect was testified to by her husband, Ben Jones, joint founder of the London CWS, following her death in 1894, aged 46. 'It is a great consolation to our children and to me', he wrote to the Guild CC, 'that she succeeded so well in making our home an earthly paradise, while at the same time she was able to do so much to promote the happiness of others.'[20]

Yet Mrs Ben Jones' record in the Guild shows a conscientious wife and mother grappling with a felt tension between the claims of public and private life. Organizationally, she owned that there was a problem: branches did not grow as fast as they might, 'as it was impossible for women to get the time they would like';[21] attendance suffered because 'we can't expect married women to attend with absolute regularity; they cannot leave the home like the men, or arrange everything to suit their meeting'.[22] Nevertheless, she clearly believed that the effort was necessary and was ready to begin, tentatively, to question traditional values as she did when she advocated public speaking for women. 'Some say that women's work is to stay at home', she argued in 1889, 'but we think that always to stay at home is to rust and become so useless that we are neither fit to be companions to our husbands nor nurses to our children.'[23] Two years later she is to be found claiming that 'women were fitted for something more besides making puddings and pies, and looking after household wants. They could find time to do that, but if they were anxious to take part in public work, they could, in connection with the co-operative movement, spare time for the benefit of other people around them.'[24]

In the 1880s the Guild was characterized by a concern for respectability, deference to convention, and an acceptance that women's proper place in the movement and in society was defined by their sex. Whilst it was accepted that Co-operative women should have greater opportunities for education and association, it was envisaged that the beneficiaries of such activities should be others; thus cautious forays beyond the home were justified in terms of possible gains for the movement, young people, children, or husbands. In the main, these early guildswomen conceived of their potential public role in the light of a philanthropic model of social service, which gave women a role outside the home but simultaneously confirmed their essentially maternal identity.[25]

While it is not surprising that the Guild at this stage actively cultivated a model of respectable femininity, the evidence does suggest that had the moderation of the 1880s been sustained, it would have remained a marginal grouping within the Co-operative movement, incapable of achieving organizational strength and stability, still less a position of national influence. In sharp contrast, the approach taken by Margaret Llewelyn Davies and the women she drew around her recognized that with the whole social and economic structure of society, the legal system, and customs and beliefs combining to enforce working-class women's subordination, one of the first tasks of an effective women's organization must be to establish the legitimacy of combating those forces.

The Guild rapidly became the source of a new and emancipatory discourse about working-class femininity. Three distinctive claims about working-class women took shape. Firstly, that they possessed a great but hitherto latent capacity for public service; secondly, that as citizens they had rights and responsibilities beyond the confines of the home; and finally, that as wives and mothers they were entitled to protection from forms of domestic abuse generally concealed by a conspiracy of silence. In each of these the Guild was effectively turning the ideology of domesticity on its head. To insist that housewives possessed an aptitude for public life subverted the notion that their social role as wives and mothers was dictated by their biology; to claim full citizenship for women problematized the sexual division of society into separate spheres of activity; to maintain that the home was an arena of hidden suffering undermined the idealized conception of the domestic sphere as the fount of all virtue.

Separate sphere ideology presupposed that while women were naturally equipped for domestic life, as were men for public activity, they were no more capable of functioning in the world outside the home than men were of bearing children. Accordingly, an essential part of the Guild's efforts to open the public sphere to women was to assert their fitness for the tasks involved, not least to the women themselves, many of whom had long internalized a belief in their own limitations derived from mainstream attitudes and enforced by their own lack of experience and formal education. In response to this need, the Guild developed practical training methods for Co-operative women, alongside a 'culture of affirmation' whose central message was that guildswomen possessed a vast, untapped capacity for public work that required only the right organizational setting to become manifest.

At the most basic level, women needed to be convinced that they could combine Guild membership with their domestic labour; the first step was to recognize how difficult and demanding that work was. While wealthier women employed servants, the majority of Co-operative women did their own housework, and running a home, caring for children and a husband, left them very little time to spare. 'Women are, as a rule', pointed out one article in *Co-operative News*, 'so hemmed in by their domestic surroundings that they have far fewer chances of becoming interested in the national affairs than men'.[26] The 1904 Guild history described members' homes as 'the workshops of many trades, where overtime abounds, and where an eight hours' day would be a very welcome reform ... Few men can realise how much drudgery and lonely effort there is in the everyday work of a housewife.'[27]

Housework and childcare could not be abolished but it could be rationalized to free time for other activities. The Guild advocated the collectivization of domestic labour and the introduction of labour-saving technology: 'Modern methods of production, namely machinery and association, should be applied to women's domestic work, and with that view co-operative societies are urged to use a portion of their capital in the establishment of co-operative washhouses, bakeries, laundries and kitchens.'[28] More immediately, the Guild encouraged greater proficiency and more effective time management. Thus even the domestic craft classes that dominated branch programmes in the 1880s could be turned to good account. Cookery lectures, clear starch classes, and so forth, noted Sarah Reddish in 1891, 'could teach them to make their homes brighter and happier. These things being done well left more time for mutual help.'[29] 'One of the things the Guild teaches, is system,' explained one member. 'To be able to attend branch meetings and conferences, and do your household duties, you must have a system in your home work. You can't loiter over it. The Guild really gives a zest to it.'[30] An 'elderly Guild member' confessed that 'I let it (housework) keep to a more convenient season, when it means a little more time to rid a little more dirt and dust and a few more microbes to kill'. Yet she also admitted that she carried out most of her Guild work 'in the small hours of the morning, when otherwise I should be in bed'.[31]

The Guild's approach, then, was not to devalue the occupation of most of its members, or to advocate domestic neglience, but rather to dignify housework as a highly skilled, if hard and often thankless, occupation. Lancashire members were said to be 'as "house proud" as any', and one guildswoman could boast that in 21 years of married life she had never bought bread.[32] Yet domestic efficiency should not become an end in itself, but afford free time for wider interests. 'Many economies of time, labour, and temper could be made', pointed out the 1892 Annual Report, 'so as to give women more leisure and freedom for other work. Much is done by our lectures in making women more efficient housewives. But the main object of the Guild is to give women a knowledge of labour questions, and make them take an active part in ... the labour movement.'[33]

The Guild held that its members were capable and hard-working women; if they could balance household budgets and carry out the range of tasks involved in housework, why should they not be fit to tackle wider social questions and participate in public life? As Sarah Reddish was quick to point out to Mr Rae, of the Co-operative Education Committee, their members were keen to learn more about all aspects of the movement, 'and to study the economic questions which many people supposed that women would not be interested in at all.'[34]

Guild training offered women a grounding in the basic procedures of public activity. Talks on such subjects as 'Women's Duties outside the Home' and 'Practical Helps to would be Speakers',[35] leaflets such as *Outline of Work with Model Branch Rules* (1891) and *How to Start and Work a Branch* (1897),[36] were supplemented by articles in the 'Women's Corner' of *Co-operative News.*[37] The practical demonstration of newly acquired skills, particularly public speaking, received special attention. In April 1897 the General Secretary congratulated the North Western Section on its work: 'Great progress had been made in bringing out new speakers.' A discussion on the subject of Factory Accidents and Compensation had 'brought out a first speech from Miss Oldfield (West Bowling, Bradford)' on her experience as a weaver.[38] By 1899 the General Secretary was pleased to request that since meetings were now generally so well managed, reports should concentrate on content rather than form: 'it is hardly necessary ... to mention such things as: That the arrangements for the meeting were very satisfactory. That the members did full justice to the tea. That the music was rendered in very good style. And that the meeting passed votes of thanks.'[39]

As the Guild began to take shape as a self-sustaining organization, the General Secretary was lavish in her praise of the membership. 'It is most encouraging', noted an early report, 'to see how the guild calls out powers that would otherwise remain latent, and helps to develop and utilise the gifts of each for the good of all.'[40] The 'intelligent interest displayed, and the very business-like way the delegates set to work to arrive at a clear and thorough understanding of the subject in hand', noted a report on Midlands district conferences in 1894, 'proved pretty conclusively how much the guild has already achieved in training women in the intelligent management of affairs having a wider significance and lying beyond the immediate circle of the home and the store.'[41] 'The guild certainly ought to grow into a structure which is good to look on, as the material from which it is being shaped is so full of beauty', Davies wrote in 1899, reflecting on the qualities she observed among guildswomen: their 'lives of unconscious heroism' and 'the great capacity – the practical wisdom and public spirit – which the guild is bringing out and turning to valuable account.'[42]

New delegates to sectional conferences were reported often to be struck by the quality of the debates, making such comments as: 'My word, I never thought that women could speak on such subjects.'[43] 'What is so remarkable about so many of the Guild members', wrote Davies in 1904, 'is that, although no longer young in years, and having had little or no early advantages, they possess a most youthful spririt; taking up new ideas, attending lectures, writing papers, and throwing themselves into a wider life with enthusiasm'.[44] As her introduction to the 1927 Guild history summed up the matter: 'It might well have been thought a hopeless task for a class of women who "never know when their day's work's done", and on whom personal claims are insistent, ceaseless, and irresistible, to organise and educate themselves and undertake public work and responsibilities. But the miracle has been accomplished, and who can say that the Guild has not justified its existence and that a great and hitherto untapped source of strength has not been added to national life.'[45]

Another task facing Guild leaders was the need to establish strong grounds for women's entry into the public sphere. During the 1890s the early Guild language of benevolent maternal influence was superseded by an unbending insistence that women, like men, were citizens, and as such had responsibilities, as well as rights. Far from being reminded of their home duties, guildswomen were increasingly urged to take their public role more seriously. At the Guild conference in Leicester in 1893, Mrs Woodward gave a paper arguing for more women to become Co-operative shareholders and to stand for election as officials. She admitted that some would object to this view: 'every breaking down of prejudice, every readjustment of ideas is accompanied by prophets of evil, foretelling dire catastrophe.' But such opposition, she insisted, would not daunt those who believed that the relation between men and women, 'should be one neither of submission nor of opposition, but what these are giving place to, namely, a cultivated sympathy and a growing feeling of comradeship. That women are worthy of taking their stand side-by-side with men, and sharing the honours and responsibilities of public life is becoming more apparent every day. Women have been content to stand back too long, and cling to old traditions and usages too pertinaciously, but they are now awakening to a sense of their capacities and duties.'[46]

The impact of such remarks comes through powerfully in an account given by Mrs Bury of Darwen, former millworker, now a housewife in her forties, of the same conference. It was, she wrote, 'a revelation'. On each of the three days of the gathering, 'my vision seemed to be widening, and my spirit felt that here was the very opportunity I had always been seeking, but never put into words. I had longings and aspirations and a vague sense of power within myself which had never had an opportunity for realisation. At the close of the meetings I felt as I imagine a war-horse must feel when he hears the beat of the drum.'[47] What Mrs Bury saw and heard at Leicester changed 'the whole course of my life for the next few years'. She believed that there 'are certain latent sparks in me which the Guild has kindled and caused to burn brightly. It has given me much greater understanding of life ... I feel more and more what an immense power united action can be ... I have heard other women say practically the same thing, and say how it has taught them to think on social questions they at one time would have passed over as outside their capacity. In words that our members often use "it has brought us out" '.[48]

Sarah Reddish, the Guild's first paid organizer, used the value of women's contribution at home to justify their right to a wider province. 'The influence and power of women in the home', she reasoned, 'are everywhere acknowledged to be great. Why should they be so much undervalued in society?'[49] Her 1894 Organiser's Report was uncompromising in its rejection of traditional femininity. 'We are told by some', she acknowledged, 'that women are wives and mothers, and that the duties therein involved are enough for them. We reply', she continued briskly, 'that men are husbands and fathers, and that they, as such, have duties not to be neglected, but we join in the general opinion that men should also be interested in the science of government, taking a share in the larger family of the store, the municipality and the State. The WCG has done much towards impressing the fact that women as citizens should take their share in this work also.'[50]

Reddish thus neatly demolished the presumption that the social segregation of the sexes reflected natural difference, asserting instead the equal responsibilities of men and women in the interlocking spaces of the national and local state, the co-operative movement and the home. Rather than being an atomized, private social unit, imprisoning women, Reddish's version of 'the family' signifies a site of sharing and solidarity in which the affective role of men, as husbands and fathers, complements that of women as wives and mothers, and in neither case diminishes the importance of the contributions of both as citizens and Co-operators.

The demand for the franchise provided a central focus for the Guild's discussion of citizenship. The vote, declared the General Secretary in 1897, was 'part of the great movement for the freedom of women, which will give them their true status in society and lead to a trustful and respectful comradeship between men and women.' 'We are tired', she continued, in a sharp attack on the feminine ideal:

> of being flattered, of being told of our wonderful 'influence' –
> of hearing that 'the hand that rocks the cradle rules the world'
> – when a moment afterwards our brains are compared with
> rabbits, and we are told that men do all the work of the world,
> and that wives 'should stay at home to wash their husbands'
> moleskin trousers.' We do not believe that the home is our
> only 'sphere', and we are suspicious when we are told we are
> 'the angels in the house.'[51]

As support for the vote among guildswomen began to grow, the tone in which the issue was discussed indicated the assumption that the justice of the claim to sex equality was comon sense. Thus a report of the Second Reading of the 1897 Suffrage Amendment Bill drily observed that 'Mr Labouchere, in an amusing speech, poured ridicule on the proposal. It had always been held since the world began that it was most undesirable that women should take an active part in public affairs as men did.'[52] A commentary the following week added: 'It is difficult to take seriously the contention that women are not fit to vote. The same could be said of many classes of male voters.'[53] Furthermore, as J. Green (Canning Town Branch) pointed out in a letter, the fact that women had been excluded from public affairs 'since the world began' was no reason not to include them in the 19th century.[54]

For the Guild, as for any organization aiming to advance the position of women, there was a need to assert women's full humanity, and to refute the traditional view that their sex rendered them incapable of rational thought and deed and therefore undeserving of rights.

The conviction that what men and women had in common outweighed the sexual differences invoked to justify women's exclusion from public life became a core value of the Guild. Arguments about 'Women's Sphere', Davies insisted in a 1904 article, were irrelevant. 'Citizenship is above sex, party, class and sect ... A citizen is a human being, belonging to a community, with rights and duties arising out of a common life.'[55] Sex discrimination was therefore a glaring injustice. As Mrs Mellor pointed out: 'No right should be taken from us simply because of sex.'[56] There was 'a great need', urged Sarah Reddish, 'for all women to join together to work for the removal of the sex disability. This was a sex question and no matter what their position in life, they ought to join together in order to remove all disability.'[57]

Yet while formal equality mattered in principle, in practice it would not have delivered many substantial freedoms to the women whom the Guild represented. Childbearing, child care, housework, and the paucity of paid employment open to working-class wives combined to make the goal of absolute equality of opportunity unrealistic. In claiming equal rights the Guild was not in the business of denying sexual difference. 'We are not', Davies assured guildswomen in 1897, 'seeking to turn women into men'. On the contrary, it was precisely because sexual differences were 'so great and so eternal' that women should 'take their place side by side with men, and have the power we claim for them in shaping our ideal society.' The skills, knowledge and distinctive qualities that women manifested in the domestic sphere should find expression in the public sphere too.

Yet this acknowledgement of sexual difference had to be qualified. As Davies pointed out: 'there are some differences that we want law and custom to diminish instead of accentuating.' Furthermore, she was at pains to disassociate herself from the idea of a 'sex point of view'. She considered that as human beings 'the aspirations of men and women are the same ... For below all differences of sex there is the great bond-likeness of human nature, and it is the complete human being, whether man or woman, whom we have in view'. Sexual differences brought 'not so much a different point of view', but 'peculiar insight, knowledge, and sympathy. And it is on this account, rather than from the notion that there is a special "woman's point of view," that women's contribution will be of special, as apart from its general, value.'[58]

The Guild's claims concerning working women's rights and capacities were not academic, but embedded in the activities of a rapidly growing movement; equally, its perceptions of its own character and purpose did not stand still but were shaped by that organizational growth. In the 1890s its priority was to legitimize working women's entry into the public sphere as part of the working-class movement; as Davies later wrote, at that stage its 'unique position' as 'the only organisation whose interests are specially those of married working women ... was only dimly seen.' But 'by degrees', as the organization gained strength and developed its own momentum, 'it became apparent that the need for reforms in the lives of the married women themselves was urgent'. This growing awareness of the wrongs of working women in the private sphere meant that in addition to being an organization *of* working women, the Guild also became an organization *for* working women, and it was in this capacity that it made 'its chief contribution to national life.'[59] Thus the Guild sought to oppose sex discrimination without surrendering the ground on which to argue that working-class women had special needs arising from their socio-economic position as well as their biology.

Guild organization provided the means by which aspects of married life that had previously been regarded as private matters for the individuals concerned were presented in the public domain as social problems with social solutions. This entailed a major assault on a pillar of Victorian domestic ideology: the piety that the home was the source of everything virtuous in society, a place of harmony in which, protected from the harsh reality outside, the wife nurtured and replenished her children and husband, morally as well as physically. Davies was well aware of both the resonance and the falsity of this idealized image of home life. As she wrote in 1911:

> It seemed as if in the past, when women married, they retired
> behind a dark curtain on which was embroidered all sorts of

beautiful sentiments about the beauty of motherhood and the sanctity of the home; but now the curtain was being withdrawn, and from the discussions that had taken place they had learned much of the sufferings of married women, the pain and misery that were going on behind the curtain.[60]

The Guild first began to analyse the situation of married women in relation to the suffrage question. In 1897 the claim of an MP that the suffrage demand lacked widespread support and was 'fostered by a stage army of a few ladies, who went about the country', elicited an angry response from a Guild member, Miss Sharp, who set out some of the reasons why married women needed the vote. For a woman, she argued:

home is not only her workshop (from which she does not get away once work hours are over) but the scene of important differences in treatment based, not upon character – which would be reasonable – but purely upon sex, and often enough in utter defiance of character. Anyone who doubts this might be asked to instance the family in which the man would honestly like to change places with the woman.

So long as 'women count for nothing in politics, their position in every other relation in life is certain to be affected by it.' Wholly governed by her husband, the quality of a married woman's life was wholly dependent upon his character. Under the 'benign guardianship' of a good man she might enjoy a 'consecrated liberty such as no outward law could give or take away', but such men were rare; without the protection of the law, without the rights of citizenship, most women lived in bondage.[61]

In that same month, echoes of John Stuart Mill again reverberated in a discussion paper, *Why Working Women Need the Vote*, by Mrs Martin, whose focus was the legal position of married women. She acknowledged that many guildswomen were 'blessed with happy homes', but then pointed out to her audience that 'we do not legislate for justice-loving men and women any more than we build prisons for honest men and women.' Did they realize that in law women had no right to custody of their children, that some men took their children away from the mother, or used this power to 'compel their wives to bear cruel treatment, immorality, and drunkenness, rather than be separated from their children'. Furthermore there were the divorce laws which enshrined the double standard by 'making immorality on the part of the wife a sufficient cause for divorce from her husband, yet expects the wife to prove cruelty in addition to immorality before she can claim divorce.'

Mill's argument was given a particular inflexion in regard to the family economy. Mrs Martin drew attention to the fallacy that married women were 'kept' or 'maintained', and therefore had no entitlement to a share of their husband's earnings. While Mill in his treatment of such issues could comfortably envisage servants dealing with the hard graft of domestic responsibilities, this woman is mindful of the workload of a wife without paid help. One would think, railed Mrs Martin, that 'housework, bearing children, and caring for them when they are born is all play. I wonder what man would think life easy if he had to be general servant, cook, nurse, washer-woman, tailoress and mother all at once.' The dependent status of married women was invidious: 'for the sake of the home the wife gives up her chance of earning, and although her work brings in no legal wage, yet it should give her a "right" to share in his wage'. Married women had no reason to expect consideration in law as long as they left men to speak on their behalf; they needed the vote so that they could exercise their influence on the legislative process.[62]

The most significant landmark in the evolution of the Guild's perspective on the domestic sphere was Rosalind Nash's 1907 Congress paper: 'The Position of Married Women'. A Guild member, and a friend of the General Secretary since their days at Girton together, Mrs Nash's central theme was the suffrage, and her starting point Mill's critique of marriage. Yet as she developed her argument, she planted seeds for future growth.

Writing in 1869, she pointed out, Mill had described the wife as the 'bond-servant of her husband'. Admittedly, there had been some advance since then: 'we might say that they have been promoted from slaves to servants' – but with the important qualification that while a servant could ask for better wages and conditions to compensate for 'living-in', a wife could not bargain with her husband over her home and her children.[63] Nevertheless, the idea that married women were entitled to more than a life of drudgery was gaining ground. However, without some intervention by the women, its progress would be slow. The main problem they faced was their isolation. 'It is difficult', Mrs Nash owned, 'for each woman separately to assert herself against the unjust claims of home'. Here, then, was an opportunity for collective action: 'the Guild can be a kind of trade union, through which, without making unpleasantness between husbands and wives, we can spread better ideas.'[64]

Meanwhile, the vote would surely be a weapon in tackling the many problems of their lives. The wife would gain formal recognition as a joint head of the family and as a citizen with rights and responsibilities. Municipal and co-operative enterprise could improve housing and community facilities to lighten the load of domestic labour. Legislation could be brought forward to secure changes which would entitle her to a share of the family income, make decisions concerning her children, and perhaps challenge the 'repulsive' divorce laws that at present made it so difficult for her to leave a cruel husband. Warming to her theme, Mrs Nash provided anecdotal evidence of the brutish treatment of married women and then drily observed that this was only through 'such glimpses that we can get an idea of what goes on in some homes, for of course, the privacy of the home is sacred.'[65]

Mrs Nash's concept of a trade union for married women crystallized the Guild's emergent identity as an organization that could 'voice the needs and rights of women, especially of married working women' and as 'the champion of a class which has now found organised expression for itself.'[66] What she did not and probably could not have envisaged when she prepared that paper was that through such collective organization the Guild could begin to break down the privacy of home life, to expose some of its darker secrets to public scrutiny, and thus strengthen the case for certain kinds of reform. Yet this is precisely what occurred as these insights and arguments began to inform the Guild's interventions on behalf of married women in the field of social policy. In its two most significant campaigns – for divorce law reform and state care of maternity – the Guild elicited written statements from members giving explicit details of marriage and childbirth which brought information about their sexual oppression into the public domain.

The evidence which the WCG placed before the Royal Commission on Divorce in 1910[67] included members' letters describing instances of sexual, physical and psychological abuse and hardship that exploded the ideal of the wife-nurturer/ husband-protector. Guildswomen told of 'cases where a woman, ill-used and kicked, has taken her husband back five times; of a diseased husband compelling co-habitation, resulting in deficient children; of excessive co-habitation, regardless of the wife's health; of a man frightening his wife during pregnancy in order to bring on a miscarriage.'[68] In 1915, with the encouragement of the Woolfs, the General Secretary published *Maternity Letters from Working Women*, an edited collection of members' letters describing their experiences of pregnancy and childbirth. Frequent references were made to attempted abortions, while phrases such as 'A Time of Horror', 'Mother Last', 'I am a Ruined Woman' and 'Men need Education' used in relation to childbearing signalled self-sacrifice, physical and mental distress, and the selfishness of husbands.[69]

Davies' introduction to *Maternity* sketched out the mixture of sexual and social oppression that defined the lives of working-class women: 'In plain language and in popular morality,' she wrote:

the wife is still the inferior in the family to the husband. She is first without economic independence, and the law therefore gives the man, whether he be good or bad, a terrible power over her. Partly for this reason, and partly because all sorts of old half-civilised beliefs still cling to the flimsy skirts of our civilisation, the beginning and end of the working woman's life and duty is still regarded by many as the care of the household, the satisfaction of man's desires, and the bearing of children.[70]

The texture of this sexual subordination was determined by social class, so that even the biological experience of childbearing was mediated by material circumstances. 'From the beginning of a pregnancy', Davies pointed out, a middle-class woman received proper medical care; 'she is not called upon to work; she is well fed; she is able to take the necessary rest and exercise.' During the labour, a doctor or nurse would be in attendance and afterwards the woman could stay in bed until she was fully recovered. 'For a woman of the middle-class to be deprived of any one of these things would be considered an outrage. Now, a working-class woman is habitually deprived of them all. She is lucky if her husband hands her over regularly each week 25s with which to provide a house, food, and clothing. It has to be remembered that the ordinary family wage leaves nothing over for the additional outlay upon maternity.'[71]

The Guild's revelations about the lives of married women clearly strengthened its case for reform. Yet there is also a sense in which it was a double-edged weapon. Potentially, the images thus evoked – of women as passive victims, patiently suffering hardship – were corrosive of the strong, capable and assertive version of working-class womanhood the Guild wished to project. Thus the price of proving need could be the negation of agency: these women obviously required help, but equally obviously were incapable of helping themselves. It is important, therefore, to notice that the Guild inflected this material in ways that buttressed its demands for women's rights, its claims about women's aptitude for public life, and its insistence on the value of autonomous women's organizations.

In its discussions of domestic abuse the Guild skilfully used both its own dignified, fully human conception of womanhood, and the mainstream ideal of domesticity, to point up the pervasive degradation. The 'hidden suffering amongst working women,' Davies pointed out at a Manchester Guild District conference in 1911, meant that 'home-life was degraded'. The current divorce laws upheld an 'unequal standard of morality', which 'did not conduce to the dignity of womanhood nor to the sanctity of home life.'[72] Even some of the most shocking information thrown up by the Guild inquiries – the extent of illegal abortion – could be used to highlight the gap between the ideal and reality and as evidence that women were rebelling against such stereotypes of femininity as maternal self-sacrifice. As an article on 'The Declining Birthrate' in the women's pages of *Co-operative News* pointed out, the 'sacrifice' expected from married women was too great: 'Many a woman, as soon as she has reason to expect another child, tries to escape by taking drugs.' In Lancashire alone there were reputed to be 1,000 people making a living from carrying out abortions. If, as the various critics of small families maintained, 'married women owe a duty to society to bear children, society must see to it that the conditions of child bearing and rearing are made more attractive to the average mother.'[73]

In the maternity benefit and divorce law reform campaigns, the Guild pressed claims about the rights and wrongs of working-class women with a confidence that reflected both conviction in the proven justice of its case and the collective strength of tens of thousands of women. A strong point to emerge was the fact that the context in which the 'hidden suffering' had come to light was the self-organization of working women, and that were it not for such organization it would still be hidden. As the introduction to *Maternity* stated, the situation of the mother had previously been overlooked, 'for the isolation of women in married life has, up to now, prevented any common expression of their needs. They have been hidden behind the curtain which falls after marriage, the curtain which women are now themselves raising.'[74]

The different facets of the Guild's radical account of working-class womanhood were set out in its 1913 pamphlet, *The Education of Guildswomen*. 'Our Guild', it stated, 'is an example of what is going on among married women. It is the reply of the married women of to-day to those who have told them that "the woman's place is at home," meaning, of course, by this that woman's only place is at home.' No longer accepting what they were told, women were now asking 'for themselves what their place is', and coming up with their own answers.[75] The guildswoman's response would be: 'My place is in the Co-operative Movement, because I am the wage spender; my place is in my Town and country, because I am a wife and mother; my place is in my Home because I am a joint maker of the family life; and I find I cannot do my work properly in any one of the three places without doing it in all.'[76]

As well as being fully aware of 'her inseparable connection with the Store, the Town Council and Parliament', the guildswoman was also conscious of the importance of social relations in the domestic sphere, reflecting 'on her own position in her home, and all that in her relations with her husband and children go to make the best family life.' On this question, she 'understands that the first need is equal comradeship of husband and wife, of brothers and sisters, and how destructive of this is the subordination which we always know is expected when we hear "A woman's place is at home".' The guildswoman thus appreciated the need for 'parity to begin at home', and she was alert to the extent to which socialization rather than biological characteristics determined the sexual hierarchy:

> Mistakes have been made from the beginning: boys have been given more chances than girls, and allowed to nourish a sense of superiority; and wives have been taught to be obedient to their husbands; while the fact that no money value is attached to the services of a woman in her home is also responsible for the position of so many women. Guildswomen are now facing the problems of marriage and divorce, of economic independence, of the moral training of their boys and girls. It is only by men and women alike studying these problems that true companionship in the home can be arrived at, and the best atmosphere created for children to be brought up in.[77]

The same sense of working women claiming their rights in public and domestic life is apparent in the reporting of the Guild's 1914 Congress, which reveals the organization in fighting form. Now a three-day, independent event, and the high point of the Guild's calendar, these notable occasions were attended by hundreds of delegates, their expenses met by Guild funds, primed to represent their branches on matters that had previously been the subject of education and debate and to approve the Guild's own lengthy *Annual Report*.[78] Also present were guests from labour and women's organizations, and a sizeable press corps. 'In the large hall at Birmingham,' reported the *Manchester Guardian*, 'under the banners of their branches, sat some 600 delegates. They are women of the working classes ... worthy representatives not only of 30,000 co-operative women, but of all the women who have borne children and lived laborious lives since Eve.'[79] The most pressing item on their agenda was the ultimatum from the Co-operative Union Central Board that the Guild either abandon its campaign for divorce law reform, or lose its annual grant. In near unanimity, delegates voted to stand firm against the Board. As Mrs Holdness (Derby) pointed out, it 'was repeatedly said that the women were the backbone of the movement; was it not time they showed the strength of that backbone?'[80]

The contrast between the 1885 meeting and the 1914 Congress registers not only the growth of numbers, organizational strength and vitality, and political substance, but also the Guild's escape from the dominant values and codes of conduct of respectable femininity. The identification of the home as a site of sexual oppression, alongside the steady emphasis on the capacities and rights of working women, crystallized the Guild's sense of its own identity and purpose, and underlined the changes since the days when Mrs Acland could define its role in terms of the benefits of women's influence from 'home to home'.[81]

The Guild's development had made married women visible and vocal. In contrast to their traditional role, concealed within the family, working-class wives, as a collective entity with views, needs and interests, had entered the public domain. Far from being careful not to stray from their proper place, guildswomen now took it for granted that they could and should participate in public debates on any and every subject, including the most controversial social issues of the day; and, if necessary, criticize officials, institutions, or politicians who were responsible for unjust and discriminatory policies. There was, too, an explicit recognition that the Guild's role was not only to contribute to the social good, but to tackle wrongs in the lives of working women. The public disclosure and discussion of the conditions of women in the private sphere had generated a profound sense of grievance, but one conjoined with a high level of consciousness of collective strength and agency. Guildswomen now exhibited an awareness of speaking not for themselves as individuals but as representatives of a wider constituency – tens of thousands of Co-operative women, who were themselves the organized expression of the interests of the millions of working-class housewives so long denied any public voice. Yet this achievement was about more than the construction of a discourse: while ideological innovation constituted an important element of the Guild project, its fullest expression was to be found in the campaigning work to which we now turn.

Notes

1. As Riley argues, an unstable, historically and discursively constructed category, see D. Riley, *'Am I That Name?' Feminism and the Category of 'Women' in History* (London: Macmillan, 1988, ch. 1).
2. C. Hall, 'The Early Formation of Victorian Domestic Ideology', in S.

Burman, *Fit Work for Women* (London: Croom Helm, 1979). L. Davidoff & C. Hall, *Family Fortunes: Men and Women of the English Middle Class 1780–1850* (London: Hutchinson, 1987).

3. G. Stedman Jones, 'Working-class culture and working-class politics in London, 1870–1900: Notes on the remaking of a working class', *Languages of Class, Studies in English Working Class History 1832–1982* (Cambridge University Press, 1983).

4. S. Kingsley Kent, *Sex and Suffrage in Britain 1860–1914* (London: Routledge, 1987, p. 16). As Brian Harrison notes, Kent's dependence upon secondary sources, and her use of post-structuralist theories of language, lead her to some bizarre conclusions in this, and in her subsequent work, *Making Peace: The Reconstruction of Gender in Interwar Britain* (Princeton University Press, 1994). See B. Harrison, 'How the female sex warriors lost their way', *Guardian*, 30 April, 1994.

5. M. Llewelyn Davies, *The Women's Co-operative Guild* (Kirkby Lonsdale: WCG, 1904, p. 21).

6. A. James & N. Hills, *Mrs John Brown 1847–1935* (London: Albemarle St. W., 1937, p. 42).

7. 'North Western Section Guild Report', *Co-operative Congress Report (CCR)*, 1894, p. 85.

8. 'Report of Women's Guild', *CCR*, 1894, p. 58.

9. 'Nottingham District Guild Report', *CCR*, 1896, p. 56.

10. J. Ruskin, 'Of Queen's Gardens', in *Sesame and Lilies* (1865) (Oxford University Press, 1936); K. Millett, 'The Debate over Women: Ruskin vs. Mill', in M. Vicinus, *Suffer and Be Still* (Bloomington: Indiana University Press, 1972).

11. 'Education and the Women's Guild', *CCR*, 1894, p. 139.

12. 'Memories of Seventy Years by Mrs Layton', in M. Llewelyn Davies (ed.), *Life As We Have Known It by Co-operative Working Women* (1931) (London: Virago 1977, p. 39).

13. MLD, *The WCG*, p. 21.

14. G.D.H. Cole, *A Century of Co-operation* (London: Allen & Unwin for the Co-operative Union, 1944, p. 216).

15. *Co-operative News*, 13 June 1885, p. 580.

16. 'Meeting of the WCG', *CCR*, 1885, pp. 71–2.

17. *Co-operative News*, 27 June 1885, p. 621.

18. 'Presidential Address, 4th Annual Guild Meeting', *CCR*, 1886, p. 89.

19. 'Presidential Address, 8th Annual Guild Meeting', *CCR*, 1890, p. 112.

20. Benjamin Jones (1847–1942), see J. Bellamy & J. Saville (eds), *Dictionary of Labour Biography*, I (London: Macmillan, 1972); MLD, *The WCG*, pp. 21–2.

21. 'Presidential Address, 8th Annual Guild Meeting', *CCR*, 1890, p. 112.

22. 'Presidential Address, 7th Annual Guild Meeting', *CCR*, 1889, p. 104.

23. Ibid.
24. 'Presidential Address, 9th Annual Guild Meeting', *CCR*, 1891, p. 112.
25. For a full discussion of 'social motherhood', see E.M. Janes Yeo, *Contest for Social Science in Britain: Relations and Representations of Gender and Class in the Nineteenth and Twentieth Centuries* (London: Rivers Oram, 1996, ch.5).
26. *Co-operative News*, 20 February 1897, p. 186.
27. MLD, *The WCG*, p. 151.
28. Catherine Webb, 'Co-operation as applied to Domestic Work', paper given at WCG Annual Meeting, Leicester, June 1893, 'Material illustrating the work of the guild and kindred interests, manuscript, typed and printed papers, photographs, erstwhile property of Margaret Llewelyn Davies (1890–?1944)', 11 vols., British Library of Political and Economic Science, 1, item 7.
29. '9th Annual Guild Meeting', *CCR*, 1891, p. 113.
30. MLD, *The WCG*, p. 151.
31. Ibid., p. 154.
32. Ibid., pp. 153–5.
33. 'Report of Women's Guild', *CCR*, 1892, p. 56.
34. 'Education and the Women's Guild', *CCR*, 1894, p. 139.
35. WCG, *Winter Circulars*, September 1894; August 1894; 'Material ...' (see note 28), 1, items 9 and 10.
36. WCG, *Outline of Work with Model Branch Rules* (Manchester: Co-operative Printing Society, 1891); WCG, *How to Start and Work a Branch* (Kirkby Lonsdale: WCG, 1897).
37. For example, 'Public Speaking, Some Hints for Guild Members (By One of Themselves)', in three parts, *Co-operative News*, 21 August 1897, p. 927; 28 August 1897, p. 950; 4 September 1897, p. 984.
38. *Co-operative News*, 10 April 1897, p. 387.
39. *Co-operative News*, 18 February 1899, p. 162.
40. 'Report of Women's Guild', *CCR*, 1892, p. 56.
41. 'Midland Section Guild Report', *CCR*, 1894, p. 66.
42. *Co-operative News*, 4 February 1899, p. 114.
43. MLD, *The WCG*, p. 46.
44. Ibid., p. 156.
45. MLD, 'Preface', in C. Webb, *The Woman with the Basket: the History of the Women's Co-operative Guild* (Manchester: The Guild, 1927).
46. Mrs Woodward (Birmingham), 'Women as Shareholders and Officials in the Co-operative Movement', paper given at WCG Annual Meeting, Leicester, June 1893, 'Material ...' (see note 28) 1, item 8.
47. MLD, *The WCG*, p. 61.
48. *Co-operative News*, 14 June 1913, p. 754; MLD, 'Special Education,

Divorce and Independence', MS article for German publication (?1933), 'Material ...' (see note 28), 1, item 42.

49. Miss Reddish, *Women's Guilds With Special Reference to their Claims on the Attention and Support of Educational Committees*, Co-operative Educational Committees' Association Annual Meeting (Bolton: Henry Smith, 1890, p. 3).

50. 'Organiser's Report, Report of Women's Guild', *CCR*, 1894, p. 58.

51. M. Llewelyn Davies, *Why Working Women Need the Vote*, paper read at the WCG Southern Sectional Conference, London, 15 March, 1897 (Manchester: Co-operative Printing Society, 1897, p. 8).

52. *Co-operative News*, 13 February 1897, p. 163.

53. *Co-operative News*, 20 February 1897, p. 186.

54. *Co-operative News*, 20 March 1897, p. 311.

55. *Co-operative News*, 12 November 1904, p. 1392.

56. *Co-operative News*, 20 March 1897, p. 311.

57. *Co-operative News*, 23 July 1904, p. 917.

58. MLD, *Why Working Women Need the Vote*, pp. 9–10.

59. 'The Women's Co-operative Guild, 1895–1916: A Review of Twenty-One Years' Work,' *WCG Annual Congress Handbook*, London, 1916, pp. 10–11.

60. *Co-operative News*, 27 May 1911, p. 667.

61. *Co-operative News*, 13 March 1897, p. 268; Mr Radcliffe Cook made the remark during the second reading of Mr Faithful Begg's Bill. Miss Sharp was a former editor of the 'Women's Pages' of *Co-operative News*.

62. Mrs Martin (Bedminster Branch, Bristol), *Why Working Women Need the Vote*, paper read at the WCG Western Sectional Conference at Gloucester, 25 March 1897 (Manchester: Co-operative Printing Society, 1897).

63. R. Nash, *The Position of Married Women* (Manchester: CWS Printing Works, 1907, pp. 3 & 5).

64. Ibid., p. 9.

65. Ibid., p. 12.

66. WCG, *Annual Report*, 1907–8, p. 4.

67. 'Miss Margaret Llewelyn Davies', *Minutes of Evidence taken before the Royal Commission on Divorce and Matrimonial Causes, Minutes of Evidence* (1912), 3 (Cd. 6481) pp. 1912–13, XX.

68. WCG, *Divorce Law Reform: The Majority Report of the Divorce Commission* (Manchester: CWS, 1913, p. 12).

69. M. Llewelyn Davies (ed.), *Maternity Letters from Working Women* (1915) (London: Virago, 1978).

70. MLD, 'Introduction', ibid., pp. 7–8.

71. Ibid., pp. 4–5.

72. *Co-operative News*, 11 March 1911, p. 299.

73. *Co-operative News*, 18 March 1911, p. 366.
74. MLD, *Maternity*, pp. 8–9.
75. M. Llewelyn Davies, *The Education of Guildswomen* (London: WCG, 1913, p. 2).
76. Ibid., p. 4.
77. Ibid.
78. WCG, *Annual Report*, 1913–14.
79. *Manchester Guardian*, 24 June 1914, Gertrude Tuckwell Collection.
80. *Co-operative News*, 20 June 1914, p. 808; WCG, *Annual Report*, 1914–15, p. 4.
81. See Chapter 1, note 19.

Chapter Four

Campaigns

The Guild's primary aim, as Sarah Reddish wrote in 1890, was 'to bring into active life the great body of women in the Co-operative movement.'[1] Its first major interventions were in the Co-operative movement itself, beginning in 1899 with the extension of Co-operation to the poor, and then, from 1905, with the Amalgamated Union of Co-operative Employees (AUCE), to secure a minimum wage for Co-operative female employees. In tandem with these campaigns ran the Guild's elaboration of an original working-class feminist agenda under the banner of its Citizenship work, and while it gave formal support to the suffrage movement, it did not, as Davies later pointed out, 'wait for the vote to tackle some of the most urgent problems of married women's lives.'[2] It was through its prominent national campaigns, for statutory maternity benefit and divorce law reform between 1910 and 1914, that the Guild established a distinctive reputation as 'a kind of trade union for married women'.

The fact that this purpose had taken some three decades to be realized underscores both the difficulties inherent in mobilizing women who 'never know when their day's work is done',[3] and the extent to which the Guild's mature identity was not preconceived but constructed through an interplay of theory and practice. While left-wing and feminist women in the Guild grasped that the organization had potential for the advancement of working women, in the 1890s there were no blueprints for either the methods, or the policies, most conducive to that end. What had been achieved by the First World War reflected painstaking organizational and educational work, a dynamic relationship between leadership and membership, and a steady accumulation of the lessons of experience. This chapter demonstrates how the evolution of that campaigning experience, in local, Co-operative and suffrage work, brought the organization to a point where it could speak with authority in the national debate on maternity provision as the representative of working women, while that which follows analyses the ways in which the divorce law reform campaign crystallized not only its distinctive form of advocacy but also the indispensability of self-government to safeguard that role.

The women who first sought to put women's rights on the Guild's agenda were well intentioned but had very little practical knowledge of the lives of the working-class housewives entering the Guild. Davies' earliest interventions in the Guild made it plain that she was not there to promote the purchasing of Co-operative groceries as an end in itself, and that it should not be used as a vehicle for recruiting passive housewives for the movement. She saw in the WCG, Cole notes, 'an ideal instrument for carrying to the working-class housewives the message of the movement for the emancipation of women'.[4] Yet in those early years, as Davies later admitted, 'the urgent need for reforms in the lives of married women themselves'[5] had not been understood. Looking outside the Guild for inspiration, the General Secretary's first step was to try to link the Guild with areas of activity that involved some inter-connection between working-class politics and women's rights.

The initial approach was to suggest that guildswomen had a duty to take an interest in efforts to improve the condition of their sex. Soon after Davies joined the Guild, she gave a talk suggesting that besides strictly Co-operative discussions, branches would do well to have lectures on 'such subjects as Women's Trade Unions' and 'Women's Suffrage',[6] and in her first speech as General Secretary she warned members that 'guild meetings must not descend into being mere "mother's meetings". There must be some educational work in connection with them, or they might as well be just parish meetings, and not co-operative at all.' She wanted the members to 'join, and feel themselves members of a large body; they must learn of each other. More *unity*, more *education* were the points she specially desired to urge.'[7]

Invited to speak at the 1892 Manchester Guild Festival, Clementina Black,[8] of the Women's Trade Union Association, directed the attention of guildswomen to the plight of women workers. They were, she said, 'the worst paid, the most in need of organisation, and the most difficult to organise'. Accordingly, 'as women, as citizens no less than as co-operators, it is your business to help in the formation of Trade Unions for women.'[9]

Davies and Black were both making certain assumptions about their audiences: firstly, that as members of Co-operative Societies they would be sympathetic to trade unionism; and secondly, that while not themselves likely to be trade-union members, they would be in a position to engage in some kind of solidarity work. The average guildswoman, then, would not be a trade unionist, although she might well be married to one. This prompted the following question: what kind of union activity might a full-time housewife get involved in? Several tentative responses may be found in the Guild's records for the 1890s.

assumptions made by MLD (margin annotation)

Strike action was exceptional, and could hardly form the basis of regular branch work. Nevertheless, during the upsurge of industrial action associated with the New Unionism from 1889–92, some guildswomen did find opportunities to make a contribution. Reports appeared of branches setting up joint meetings with women's unions, and assisting strikers. Battersea Guild was reported to have been active in improving wages and conditions in a local glove factory; a Bristol branch supported young women workers in a sweet factory who were demanding the right to join a union.[10]

As well as supporting women workers, guildswomen could support their husbands. In 1893, during the first large-scale action led by the Miners' Federation (400,000 men came out), the Guild drew attention to the part played by women. Some employers, stated the *Annual Report*, believed 'that the men would have gone in at a reduction if it had not been for the women.' The 'principle spokeswoman' during the strike was the Guild's Airedale District secretary, Mrs Dickenson, a miner's wife, who addressed mass meetings around Leeds and a large rally in St James's Hall, London, where, she later wrote, illustrating the strength to be derived from organization, she gained confidence from the sight of familiar Guild faces in the audience.[11]

Where unions were weak or non-existent, the Guild supported legislative intervention. During the 1890s it established close links with the Women's Industrial Council,[12] and officials collected information for Clara Collet at the new Labour Department of the Board of Trade.[13] It also published a series of papers on such questions as: 'Hours of Work for Women', 'Overtime for Women', ' Homework', and 'Women as Inspectors'.[14] Sarah Reddish, one of the Guild's most experienced trade unionists, toured Co-ops in the Midlands speaking on the Workmen's Compensation Act; after one such meeting, a woman approached her 'holding up a maimed hand, and saying how she had suffered pain and monetary loss in her early life, and she blessed me for the words I had spoken in the workers' cause.'[15]

This close attention to legislative developments underlined the need for working women to secure effective representation. 'When the next chance of amending the Factory Acts presents itself,' the General Secretary wrote in 1896, 'we shall be able to say what working women wish done on these matters, and shall not be left entirely at the mercy of such remarks as Mr Matthews (a former Home Secretary), who said during the progress of the present Act through the House of Commons, "I have my own opinion of what working women think, and to such opinion I shall always adhere." '[16]

The most obvious entry-point into the wider labour movement for the Guild was through the Co-operative movement itself, where as members of Societies guildswomen were technically employers. During the 1890s efforts were made to ensure that only union-made goods were stocked in the stores;[17] and some branches attended the quarterly meetings of the Societies to vote for such measures as early closing. In all such cases, the 1899 *Annual Report* noted 'our women have been on the forward side.'[18] In the 1900s, as we shall see below, joint work with the AUCE brought the Guild further toward the 'natural alliance' urged by Clementina Black in 1892.

In the course of the 1890s the Guild introduced subjects for study and discussion throughout the whole organization, adopting the separate headings 'Co-operation' and 'Citizenship' to broaden its field of action. Davies had been in office for a whole decade, however, before the organization reached a point where properly co-ordinated national initiatives were feasible. These began in the early 1900s with two Co-operative issues – the 'Extension of Co-

operation to the Poor', and a 'Minimum Wage for Female Co-
operative Employees'. As well as giving considerable impetus to
the development of the Guild's campaigning methods, these two
interventions both involved a reassertion of the Owenite
commitment to trading practices with social rather than narrowly
commercial benefits, and as such won the Guild a reputation as
'the left wing' of the Co-operative movement.[19]

The 'Extension of Co-operation to the Poor', which consumed
much of the energy of the national office from 1899 to 1904, was
the Guild's boldest attempt to build into the movement an explicit
project of social reform. Its goal was to extend the most
progressive aspects of Co-operation – democratic association
and non-profit making trade – to the unskilled and casually
employed working-class. As Davies argued, through Co-
operation, trades unionism, friendly societies, and building
societies, the 'gospel of self-help has done inestimable work.
Those who grasp the powerful weapon of organisation have
splendid chances of preservation and victory. But what of those
who, from various causes, have not grasped it? Who are not only
weaponless, but are too weak to carry the weapon, even if offered
them.' Instead of leaving the poor to charity, she held that Co-
operation should use some of its strength and ingenuity 'to forge a
weapon on our own pattern,'[20] so as to free poor neighbourhoods
from all that trades on 'ignorance, poverty and misfortune'.[21]

Inspired by the remark of a delegate at the 1899 Co-operative
Congress that no agency was better qualified than the Guild to
increase membership among the poor, the Guild 1899 Winter
Circular included the topic: 'Through what Forms of Co-operation
we can Hope to Reach the Poorest Class'; while the autumn
Sectional Conferences discussed 'Co-operation in Poor
Neighbourhoods', the first of a series of carefully researched
papers from the General Secretary on the subject.[22] Undeterred by
official resistance to a joint WCG, CWS and CU initiative, the
Guild managed to secure CU funds to conduct its own investigation
and make recommendations. The inquiry, from December 1901 to
February 1902, featured two elements that were to be characteristic
of Guild campaigns under Davies' leadership: a social-scientific
concern to establish and then broadcast the facts of the matter; and
a pronounced sensitivity to the perceptions and experience of

women. Guild investigators visited the poorest areas of Sheffield, Bury, York, Newcastle, Sunderland, Plymouth and Bristol, met with local residents, Co-operative and municipal officers, and convened special conferences of Guild branches and Society management committees. In their reports, Guild investigators demonstrated their sensitivity to the nuances of gender relations. They noted an interesting dichotomy: the speeches of 'the women showing the difficulty of shopping on low wages, those of the men recounting the miraculous thrift of their early family life.'[23] Women, Davies observed, understood, 'as few men do, that high prices are an insurmountable barrier to loyalty or membership'.[24]

Drawing on existing good practice, the Guild advocated more stores in poor neighbourhoods – 'People's Stores', with coffee shops, selling cheap, wholesome food, including cooked meat (many slum homes were not equipped with ovens) in small quantities. Entrance fees, high dividends, and high prices – all such barriers to those on low incomes should go. Profits should be used to reduce prices, rather than increase dividends, and small savings and credit facilities – penny banks and 'reformed pawn shops' or loan departments – provided. More adventurously, the Guild proposed 'Co-operative Settlements', with a 'special Propagandist Committee of resident workers' to spread Co-operative principles, provide a social centre 'to attract from the public-house', and a forum for 'Co-operative activity in the district.'[25] Supported by the store, these would be economically self-sufficient and socially constructive in ways that would distinguish them from the moralizing mainstream of charitable settlement work.[26]

This radical overhaul of Co-operative practices and philosophy met with a mixed reception. In some quarters, proposals that questioned the movement's secure base in the skilled working-class engendered hostility; elsewhere there was agreement as to the desirability of the end in view, but an unwillingness to furnish the means: 'co-operative mission work for women always meets with the approval of the men!', Davies noted. 'But it sometimes seems to be expected that bricks can be made without straw.'[27] There was support from the more progressive Societies; many reformed their trading practices, and one – Sunderland – opened a Settlement at its Coronation Street branch, in a slum district of the city, in 1902.

For two years the Settlement flourished. It was attractively furnished and equipped with modern facilities, including a meeting hall with a kitchen, and accommodation for the resident workers.[28] Several guildswomen worked as volunteers, including Davies for the first three months; in January 1903, the Society employed Miss Partridge, a Guild member, for one year as a resident worker at 25s a week (the equivalent of a male manual workers' wage), while Davies undertook to bear the cost of a second worker for a year.[29] By January 1904, the store was covering the costs of the Settlement, and paying a dividend of two shillings in the pound, and in Davies' judgement the resident workers were succeeding in winning the trust of the local people. The Society voted to make the project permanent with two appointed resident workers. In the following months, however, tensions developed between the Society's directors and the workers, who alleged that they were being 'unduly interfered with' and resigned. Despite indications that the Settlement was improving the store's volume of trade, and doing valuable propaganda work, the September quarterly meeting of the Society followed the directors' advice and voted to close the Settlement.[30] There were no further Co-operative experiments with social centres and resident workers.

The Guild interpreted the short-lived success of the Coronation Street project as proof that, if Co-operators so chose, they possessed, 'to an almost unlimited degree, the power to raise the whole standard of individual and social life in poor areas.'[31] But the attempt, as Cole put it, to 'mingle storekeeping, if not with philanthropy ... with social service', revealed a gulf between the Guild and the official movement which could not be bridged. Co-operation had become embedded in the self-help culture of the skilled working class by virtue of a reliance upon commercial viability that was threatened by poverty;[32] the prospect of taking the poor on board induced unease: 'It was not "independent"; it was not the sort of self-help they were used to; it savoured too much of soup and blankets even if the poor paid for the soup and blankets.'[33]

Despite the failure of this vision of a Co-operation remodelled to empower the poor, the Sunderland experience undoubtedly helped to strengthen the Guild's sense of itself as a force for progressive change, in the movement and in the wider world, and gave Davies and her fellow-workers a useful education in slum life. In particular, they were exposed to some of the harsher realities of married women's lives, not simply having to make ends meet but also suffering brutality. Davies privately noted a visit to a woman, stone deaf and in bed, 10 days after delivering a still-born child. Her husband of 20 years had died 8 weeks previously: 'he treated her shamefully when drunk, & brought her to poverty. She made me feel *the lumps, like walnuts* in her head where he had whacked her with "anything handy" '.[34] An awareness of this kind of suffering must have informed certain of Davies' attitudes to the divorce question a few years later.

The Guild's next major initiative to activate the movement's social conscience – the campaign for a 'Minimum Wage for Co-operative Female Employees' – achieved a neat convergence of issues of Co-operation, trade unionism and women workers' conditions. The Guild's scrutiny of the Co-operative movement's record as an employer, in part a logical extension of the trade-union principles it had nurtured since the early 1890s, was sharpened by a vigorous national anti-sweating campaign.[35] The 1906 'Sweated Industries Exhibition',[36] featuring live workers, was visited by many guildswomen; Congress that year included a small display of 'sweated' goods, a lecture on the subject by Gertrude Tuckwell of the WTUL, and a resolution in favour of a legal minimum wage for women. Guild inquiries soon revealed that while the AUCE had already advanced the demand for male workers, women workers' need for a living wage was unrecognized.[37] Research revealed it to be an urgent imperative: one manageress of a store taking £400 a week received only 13 shillings a week; a 20-year-old had been employed for three years on 5 shillings a week before a recent increase to 8 shillings.[38]

Working closely with the AUCE in an alliance which produced a sixfold increase in female membership between 1907 and 1912,[39] the Guild instigated a two-pronged campaign for fixed wage scales, aimed at local Societies through branch activity, and at the CWS through a petition. Delegates to the 1909 Co-operative Congress recommended (Congress did not have the power to impose the measure) the implementation of a minimum wage scale in all Societies. By 1910, over 500 Societies had done so for men, but only eight for women. However, as a result of the Guild's efforts this number began to increase, to over 60 in 1911 and more than 250 by 1913, with many others considering the question.[40]

Meanwhile, the CWS petition was presented in March 1910, urging the reform as a step towards 'a living wage' and 'the principle of equal pay for equal work', at the same time accenting the rights and responsibilities of guildswomen in the matter: as Co-operators, keen to be model employers; 'as *Purchasers* and *Propagandists*', wanting goods produced under the optimal conditions; and 'as *Mothers* and *Workers*' responsible for the creation of 'a higher standard of life among women.'[41] Despite 13,337 signatures of guildswomen, and cogent evidence, the CWS directors were not convinced of the need for change. The Guild then sought to apply pressure through CWS customers, mailing all shareholding Societies, distributing leaflets to delegates at CWS quarterly meetings, and appealing to Societies to submit resolutions.

At the CWS quarterly meeting in December 1911 a minimum wage resolution was defeated by 1,523 to 978, and a period of intensive lobbying began to convert the requisite number of voters. Just before the December 1912 quarterly meeting the directors decided to adopt the scale for women distributive workers, and shortly afterwards the quarterly meeting voted for its full implementation, spurred on by the prospect of a worthy act to mark the 1913 CWS Jubilee celebrations. To have converted a defeat of 545 votes into a majority of 130, commented the Guild Annual Report, showed 'very satisfactory educational progress in a year's time'.[42]

During the campaign strong feminist arguments were advanced in support of the claims of women workers. An AUCE member wrote to *Co-operative News*, pointing out that since girls were not taught the importance of combination, there was a great need for the organization of women workers to be carried out 'by women teaching women'.[43] Davies protested to the CWS directors that a self-supporting woman could not survive on 13 shillings a week; at Lewes District Conference in October 1909, Mrs Wimhurst (Lewes) argued that co-operators 'ought not make it compulsory for girls to marry if they did not want to (laughter). Girls were very often compelled to marry because the wages they received were so low that they felt compelled to accept the first offer from a decent man (laughter).'[44]

   The main focus of organized feminism prior to the First World War was the demand for the vote.[45] The oldest of the active suffrage societies could trace their origins back to the 1867 Reform Act, and this staple of the equal rights agenda surfaced intermittently through the remaining decades of the century. By the early 1900s 'the Cause' had the support of a range of constituencies from the Lancashire mill workers, through the WCG, to the more genteel circles of Temperance and Liberal women,[46] and the hard core of suffrage societies, federated as the umbrella NUWSS in 1897, and multiplying to an affiliated membership of 50,000 by 1909. The efforts of these different strands of constitutional suffragism were variously publicized, contradicted, or even submerged by the increasingly militant campaigns of the WSPU, which from its northern socialist origins in 1903 mutated into a socially exclusive corps of martyrs under the autocratic leadership of Christabel Pankhurst, generating along the way splinter groups of more democratic militants.[47]

   Although support for the suffrage demand was, from the outset, high on Margaret Llewelyn Davies' agenda for the WCG, it was not until 1904 that Guild Congress formally adopted this position. Many guildswomen were unsure about the propriety of such an unequivocal claim to a place in this masculine domain; even in 1908 the General Secretary noted 'a section of our members who have not seen the connection between the vote and their home and store, while some branches have refused to take part in our campaign'.[48] The 1904 Congress vote was part of the wider 'women's suffrage revival' of the early years of the century[49] but also the product of an extended, gradual process of internal education, discussion, and activity which enabled Guild members to grasp the various ways in which their lives were affected by the legislative process. The Guild's opposition to a new tax on sugar, and its defence of free trade[50] alerted its members to their parliamentary concerns as Co-operators while its investigations into the conditions of women workers also highlighted their needs for representation. The most direct route to the 1904 Congress vote, however, was through direct involvement in suffrage agitation, and in municipal politics.

The Guild's organic links with the suffrage movement consisted in both the presence of middle-class feminists like Davies and Rosalind Nash,[51] and the close relationship between the Lancashire and Cheshire guilds and the working-class suffragists in the textile industry.[52] The Guild was used in the collection of signatures for 'An Appeal from Women of all Parties and all Classes', launched in the summer of 1893; it contributed only 2,200 of the 250,000 total but the General Secretary was confident that more could have been achieved 'had we made the appeal more widely known among our members.'[53] In 1897, prompted by the successful second reading of Mr Faithfull Begg's women's suffrage Bill in February,[54] four of the Guild Sectional Conferences took the subject 'Why Working Women Need the Vote', and the discussions and votes showed that many guildswomen were ready to 'press their claims to citizenship'.[55]

Sarah Reddish, a prominent figure in the North of England Women's Suffrage Society, was the most visible embodiment of the Guild's association with 'our sisters in the textile trades in urging their just rights to the mark of citizenship'; in 1901 she led the deputation to the House of Commons which presented the Lancashire female textile workers' petition of almost 30,000 signatures.[56] Many other Guild members were involved in the small suffrage societies that began to appear in the mill towns, and Guild branches were active in passing resolutions, lobbying trades councils and MPs, and generally pressing for reform.

For the many Co-operative women who joined the Guild not fully committed to the suffrage, the way into politics was through the local state. The desirability of guildswomen standing for municipal office was endorsed at the 1892 Manchester Festival; in 1894, 45 stood in Poor Law elections, 22 successfully (a number which increased to 36 in 1898).[57] Early anecdotes testify to the different kinds of prejudice encountered by these pioneering candidates. Rotherham Guild found a member of the Women's Liberal Association 'a very suitable candidate', and yet her nomination was rejected by the 'Gentlemen's' Liberal Association: they wanted 'a "lady" and not a "woman"!'[58] In Bolton, when Sarah Reddish was nominated for co-option onto the School Board, 'rather far-fetched arguments were brought to show that Miss Reddish, though "not personally unwelcome," was unwelcome by reason of her being a woman.' She was vindicated at the next regular elections, winning a seat with 12,418 votes and coming sixth out of 18 candidates.[59]

This activity made the Guild especially alert to the erosion of women's already minimal citizenship rights by local government reorganization at the turn of the century. The 1899 London Government Act abolished parish vestries, on which women had had the right to sit, and created Borough Councils, from which they were excluded. The Guild CC asked all branches to write to their MPs protesting 'the injustice of taking from women the small rights they already possess', and to support the London Borough Councils (Women's Disabilities Removal) Bill. However, despite vigorous lobbying the Bill fell at its second reading, leaving, as the General Secretary noted, 'another injustice to women' still to be wiped out.[60] The 1902 Education Act replacing School Boards with local education authorities was condemned by Guild Congress as 'undemocratic and reactionary', firstly because it contained 'no provision for the direct election of women on to the education authority', offering only co-opted seats; and secondly, for taking 'the control of education out of the hands of the people', allowing schools rate support 'without ensuring popular control.'[61] It was this interference with local democracy that finally convinced the Guild CC that it would be appropriate to bring the matter of parliamentary representation before the whole organization at Congress in 1904.[62] As Davies commented: 'this treatment of women is not taking place without effect. Women have been roused, and they realise the weakness of their position without a vote.'[63]

The 1904 Guild Congress approved, with only 12 dissentients, a resolution moved by Sarah Reddish calling for the enfranchisement of women on equal terms with men.[64] Explicit support for the suffrage movement immediately drew the Guild into the complicated debate that was under way about sex, class, and electoral reform. A strong body of opinion in trade-union and Labour Party circles opposed the extension of the suffrage to women on the same terms as it was currently available to men, on the grounds that it would strengthen the anti-Labour vote, and was only prepared to support full adult suffrage. In 1905 this position was adopted by the Labour Representation Committee,[65] and in the same year the Adult Suffrage Society was formed. Yet while purporting to be concerned with strengthening the working-class franchise, it was more active in orchestrating opp limited female suffrage bills than in agitating for a wider use.

In the Guild this debate found expression in the conflict between working-class suffragists and active Labour women. In the 1904 Guild Congress debate, Gertrude Tuckwell (WTUL) declared that she was in the 'horrible position of differing from Miss Reddish'. The WTUL's priority, she claimed, was 'the working women, and they wanted to put the power into the hands of the people who were suffering. They did not want to put power into the hands of the property-owning class, who had had it too long already.' In a similar vein, Mrs Gasson, a guildswoman, pointed out that if the vote was won on the same terms as men, many of them would not qualify as they were neither householders, owners, occupiers or lodgers.' Mrs Moussey (Liverpool) asked if women had the vote on the same terms as men, would women earning 10s a week have the right to vote, and was answered by Mrs Bury that she would if the working man on 10s a week had the vote. The majority of delegates were agreed with Sarah Reddish's view that even a limited female franchise had tactical advantages. They all wanted adult suffrage, Reddish emphasized, the question was: 'how were they to get it? They had no political power.'[66]

Ada Nield Chew, a WTUL organizer,[67] reopened these differences a few months later in a letter to the women's pages of *Co-operative News*. She accused the Women's Suffrage Societies of concealing from working women the true nature of the 'class and property Bill' currently being considered, which, if passed, would enfranchise not one working woman in 50, married or single. 'So women who would not benefit at all are to work for and support a measure which would only benefit rich women, on the understanding that their turn will come some day.'[68]

In response, Davies confirmed womanhood or adult suffrage as the Guild's aim and returned to the question of which policy was most likely to achieve this. Some, she argued, including Mrs Chew, believed that only an adult suffrage bill would do. By contrast, the WCG and the textile women trade unionists maintained 'that as men have not abolished a property qualification for themselves, it is a mistake to cut ourselves off from being able to support any measure which we considered satisfactory as a step towards adult suffrage.' Admittedly, it was difficult to predict accurately the number of women who would qualify for the vote on the same terms as men. But it seemed probable that working women would outnumber the wealthy.[69] Of greater importance than the numbers game, however, was the need to secure women's right to the vote in principle so that future reform would bring adult rather than manhood suffrage.[70] Accordingly, the Guild CC's 'Manifesto on the Enfranchisement of Women' reserved the right to support any bill that did not disqualify married women, and was likely to enfranchise a large proportion of working women.[71]

The 1904 Congress vote opened the high point of Guild suffrage activity. Its immediate objective was to win the equal rights position at the Co-operative Congress. In regard to Co-operators, the initial response was not auspicious. In 1906 the Co-operative Union executive excluded a woman's suffrage resolution from the Congress agenda because it was 'political', an 'unsympathetic official attitude' deplored by the Guild, not only because of the vote's importance to women but because the decision ignored the fact that the movement's national position would be strengthened by reform which enfranchised the large number of female Co-operators.[72] The Guild then embarked upon a two-year propaganda campaign, leafleting the Societies, and conducting a postal ballot of members' husbands, the results of which showed overwhelming support for the enfranchisement of married women.[73] As Davies observed when the question was debated at the 1908 Co-operative Congress, even in their own movement, which they recognized to be 'exceptionally just and generous to women', it was only through 'extreme watchfulness and distasteful self-assertion' that women's needs were considered.[74]

At the 1908 Co-operative Congress, Mr Tweddell, Chairman of the Parliamentary Committee, and a good friend of the Guild, moved the resolution calling for a Government bill to enfranchise women. It was passed almost unanimously, 'only one voice being heard in opposition.'[75] Yet the terms of the debate reflect tensions that were being generated both by militancy and the implications of female enfranchisement on a strict property qualification. Seconding the resolution, Mrs Hodgett (Lincoln), found it expedient to begin by stating that 'she was not a militant suffragette.' She represented '25,000 trained co-operative women', and asked delegates to 'show to the world their earnest desire that co-operative women should be entrusted with the full rights of citizenship, just as they enjoyed those rights in the co-operative State within a State.'[76] Mr Redfearn professed himself partly in agreement with the resolution but wanted to know precisely what was meant by giving votes to women. He insisted that 'the Women's Political Union themselves, those militant suffragettes' were satisfied with the terms of the recent limited franchise bill of Mr Stanger.'[77] Davies replied that 'the property question in relation to the vote was not nearly so important' as the great need for the vote to tackle the many 'grave injustices, hardships, and miseries' in women's lives.[78] Closing the debate, Mr Tweddell reminded delegates that the resolution 'simply pledged Congress to the principle of women's suffrage'. If they were 'to discuss all the side issues, whether it should be a property or any other qualification, they would not get through the discussion until the morrow.'[79]

Alongside the Guild's feminist intervention in the Co-operative movement ran its efforts to represent Co-operative women in the suffrage movement. Branches were asked to write to parliamentary candidates and MPs, and to oppose anti-suffrage electoral candidates, while the pressure for local enfranchisement was sustained.[80] The WCG established a separate Women's Suffrage Fund, and began to collaborate with the suffrage societies in lobbying MPs for their support of private members' bills, leafleting, petitioning, passing resolutions, and participating in deputations to the House of Commons, demonstrations and processions.[81] During the 1906 election campaign, the Guild sent to all cabinet ministers copies of a 'united manifesto' demanding the parliamentary franchise for women, with signatures from labour, political, and temperance organizations including the Women's Liberal Federation, the North of England Weavers' Association, and the ILP.[82]

As well as emphasizing broad-based support for the suffrage demand, the Guild also sought to extend its scope. The proposal that occupiers' wives should qualify for the vote, set out in a letter to the press from the General Secretary in December 1906, elicited a favourable response from a Liberal MP, W.H. Dickinson, who was introducing a Women's Enfranchisement Bill. The Guild sent a memorandum on the subject to MPs but for 'tactical reasons' the measure was not included, and although there were plans to bring it forward as an amendment at committee stage, the Bill fell for want of time at its second reading in March 1907.[83] Dickinson's second attempt – Enfranchisement of Women No. 2 – was brought in at the end of the 1907 session, and did include the wives of voters,[84] but made even less progress than its predecessor. Mr Stanger's Bill in 1908 – of which Mr Redfearn was so dismissive in the Co-operative Congress debate that year – was confined to the removal of sex disability from the existing franchises and aroused little enthusiasm from guildswomen. In 1909, however, the Howard Bill, which also passed a second reading but got no further, sought to give residential suffrage to men and women, and a Guild memorandum was dispatched to MPs, stressing its support for 'a larger measure than Mr Stanger's Bill of last session.'[85]

Yet the Guild's attempt to hold together feminist and working-class interests in the suffrage movement by extending the suffrage qualification was under strain. The 'tactical reasons' that prevented the inclusion of voters' wives in the original Dickinson Bill referred to the conviction of many suffragists that any measure toward adult suffrage would weaken the chances of such a bill. Mrs Fawcett viewed the Howard Bill as 'practically universal suffrage', and recorded that it 'alienated all Conservative and much moderate Liberal support, and was taken in the face of the strongly expressed protests of all the suffrage societies.'[86] This kind of attitude created hostility among working women who were being asked to support limited bills from which they would not immediately benefit.[87] At the same time, the growing momentum of WSPU militancy was splitting the suffrage movement and alienating many working-class women from broad sexual solidarity.[88]

Irritation at the NUWSS's attitude to the Howard Bill and the 'reaction against militancy'[89] both found expression at the 1909 WCG Congress, which resolved that only adult suffrage would be 'consistent' with the Guild's democratic aims of establishing equality between 'men and women, married and single, rich and poor.'[90] As the vote – 238 to 232 – makes plain, the issue was closely fought, turning around tactical as well as ideological differences. Nevertheless, the formal refusal of any reform short of adult suffrage implied an indefinite deferral of women's political rights. Neither the Liberals nor the Conservatives had any reason to introduce adult suffrage, and Labour – the only party with a strong electoral interest in such reform – had ignored the matter until roused by the women's agitation, and still seemed more intent on orchestrating opposition to a limited female suffrage than on pressing for adult suffrage.

Determined to keep alive the claims of women while honouring the Guild's decision to enter the adult suffrage camp, in the same year Davies was prominent in the foundation of the People's Suffrage Federation. Its aim was to obtain 'the Parliamentary vote for every adult man and woman', with only a short residential qualification.[91] Davies herself refused to criticize the WSPU.[92] Interviewed by *The Woman Worker*, she stressed that it was thanks to their agitation that the women's interests would not be ignored. Nevertheless, she faithfully represented the Guild's official position. 'The Limited Bill is so obnoxious to us,' she explained, 'We feel that a personal, and not a property basis, is the only democratic one. Any property or tenancy qualification would place the working-class women at a disadvantage.'[93]

The PSF immediately became the organizational means by which guildswomen continued to be active in the suffrage campaign, transferring, as Davies put it, the Guild's aim of 'Equal Fellowship of men and women' to the 'suffrage platform.'[94] By 1911, 68 WCG branches had affiliated to the PSF,[95] and Guild Congress that year featured an evening meeting in which Margaret Bondfield – for the PSF – debated a speaker from the National Association for Opposing Women's Suffrage.[96] The PSF gained support from the other working-class women's organizations – the WLL, the WTUL, the NFWW, the Railway Women's Guild – and many ILP branches. Also involved were leading labour and socialist women – Margaret Bondfield, Mary Macarthur, and Margaret Macmillan, left-wing politicians and academics such as Arthur Henderson, George Lansbury, Bertrand Russell, the Webbs, and a number of enlightened Liberals.[97] It was thus well placed to bring pressure to bear on Liberal MPs, the PLP and the Labour Party, to take the women's cause more seriously, and to outflank the anti-feminist camp within the Labour Party. More than two years of patient effort by the PSF was thus a key factor in securing by a large majority the backing of the Labour Party Conference in 1912 for a resolution stipulating that 'no Bill can be acceptable to the Labour and Socialist Movement which does not include women'.[98]

The 1912 vote opened a period of close collaboration between the NUWSS and the Labour Party,[99] which drew the Guild back into the mainstream of suffrage agitation, its efforts now co-ordinated by the Citizenship Sub-Committee that was formed that year.[100] Guild branches pressed MPs to vote for amendments to the 1912–13 Reform Bill that would 'enfranchise married women.'[101] Early in 1913 the Guild CC joined with the NUWSS, the WFL, the WSPU, and the WLL in condemning the Speaker's ruling against the women's suffrage amendment, and demanding a government sponsored adult suffrage bill as the only measure capable of restoring 'the lost confidence of the women'.[102] Guildswomen joined the NUWSS-organized Women's Suffrage Pilgrimage to London in July 1913.[103] Although mass suffrage agitation lapsed with the outbreak of war, when franchise reform again appeared on the political agenda in 1917, the Guild was among those women's organizations alert to the need to press the women's case,[104] and then to sustain the momentum of citizenship work for women after the vote was won. 'The terms of enfranchisement have given the vote to practically all co-operative women', declared the 1918 Guild Annual Report, 'while the decision of co-operators to take political action turns the movement into the political organisation specially suitable to voice the reforms desired by married women.'[105]

It followed from the WCG's view of the vote as a weapon for reform, rather than an end in itself, that however valuable the franchise might eventually prove to be, there was much that the Guild could accomplish in the interim. The Citizenship Sub-Committee's brief 'to watch and initiate legislation and administration in the interests of married working women',[106] was a formal registration of the role that had been maturing within the organization since the 1890s. By 1912 this included the Guild's heavy involvement in the campaigns for divorce law reform and maternity care, both of which by now overshadowed its support for the suffrage movement, and focused on its special character as an organization of married women.

As such, the Guild had a particular interest in the public debate about maternal and infant welfare that gained momentum following the Boer War;[107] and its role in these proceedings is in itself a measure of the national recognition it had achieved as the representative of this constituency. Its campaigns to improve the care of maternity reveal two overarching concerns: firstly, to prioritize the needs of the mother; secondly, to shift some the financial burden of maternity from the family to the state.

In 1910, when the preparation of national insurance legislation was announced, the Guild applied to the Chancellor of the Exchequer for information about the provision being made for women, and was invited 'to send a private and informal deputation'. By way of preparation, the national office undertook a brief survey of the conditions of maternity. With its base in the consumers' Co-operative movement, the Guild was acutely aware of the dynamics of the family economy and the daily struggle to make ends meet that was the norm for many working women. When a baby was born, the situation worsened: the findings of the Guild's inquiry into the question showed 'that the great mass of wage earners are unable to provide adequately, and that the provision is usually at the cost of the woman.'[108] In one case, the husband had been thrown out of work when his wife was preganant with their seventh child, and she had been obliged to work long hours at home as a sewing machinist; the baby was born deformed and lived only a month, while she never regained her strength. Another couple was trying to live on the 18 shillings a week earnt by the husband and the few shillings the wife made as a machinist: none of their five children had survived. A woman had died giving birth to her fourth child, while a family with six children was trying to live on 25 shillings a week, when rent alone cost 8 shillings.[109]

Guild officials were already convinced of the need for a national system of maternity care, detached from insurance altogether, since those in greatest need were not eligible for benefits. This view was expressed by the Guild deputation to the House of Commons in March 1911, in its meeting with the Attorney General, Sir Rufus Isaacs, standing in for Lloyd

George.[110] Mrs Layton, drawing on her experience as a midwife, explained that even when the husband gave everything he could from his wages, the only way a woman could pay for her confinement was by 'going short herself, as the man had to be kept going for the work's sake, and it would break her heart to starve the children.' Sir Rufus asked her what sum of money was required. 'I told him that nothing less than £5 would see her through comfortably. He said that such an amount was impossible,' and suggested 30 shillings.[111]

The news, a few weeks later, that a bill would be introduced during the forthcoming session of Parliament galvanized the Guild into action. At short notice the spring Sectional Conferences were reorganized to facilitate a full discussion of married women's needs in relation to state insurance so that they could make their own proposals. 'Up to the present', Davies told delegates at a conference in Manchester, 'little public thought had been given to married women's conditions and needs, and the urgency of providing for maternity had not been realised.' The additional costs involved in childbirth, estimated at between £3 and £5, were way beyond average earnings. Noting the drawbacks of a contributory scheme, which excluded those most in need, Davies pointed to the advantages of a standard municipal scheme of maternal medical care, funded by the central state. In the short term, the Sectional Conferences called for the new scheme to make provision for married women's sickness, invalidity and maternity needs. 'If the State could provide for Dreadnoughts, and pensions for those who served in the Army', Mrs Haworth (Accrington) commented, 'then why not raise the ideals of motherhood?'[112]

When the National Insurance Bill was published, the Guild gave a qualified welcome to a measure which indicated a 'new realisation of the common responsibility of the whole nation for some of the worst results of our social and industrial conditions', and to the clause which provided maternity benefit for the wives of insured men and for married women who were insured in their own right. Although 'small in amount', commented the women's pages, 'it is a beginning which may be developed into more complete provision.' Yet Lloyd George's exclusion of 'non-working' women from general health cover was denounced as 'a most serious blot on this scheme' and a massive undervaluation of their work, ignoring

112

as it did the vital importance of their endless hard work caring for the home and bringing up the family. The mother 'cooks, cleans, washes, bakes, makes and mends clothes'; if she became ill, family life disintegrated; hence there was enormous pressure on her to sacrifice her own health and keep going.[113]

In her report to Congress that year, the General Secretary accentuated this point. In the Bill, she explained, 'Mr Lloyd George spoke of married women who were not wage earners as non-workers. ("Oh", and laughter). Mr Lloyd George needed a little reminder of the fact that they were workers. (Hear, hear.) They had to make a great stir, and show the Chancellor of the Exchequer that women who remained at home were workers, and that their work was as arduous as any other kind of work and just as valuable. (Hear, hear.).'[114] Delegates unanimously resolved that married women should be eligible for the two-penny state contributions, and that non-waged women who could afford to pay their own contributions should be admitted to the scheme. Modifications of the proposed system of maternity benefits were also passed, including the demand that the 30-shilling cash payment should be the property of the mother. As one practically minded delegate observed, maternity benefit would not eradicate the need for a living wage, 'but meanwhile the babies kept being born. A patch was better than a hole.'[115]

The Guild national office promptly busied itself making the 'great stir'. During the various stages of the Bill's passage, it worked with the WLL, the NUWW, and other women's groups, organizing deputations to Lloyd George, the lobbying of MPs and the Co-operative Parliamentary Committee, national and local public meetings, and letters to the press. The 'sense of injustice', wrote Davies and Harris in a letter to the *Westminster Gazette*, which broadcast the issue to a wider audience, 'rests on the fact that the claims of married women are unrecognized as regards medical, sick sanitorium, or disablement benefits unless they happen to be wage earners. Non-wage-earning women form an army of six to seven million of workers in the home, from whom life extracts more than any other class, perhaps, and who are humorously described as "non-workers" in the memorandum on the Bill.' These women should be fully entitled to the state contribution since 'provision for the needs of the whole family is the joint work of both parents, the man's wages and the woman's domestic labour (which has its direct money value) being equally indispensable.'[116]

As a result of this agitation – Lloyd George 'made a kind reference in the House of Commons to the work done by the General Secretary'[117] – specific sections of the Bill were redrafted to give married women the option of paying into the scheme, although qualifying for only half the state contribution in the absence of an employer's share. Mindful of the potentially 'disastrous' impact of married women's health problems on the funds of an insurance society, the Chancellor could not see his way to making them eligible for full sick pay. Furthermore, the 30-shillings maternity benefit was to be the husband's property unless the wife had separate insurance, with a safeguard (clause 19) that men who spent the money for some other pupose would be liable to prosecution.[118]

This question of the ownership of maternity benefit became the subject of a major Guild campaign in 1913 during the passage of the amending Bill.[119] With the firm backing of Congress in the matter, the Citizenship Sub-Committee arranged for the Commissioners drafting the Bill to receive a Guild deputation at a meeting which witnessed 'prolonged and animated discussion'. The Guild's main contention was that the current check against abuse of the system – prosecution under clause 19 – could not achieve its purpose: 'what women needed at such a time', argued the General Secretary, 'was the maternity benefit and the wages that their husbands could bring in rather than imprisonment', while Mrs Layton, a former midwife, was emphatic about 'the importance of handing the cash direct to the woman and making it her property'.[120]

Despite a sympathetic reception, the Guild's points were not included when the Bill was published. Pressure therefore had to be applied at the committee stage. 'I have been so extremely busy', Davies wrote to Leonard Woolf, 'having got landed in quite a big campaign over the Maty. [sic] benefit – begun without the faintest hope of success, but gleams have appeared, and we are now straining every nerve.'[121] Guildswomen were asked to send resolutions and letters to MPs; examples of cases where the benefit had been spent by husbands were collected from members and sent to Liberal, Labour, and Unionist MPs;[122] support was obtained from the Co-operative Parliamentary Committee, and letters and articles despatched to the press.[123]

To spearhead this activity, Guild officials attended the relevant sessions of the Parliamentary Standing Committee to press their case.[124] This mainly engaged the General Secretary and Miss Bondfield, but the whole of the CC was there for the first discussion of maternity benefit since it coincided with their scheduled meeting. Their presence would have made an interesting difference to the proceedings: gathered in the large committee room upstairs in the House of Commons were the 80 MPs on one side of the low wooden barrier, and on the other the visitors, predominantly representatives from the various industrial, friendly, and trade-union societies watching over their interests with their legal advisers. For the guildswomen, the overwhelmingly masculine character of the occasion underlined the need 'not only for women to be present to watch Bills in which they were interested', but also to sit on the committees.[125]

The guildswomen witnessed the chief opposition to their position coming from the 'five Labour men' on the Committee. They took, it was reported, 'a definite line against the view that it should be her property',[126] George Roberts MP expressing his 'abhorrence against the unnecessary intervention of the State between a man and his wife.' Despite such objections, however, the Committee eventually recommended that the Benefit should be the legal property of the wife.[127] But when the Bill reached the Report Stage, the Labour members again moved that the legislation should authorize receipt by either the husband or the wife.[128] Unwilling to accept this 'undermining in practice of what we have gained in principle', Guild officers rose to the challenge of explaining their position to the whole House. The General Secretary urged branches to write again to MPs;[129] a fresh memorandum was prepared; and in less than a week's frenzied activity, a petition was drawn up, signed by 700 women with 'practical knowledge of administration and public work ... members of town councils, boards of guardians, insurance committees, nursing and midwives' associations, women sanitary inspectors and health visitors, etc.',[130] and sent with a covering letter to all MPs and to the press.

When the matter came to the Commons,[131] 'interest in the House was great.' As had been the case in the Standing Committee, 'the Members were left free to vote ... no Government Whips being put on.' Once again, the exception to this party-political agnosticism was Labour, led by George Roberts: 'I should have regarded it as a gross insult and an unwarrantable reflection on my character', he pronounced, 'if Parliament had said, "We cannot trust you with 30s, and you shall not touch the benefit which comes into your home".'[132] Supporters for the husband's right of receipt included Lloyd George and Masterman, but there were some powerful interventions against them. If there were men, stated Mr Beck, 'whose pride of manhood is outraged by the fact that the 30s is conveyed directly to their wives, then I say those men do not deserve the encouragement of this House.'[133] Mr Snowden believed that Mr Roberts 'heartily approves of the last part of the tenth commandment. He would place the man's wife in the same category as the man's ox and the man's ass.'[134]

When it came to the vote, after more than two hours of debate, the Labour amendment was carried by nine votes, although Davies was of the opinion that the Honourable Members were 'so astray without their shepherds that some got into the wrong lobby, and it seems probable that we should have won had the MPs realised what they were doing.' Fortunately, there was a fall-back position. Lord Robert Cecil, 'who had previously received a small Guild deputation', further amended the clause so that the husband would receive the benefit only 'if authorised by her', to test 'whether there is a genuine desire to save the money for the woman.' This provided further opportunity to rehearse the contending points of view but eventually the amended clause was carried by 186 ayes to 165 noes.[135]

This was a splendid victory, and the General Secretary was pleased to quote some of the tributes from the press: 'We take off our hats to Miss Llewelyn Davies and Miss Bondfield', announced the *New Statesman*, 'in recognition of a singularly successful campaign on behalf of married women.' 'If the House of Commons had gone about women's suffrage,' stated the *Manchester Guardian*, 'it could not have done anything better than its debate on the maternity benefit.'[136] The Guild itself hailed the measure as 'the first public recognition of the mother's place in the home, and the first step towards some economic independence for wives.' It constituted a recognition of two things: firstly, that 'the wife, by her work (though unpaid) in the home, contributes to the support of the family;' secondly, 'that just as an employed woman's earnings are her own, so money due to a woman as mother shall be legally hers.' Underlining the feminist significance of this development, it was noted that another point had thus been added 'to the Wives' Charter, of which the first was the Married Women's Property Act.'[137]

Yet there was also the opposition of the Labour men to be registered: 'what can be said', the Guild reporter commented despairingly, of a Labour member 'who argued that to insist on the money being paid to the woman was an insult to the working man? This is an attitude of mind confined to a type of people whom we recognise as "archaic".'[138] Here was an instance of precisely the kind of masculine assumption of responsibility for the dependent wife that the Guild was trying to challenge, partly because it denied the woman any financial autonomy, but also because it left her so vulnerable in cases where the husband's provision was not adequate. The conviction of Labour members that for better or for worse, relations between man and wife were inviolable was very marked. Indeed, J.H. Thomas even went so far as to argue that 'in a home where there is a bad husband', the measure would exacerbate the situation: the wife 'knows what is likely to take place and the misery that must result on her refusal to make this his property.'[139] That such positions could command the loyal support of Labour women was indicated in the WLL's statement, read to the Standing Committee by Ramsay Macdonald, that 'this is not a matter on which we feel very strongly.' Summing up the Labour view, Macdonald explained that 'we regard this as family benefit'. It was 'not the property of the mother exclusively'.[140] The belief that the extension of any rights to the wife must subtract from the status of the husband dovetailed with trade-union concerns about the effect of cash benefits on wage levels and collective bargaining, and reflected an enduring body of opinion in the labour movement that was to surface again in the 1920s over family allowances and birth control.

In 1913 the work for maternity benefit led the Guild straight into a campaign to establish a national scheme – for which all women would be eligible – of state-funded, municipal maternity centres, administered by the public health authorities. These proposals were set out by a private deputation to Herbert Samuel, President of the Local Government Board, in October 1913, and were 'sympathetically received'.[141] Any doubts about the progress of this area of work were removed with the outbreak of war. While 'most social reform work became impossible', the mass slaughter of trench warfare generated a heightened concern for future generations which 'raised to still greater importance' maternal welfare.[142] In 1915 the municipalities were empowered to set up maternity committees, to include representatives from working women's organizations, and many Guild branches found 'a perceptible change in the attitude of many health authorities, and a marked improvement in their readiness to consider schemes.'[143]

The Guild made a further contribution to public awareness of this question with the publication of *Maternity: Letters from Working Women* (1915), consisting of 386 letters from current and former Guild officials, giving their experiences of childbearing, with an introduction by Margaret Llewelyn Davies. 'A book of notable interest and singular distinction', wrote *The Times* reviewer, 'on the distresses, hardships, suffering, and enfeeblement, which poverty and maternity between them inflict on women.' It made a great impression on the reading public, going into a second edition within three months.[144] In his preface, Herbert Samuel expressed regret that 'an unwise public reticence' had prevented the 'public mind' from realizing the existence of such 'urgent social problems.'[145]

As well as providing details of the variety of ways in which women bore the cost of childbearing,[146] the letters contain a number of references to the use of 'artifical means' to prevent conception, and to abortion.[147] In her introduction to *Maternity*, Davies identified the 'deliberate limitation of the family' as the main cause of the declining birth rate, adding that while some viewed this development as 'the suicide of a nation and the doom of a race', others regarded it as 'the clearest solution of the inextricable tangle in which the industrial system has enmeshed humanity'.[148]

The Guild office also used information supplied by guildswomen as part of its submission to the Government Food

Prices Committee in 1916, to prove 'the serious under-consumption arising from the high prices among many classes, and especially the effect on mothers and young children.' Similar material was sent to the press, to publicize both the adverse effects of wartime profiteering and the justice of workers' demands for higher wages. An article by Davies in *The Star* in August 1916, for example, entitled 'How the Poor Live Today told by themselves', gave details of two struggling mothers, one of whom had lost her twin babies through 'want of nourishment'.[149]

Evidence of this kind helped to sustain pressure for a comprehensive national maternity scheme, and the Guild continued to monitor legislative developments, especially the progress of the Maternal and Infant Welfare Bill. In May 1917 a Guild deputation to the President of the Local Government Board, Lord Rhondda, put forward detailed proposals. Guildswomen from each of the sections made separate points about local conditions, 'one Welshwoman telling Lord Rhondda of what went on in his coalfield'; the peer listened patiently for an hour and a half, having said at the outset that he could only spare 30 minutes, and finally admitted that he 'had no idea there was such a well organised body of working women as the WCG.'[150] The 'long delayed' Maternity and Infant Welfare Act was finally passed in the summer of 1918, empowering but not compelling local authorities to make a range of provision, including maternity homes and home-help services; Guild branches were urged to seek representation on the maternity committees that the authorities making such provision were now required to form.[151]

In less than a decade, state provision for maternity had grown from being a relatively small feature of the new National Insurance scheme to become a rapidly expanding, if not mandatory, element of local authority welfare provision, in which many Guild branches soon became active. The further potential of statutory provision for married women was indicated by the wartime experimental scheme of Separation Allowances. The 'valuable results of a regular, reliable sum of money being at the mother's disposal' strengthened the case for a scheme of Motherhood or Family Endowment, which in the immediate post-war years became a major element in the Guild's demands.[152]

The Guild's campaigning work from the 1890s to the First

119

World War showed that even disenfranchised working women could, if properly organized, intervene effectively in both the working-class movement and the legislative process. The Guild's efforts to shape Co-operative policy, and to secure national reforms in the interests of working-class wives, generated radical ideas about the Co-operative women and their place in society, but were grounded in the practical mobilization of those women as a force for change. Gathering evidence to prove the justice of the case, passing resolutions, preparing and distributing leaflets and memoranda, arranging deputations, petitioning, synchronizing local and national interventions, using the press for publicity – all these required a high level of organizational efficiency, as well as a sophisticated understanding of the workings of the target institution and the best points at which to apply leverage. The methods that the Guild used in the committee rooms and chambers of Westminster were first honed in the boardrooms and conference halls of the Co-operative movement, and in both contexts produced a growing sense of agency in its membership. This found its most militant expression in the Guild's involvement with the issue of divorce law reform, and the next chapter traces the process by which the rank and file of the Guild entered into a dispute with the officials of the Co-operative movement over their right to operate not simply as an appendage of Co-operative trading, but as 'a great and growing movement, controlled by its members, expressing their needs and aspirations, fighting their battles and winning a place for married women in the counsels of co-operation and the nation.'[153]

Notes

1. Miss Reddish, *Women's Guilds With Special Reference to their Claims on the Attention and Support of Educational Committees,* Co-operative Educational Committees' Association Annual Meeting (Bolton: Henry Smith, 1890, p. 4).
2. 'Peaceful Campaigns by Two Old Campaigners', typed MS, 1933, 'Material illustrating the work of the guild and kindred interests, manuscript, typed and printed papers, photographs, erstwhile property of Margaret Llewelyn Davies (1890–?1944)', 11 vols., British Library of Political and Economic Science, 1, item 41.

3. MLD, 'Preface', in C. Webb, *The Woman with the Basket: the History of the Women's Co-operative Guild* (Manchester: The Guild, 1927).

4. G.D.H. Cole, *A Century of Co-operation* (London: Allen & Unwin for the Co-operative Union, 1944, p. 217).

5. WCG, 'The Women's Co-operative Guild, 1895–1916: A Review of Twenty-One Years' Work', *Annual Congress Handbook*, London, 1916, p. 10.

6. Miss Llewelyn Davies, 'Branch Work of the Women's Guild', Open Guild Meeting, *Co-operative Congress Report (CCR)*, 1888, p. 107.

7. 'Speech of newly-elected General Secretary, 7th Annual Guild Meeting', *CCR*, 1889, p. 106.

8. Clementina Black (1854–1922) trade union organizer and suffragist, see N.C. Soldon, *Women in British Trade Unions 1874–1976* (Dublin: Gill and Macmillan, 1978, p. 29).

9. Clementina Black, *A Natural Alliance* (London: Co-operative Printing Society, 1892, p. 8).

10. 'Report of Women's Guild', *CCR*, 1893, p. 56; WCG, *Annual Report*, 1892–3, p. 18.

11. 'Report of Women's Guild', *CCR*, 1894, p. 60.

12. Formed in 1894 to carry out systematic investigation into the condition of industrial women and promote reform; Clementina Black was one of its active members. See G. Holloway, 'A Common Cause? Class Dynamics in the Industrial Women's Movement, 1888–1918', Sussex University D.Phil. thesis, 1995, pp. 54–61.

13. WCG, *Annual Report*, 1892–93, p. 19.

14. WCG, *Investigations Papers* (Kirkby Lonsdale: WCG, 1895).

15. *Co-operative News*, 1 April 1899, p. 339.

16. WCG, *Annual Report*, 1895–6, p. 9.

17. In 1894 the Hatters' and Trimmers' Union secretary wrote thanking the Guild members for their efforts to ensure that only goods bearing the legend 'This Hat Union Made' were supplied by Co-op stores, M. Llewelyn Davies, *The Women's Co-operative Guild* (Kirkby Lonsdale: WCG, 1904, p. 125).

18. WCG, *Annual Report*, 1898–9, p. 7.

19. MLD, 'Co-operation at the Fountainhead', *Life and Labour*, Chicago, **K**, no. 7 (September 1920), pp. 199–202, 'Material ...' (see note 2), **1**, item 25.

20. Miss Llewelyn Davies, WCG, *A Co-operative Colony: Papers reprinted from Co-operative News, dealing with a scheme of Co-operation for poor neighbourhoods* (Manchester: Co-operative Newspaper Society, 1900, pp. 4–5).

21. WCG, *The Extension of Co-operation to the Poor: Report of an Inquiry made by the Guild, December 1901, January & February,*

1902 (Manchester: Co-operative Newspaper Society, 1902, p. 3).

22. *Co-operative News*, 5 August 1899, p. 878; MLD, *The WCG*, p. 76; WCG, *Annual Report*, 1899–1900, pp. 6–8; M. Llewelyn Davies, WCG Woolwich Congress, June 1900, *A Co-operative Relief Column or How to Adapt Co-operation to the Needs of Poor Districts* (Manchester: Co-operative Newspaper Society, 1900); MLD, *A Co-operative Colony.*

23. WCG, *Extension of Co-operation*, p. 25. The conference took place in York.

24. MLD, *The WCG*, p. 81.

25. Ibid., p. 77.

26. In this, Davies was influenced by the Chicago settlement worker, Jane Addams (1860–1935), whose book *Democracy and Social Ethics*, New York, 1902, emphasized the need for democratic and constructive relations with the poor; see A. F. Davis, *American Heroine: The Life and Legend of Jane Addams* (New York, OUP, 1973, p. 127); MLD, *The WCG*, p. 95; E.M. Janes Yeo, *Contest for Social Science in Britain: relations and representations of gender and class in the nineteenth and twentieth centuries* (London: Rivers Oram, 1996, pp. 268–71).

27. MLD, *A Co-operative Relief Column*, p. 16.

28. For more detailed accounts of the Sunderland Co-operative Settlement see MLD, *The WCG*, pp. 82–95; 'Material ...', (see note 2), 2–6.

29. *Co-operative News*, 26 November 1904, p. 1448.

30. Cole, op. cit., p. 223; 'Report of Women's Guild', CCR, 1904, p. 171.

31. MLD, *The WCG*, p. 95.

32. Cole, op. cit., p. 71.

33. Ibid., p. 223.

34. MLD, MS Notebook, 'Printed and MS material connected with propaganda work organised by the Coronation Street branch of the Sunderland Co-operative Society', 'Material ...' (see note 2), **2**, item 7, emphasis in original.

35. For details see Soldon, op. cit., pp. 63–8. The agitation led eventually to the 1909 and 1918 Trade Boards Acts to regulate wages and conditions in non-unionized trades.

36. Based on a similar Berlin exhibition in 1906, it continued for six weeks, and received 30,000 visitors. A key organizer was Mary Macarthur. Soldon, op. cit., pp. 64–6.

37. 'Report of Women's Guild', CCR, 1907, p. 154; see P. Redfern, *The Story of the CWS: the Jubilee History of the Co-operative Wholesale Society Ltd. 1963–1913* (Manchester: CWS, 1913, for this campaign from the point of view of the CWS Directors).

38. 'Report of Women's Guild', *CCR*, 1908, p. 145.
39. From about 500 in 1907 to 3,000 in 1912, 'Report of Women's Guild', *CCR*, 1910, p. 229; 1912, p. 180.
40. Ibid., 1909, p. 397; 1913, p. 238; 1911, p. 193; 1910, p. 229.
41. WCG, *Petition to the Co-operative Wholesale Society, Minimum Wage for Women Employees*, n.d.
42. 'Report of Women's Guild', *CCR*, 1913, p. 238; 1912, p. 181; Redfearn, op. cit., p. 363. Redfearn gives the total vote as 1,104–1,243, a majority of 140 not 130.
43. *Co-operative News*, 20 January 1911, p. 79.
44. *Sussex Daily News*, 28 October 1909, Gertrude Tuckwell Collection.
45. The subject of a vast literature, in particular, Ray Strachey, *The Cause* (1928) (London: Virago, 1978); E.S. Pankhurst, *The Suffragette Movement: an Intimate Account of Persons and Ideas* (1932) (London: Virago, 1977); R. Fulford, *Votes for Women* (London: Faber, 1957); C. Rover, *Women's Suffrage and Party Politics in Britain*, 1866–1914 (London: Routledge and Kegan Paul, 1967); Liddington and Norris, '*One Hand Tied Behind Us': the Rise of the Women's Suffrage Movement* (London: Virago, 1978); L. Garner, *Stepping Stones to Women's Liberty Feminist Ideas in the Women's Suffrage Movement 1900–1918* (London: Heinemann Educational Books, 1984); S. Holton, *Feminism and Democracy: Women's Suffrage and Reform Politics in Britain, 1900–1918* (Cambridge University Press, 1986); D. Rubinstein, *A Different World for Women: the Life of Millicent Garrett Fawcett* (New York: Harvester, Wheatsheaf, 1991).
46. The Women's Liberal Association split from the official Women's Liberal Federation over the issue in 1893.
47. The Women's Freedom League split from the WSPU in 1907 in protest at the lack of democracy; in 1912 Sylvia Pankhurst founded the East London Federation of Suffragettes; the NUWSS began distancing itself from the Militants in 1908. See Garner, op. cit., for a political analysis of these shifting relationships.
48. 'Report of Women's Guild', *Co-operative Congress Report (CCR)*, 1908, p. 147.
49. Ibid., 1905, p. 175.
50. WCG, *Annual Report*, 1901–2, p. 11; 1904, p. 173.
51. Personally connected with prominent suffrage activists such as Helena Swanwick (see Chapter 1, note 40) with whom they were at Girton in the 1880s.
52. See Liddington and Norris, op. cit., for a detailed picture of the overlapping circles of women's unions, suffrage societies, and WCG branches in Lancashire and Cheshire at the turn of the century.

53. 'Report of Women's Guild,' *CCR*, 1894, p. 61; Liddington & Norris, op. cit., pp. 76–7.
54. The first to do so since 1886; the Bill was 'talked out' at committee stage in July 1897.
55. *Co-operative News*, 10 April 1897, p. 387; 17 April 1897, p. 410; see also chapter 3. This support from an organization of '10,000 of the most capable and thoughtful of working women of the country' was duly registered: see, H. Blackburn, *Women's Suffrage: A Record of the Women's Suffrage Movement in the British Isles* (1902) (New York: Kraus Reprint Co., 1971, p. 211.
56. WCG, *Annual Report*, 1901–2, p. 5.
57. MLD, *The WCG*, p. 135; WCG, *Annual Report*, 1892–3, p. 7; 1894–5, p. 24; 1897–8, p. 8.
58. WCG, *Annual Report*, 1897–8, p. 8.
59. Ibid., 1899–1900, pp. 18–19.
60. Ibid., p. 18; 1900–01, p. 14.
61. Ibid., 1901–2, p. 12; 1903, p. 166.
62. Rosalind Nash, 'The Co-operator and the Citizen', Brougham Villiers (ed.), *The Case for Women's Suffrage* (London: Fisher & Unwin, 1907, p. 71).
63. MLD, *The WCG*, p. 141.
64. 'Guild Congress Supplement', *Co-operative News*, 23 July 1904, p. 917.
65. By a majority of 483 to 270, J. Liddington, *The Life and Times of a Respectable Rebel: Selina Cooper 1864 to 1946* (London: Virago, 1984, p. 166).
66. 'Guild Congress Supplement', *Co-operative News*, 23 July 1904, p. 917.
67. Ada Nield Chew later revised her position, see D. Nield Chew (ed.), *The Life and Writings of Ada Nield Chew* (London: Virago, 1982); G. Holloway, 'A Common Cause? Class Dynamics in the Industrial Women's Movement, 1888–1918', Sussex University D.Phil. thesis, pp. 154–7.
68. *Co-operative News*, 10 December 1904, p. 1507.
69. See Liddington, *Selina Cooper*, pp. 143–5, 160–3 for further claims and counterclaims on this question.
70. *Co-operative News*, 17 December 1904, p. 1559.
71. 'Report of Women's Guild', *CCR*, 1905, p. 176.
72. WCG, *Annual Report*, 1906–7, p. 14.
73. 'Report of Women's Guild', *CCR*, 1909, p. 167. Of the 1,626, 1,346 were in favour of married women having the Parliamentary vote, 170 believed the vote should go to rate-paying women only, 16 were doubtful, and 94 opposed to the female franchise.
74. 'Discussion on Report: Women's Suffrage', *CCR*, 1908, p. 357.

75. Ibid., p. 353 and 358.
76. Ibid., p. 355.
77. Ibid., p. 356. Henry York Stanger, Liberal; the Bill passed its second reading in February 1908 but made no further progress.
78. Ibid., p. 357.
79. Ibid., p. 358.
80. *Co-operative News*, 29 October 1904, p. 1338.
81. 'Report of Women's Guild', *CCR*, 1905, p. 176; 1906, p. 161; 1907, p. 154; 1909, p. 167.
82. Ibid., 1906, p. 161. See also Pankhurst, op. cit., p. 196. Pankhurst comments that 'such efforts were virtually unnoticed by any save the signatories.'
83. 'Report of Women's Guild', *CCR*, 1907, pp. 154–5.
84. Ibid., 1908, p. 147.
85. Ibid., 1909, p. 168.
86. M.G. Fawcett, *Women's Suffrage: A Short History of a Great Movement* (London: T.L. & E.C. Jack, 1912, p. 70).
87. See Holton, op. cit., pp. 60–2 for a fuller discussion.
88. See H. Mitchell, *The Hard Way Up: the Autobiography of Hannah Mitchell Suffragette and Rebel* (1968) (London: Virago, 1977, chs 11–16); see also Liddington & Norris, op. cit., ch. 11; Liddington, *Selina Cooper*, ch. 12.
89. Rover, op. cit., p. 161.
90. *Oldham Chronicle*, 26 June 1909, Gertrude Tuckwell Collection.
91. WCG, *Annual Report*, 1909–10, p. 11. See Holton for the significance of democratic suffragism in the wider movement, op. cit., ch. 3.
92. 'I've always felt all the talk about militancy having really put back the movement all nonsense.' MLD to L. Woolf, Sunday, n.d. (?1913), Monks House Papers, University of Sussex.
93. *The Woman Worker*, 10 November 1909, p. 437.
94. Ibid.
95. 'Report of Women's Guild', *CCR*, 1911, p. 197.
96. *Co-operative News*, 1 July 1911, p. 855.
97. *The Woman Worker*, 1 December 1909, p. 504; 'Report of Women's Guild', *CCR*, 1910, p. 231; Mary Macarthur and MLD, memorial to Gladstone in 1909, setting out the PSF's objects; Gladstone Papers, **LXXXIII**, British Museum Add. MS 46067 f. 331 (1909).
98. Garner, op. cit., p. 1.
99. Liddington & Norris, op. cit., p. 247; Liddington, *Cooper*, ch. 1.
100. WCG, Central Committee Minutes, 22 and 23 August 1912. Its members were Margaret Bondfield, employed as secretary three days a week, the General Secretary, Mrs Barton and Mrs Wimhurst (CC members).

101. 'Report of Women's Guild', *CCR*, 1913, p. 240.
102. *Co-operative News*, 8 February 1913, p. 180.
103. *Co-operative News*, 9 August 1913, p. 1003.
104. CC to attend Adult Suffrage Demonstration; main priority to press for women's inclusion in the Bill, and then think about enlarging qualifications; CC Minutes, 12 January, 9 and 10 February, 5 March 1917.
105. WCG, *Annual Report*, 1917–18, p. 2.
106. CC Minutes, 22 and 23 August 1912.
107. See J. Lewis, *The Politics of Motherhood: Child and Maternal Welfare in England 1900–1939* (London: Croom Helm, 1980).
108. 'Report of Women's Guild', *CCR*, 1911, p. 198.
109. *Co-operative News*, 15 April 1911, p. 481.
110. *Co-operative News*, 1 April 1911, p. 409. The interview took place on 15 March 1911; the Guild was represented by the General Secretary, the Assistant Secretary, Mrs Eddie, Mrs Green, Mrs Harris, Miss Kidd, Mrs Layton, and Mrs Scott.
111. 'Memories of Seventy Years by Mrs Layton', in M. Llewelyn Davies (ed.), *Life As We Have Known It by Co-operative Working Women*, *Introductory Letter by Virginia Woolf*, (1931) (London: Virago, 1977, p. 49).
112. *Co-operative News*, 15 April 1911, pp. 481–2.
113. *Co-operative News*, 13 May 1911, p. 600.
114. *Co-operative News*, 24 June 1911, p. 809.
115. Ibid.
116. *Co-operative News*, 12 August 1911, p. 1044 (quoting letter from the General Secretary and the Assistant Secretary, Lilian Harris, published in the *Westminster Gazette*).
117. 'Report of Women's Guild', *CCR*, 1912, p. 181.
118. *Co-operative News*, 14 October 1911, p. 1319.
119. The Guild secured two other changes in the administration of maternity benefit: the abolition of 'prescribed fees' involving the compulsory attendance of a doctor, and the entitlement of insured women to 4 weeks sick pay during confinement, *Co-operative News*, 16 August 1913, p. 1039.
120. *Co-operative News*, 28 June 1913, p. 827; the Guild was represented by the General Secretary and the Assistant Secretary, Miss Bondfield, Mrs Layton (a midwife), Mrs Withers (a nurse); the Commissioners present included Mr Masterman, Sir Robert Morant, Sir Claude Schuster, Miss Mona Wilson, Sir John Bradbury, and Mr Shackleton.
121. MLD to L. Woolf, Sunday, n.d. (?August 1913), MHP.
122. *Co-operative News*, 23 August 1913, p. 1083.
123. *Co-operative News*, 2 August 1913, p. 975; including *The Times*,

Daily Citizen, Westminster Gazette, Daily News, Daily Chronicle, Votes for Women, Cotton Factory Times, Reynolds News.

124. National Insurance Act (1911) Amendment Bill Standing Committee C, 'A Bill to Amend Parts I and II of the National Insurance Act 1911, 22 July–31 July 1913', *Parliamentary Debates, Commons, Official Report Fifth Series*, **LVI**, Seventh volume of Session, 56 H.C. Deb.5s (London: HMSO, 1913).

125. *Co-operative News*, 23 August 1913, p. 1083.

126. Ibid.

127. National Insurance Amendment Bill, Standing Committee, op. cit., p. 3102.

128. *Co-operative News*, 23 August 1913, p. 1083.

129. *Co-operative News*, 19 July 1913, p. 916; 23 August 1913, p. 1083.

130. 'Report of Women's Guild', *CCR*, 1914, p. 254.

131. *Parliamentary Debates, Commons, Official Report Fifth Series*, **LVI**, Seventh volume of Session, 56 H.C. Deb.5s (London: HMSO, 1913, pp. 1537–44).

132. Ibid., p. 1501.

133. Ibid., p. 1507.

134. Ibid., p. 1533.

135. Ibid., pp. 1537–44.

136. *Co-operative News*, 16 August 1913, p. 1039.

137. *Co-operative News*, 23 August 1913, p. 1084.

138. *Co-operative News*, 16 August 1913, p. 1038.

139. *Parliamentary Debates*, p. 1541.

140. Ibid., pp. 3114–5. For the WLL's opposition to cash payments, see C. Collette, *For Labour and For Women: The Women's Labour League, 1906–1918* (Manchester University Press, 1989, p. 115). Collette states that the League 'had never been willing to restrict women to the home.' She does not explain how, given married women's low levels of employment, cash payments might have such an effect. Despite her experience on the Guild Citizenship Sub-Committee in 1914, Margaret Bondfield told a special Labour Party Conference that paying an allowance 'directly to the mother was a patronising interference with working families', J. Macnicol, *The Movement for Family Allowances, 1918–45* (London: Heinemann, 1980, pp. 142–4). Similarly intent upon justifying the Labour women's 'aloof' position on maternity, Thane rehearses the argument that payment to the wife risked antagonizing a brutal husband, but omits to mention that this echoed the Labour MPs, claiming instead that it evinced the Labour women's acknowledgement of the indivisibility of class and gender, P. Thane, 'Visions of gender in the making of the British welfare state: the case of women in the British Labour Party and social policy,

1906–1945', in G. Bock & P. Thane (eds), *Maternity and Gender Policies: Women and the Rise of the European Welfare States, 1880–1950s* (London: Routledge, 1991, p. 101).

141. *Co-operative News*, 25 October 1913, p. 1423; 'Report of Women's Guild', CCR, 1914, pp. 254–5.
142. 'Report of Women's Guild', CCR, 1915, p. 255.
143. Ibid., 1916, p. 351.
144. Ibid., 1916, p. 352.
145. Herbert Samuel, 'preface', in M. Llewelyn Davies, (ed.) *Maternity Letters from Working Women* (1915) (London: Virago, 1978).
146. The letters also demonstrated, *inter alia*, that their position in the 'respectable' working class did not exempt Guild members from the insecurities and material hardships of low wages, unemployment and bad housing. Of the 160 letters that were published, 124 gave details of the husband's weekly income: 46 averaged £1 or less; 42 under 30 shillings; 29 between 30 shillings and £2; and 7 over £2. Thus only about one-third of the respondents fell into the category identified by the Fabian Women's Group, in their contemporary Lambeth study, of an income level likely to ensure the nursing or expectant mother sufficient care and nourishment; M. Pember Reeves, *Round About a Pound a Week* (1913) (London: Virago, 1979, pp. 8–9). The study was carried out between 1909 and 1913; the critical threshold was inititally set at 26s but raised to 30s after two years.
147. MLD, *Maternity*, p. 61.
148. Ibid., p. 13.
149. 'Report of Women's Guild', CCR, 1917, p. 294; *The Star*, 22 August 1916, Gertrude Tuckwell Collection.
150. 'Report of Women's Guild', CCR, 1918, p. 368; 'Memories of Seventy Years by Mrs Layton', in MLD (ed.), *Life As We Have Known It*, p. 50.
151. 'Report of Women's Guild', CCR, 1918, p. 368; 1919, p. 306; M. Llewelyn Davies, 'The Claims of Mothers and Children', in M. Phillips (ed.), *Women and the Labour Party* (London: Headley Bros., 1918, p. 32).
152. MLD, 'Claims of Mothers', op. cit., p. 33.
153. *Co-operative News*, 23 August 1913, p. 1083.

Chapter Five

Conflict

The Guild's efforts to secure reforms in the interests of working women, and its ideological reconstruction of their rights and wrongs, converged most powerfully in its campaign for divorce law reform. Originating in 1910 with an invitation to submit evidence to the newly formed Royal Commission on Divorce and Matrimonial Causes, this agitation was significant at a number of levels in shaping the Guild's identity as a self-governing women's organization with a strong feminist agenda. First, it opened up a space within the Guild in which women's oppression in bad marriages could be publicly acknowledged and politically articulated. This public recognition of private misery fused the feminist theory of the more progressive Guild leaders with the experience and knowledge of the rank and file in a way that clarified the organization's sense of purpose, what it was, and what it was fighting for. Secondly, the external challenge to the Guild's freedom to pursue this work in 1914, from the male leadership of the Co-operative Union urged on by a Catholic lobby, served to strengthen the determination of guildswomen to defend their democratic rights, not just over divorce reform, but as a basic condition of the Guild's existence. In asserting this right, they would have been fuelled both by a belief in the legitimacy of their cause and by a growing sense of collective strength.

The stand taken by the WCG on divorce law should be seen not only as a key stage in the Guild's own development, but in relation to the industrial unrest of rank-and-file trade unionists and the pressure of a mass suffrage movement, working from 1912 onwards in alliance with the labour movement. In this context, the Guild's advocacy of the rights of married women may be interpreted as one element of rising grass-roots militancy. Equally, within the Guild the knowledge of labour and feminist activity provided a sense of wider social forces moving towards shared objectives, increasing the confidence and determination of its members to press for their demands.

In 1910 the General Secretary was invited to give evidence before the newly appointed Royal Commission on Divorce, charged with looking into legislation that had been framed in 1857, and which not only discriminated against women, but put divorce out of the reach of all but the wealthy. At its meeting in May the CC discussed the subject at length and identified the key issues which it raised for the Guild. The need for equality was brought out. This meant two things: an end to the double standard enshrined in the 1857 Act, which allowed men to divorce their wives for adultery, while women had to prove desertion or cruelty in addition to adultery; and a reduction in the cost of divorce proceedings to make it feasible for working-class couples who at present could only afford a legal separation, with no possibility of remarriage. Attention was drawn to the need for an extension of the currently limited grounds for divorce,[1] and financial implications considered: women's inability to pay for divorce and the frequent failure of men to maintain wife and children after separation.[2]

Although virtually unanimous in their views, the General Secretary and the CC had too much respect for democratic procedure to offer their own progressive opinions to the Commission on behalf of the WCG. Conscious of the religious and moral taboos surrounding the subject, however, they were uncertain about the kind of response it would elicit from the membership. Their approach was to test the opinion of the whole organization. It was agreed that 'where possible, the views of members and Branches should be obtained and sent to the General Secretary'; a branch circular went out with questions on sexual equality, costs, and the desirability of female jurors, and a CC resolution was submitted to Congress condemning the sexual inequality of the existing divorce laws and calling for cheaper proceedings.[3]

At Congress, the CC was prepared for a range of objections and reservations. A senior guildswoman moved the resolution 'in a weighty and restrained speech, with a grave sense of the difficulty and responsibility of her task.' She was seconded by a midwife who 'spoke from intimate personal knowledge of the lives of women. The audience listened with great attention and a discussion was fully anticipated.' Instead, in what must have been an impressive demonstration of unity, 'not a single delegate rose to speak. They were prepared to vote instantly'. The hundreds of women were united in their belief that the existing system was wrong: 'a forest of hands showed itself immediately and silently. There were only five raised against it.'[4] Here was emphatic evidence that working women, often supposed to be the group most in need of the protection of unbreakable marriage vows, wanted, as one journalist put it, 'cheap and easy divorce'.[5]

If the leadership needed further proof that they were not in advance of the membership on this issue, the replies from 429 branches told the same story: 414 supported equality between men and women, 361 a reduction in the costs, and 310 the introduction of women jurors. The more detailed responses revealed support for state relief of divorce costs if needed, and extension of the grounds to include persistent refusal to maintain, insanity, desertion for two years, cruelty, three-year separation, mutual consent, and serious incompatibility.[6] This was, indeed, a radical reform programme, one so advanced that in its entirety was not to become law until the late 1960s.

When Davies and Mrs Barton, a Guild official from Sheffield, appeared before the Commission in October 1910, Davies' submission included 131 'manuscript letters' from guildswomen, 'often many pages long, laboriously written after thought and consultation'.[7] Their content explained why divorce had elicited greater 'strength and earnestness of feeling' than any other subject in the Guild's history: nearly every woman had first or second hand knowledge of unhappy marriages. 'Shall I continue with all this?', Davies asked as she came to the individual submissions. 'Yes', came the reply, 'I think this is so valuable we ought to have it all.'[8]

There followed a litany of the 'hidden suffering'[9] endured within failed marriages. The most shocking cases described violence, marital rape, forced miscarriage, and abortion: evidence that the women bore the 'great mass' of the suffering. No woman, Davies observed, 'could inflict on a man the amount of

131

degradation that a man may force on a woman.'[10] 'My cousin', wrote one member, 'married a man who has behaved most brutally towards her, has broken her teeth, blacked her eyes, and bruised her body, and I believe is not kind to the children ... he has killed every spark of love she had for him, but she must put up for the children's sake.' Another described women who always tried to induce an abortion on discovering that they were pregnant, because 'the husband will grumble and make things unpleasant, because there will be another mouth to fill and he may have to deprive himself of something'. In one case, the husband 'always thrashes his wife and has put her life in danger in his anger on discovering her condition.'

There were instances of syphillitic men infecting their wives and children: 'Husband physically rotten', one member reported tersely, 'through bad life previous to marriage. Compelled wife to cohabit – result three children with sore eyes and ears, and mentally deficient.'[11] Marital rape was a recurring theme. 'I felt so degraded', wrote one member. 'I had not the same privilege as the beasts of the field. No one can possibly imagine what it is unless you go through it, to feel you are simply a *convenience* to a man.'[12] Another hinted at internal injuries following post-natal rape and a near-fatal abortion attempt:

> Babies came rather fast. Then I got told I was like a rabbit for breeding and drugs was obtained, as he did not want children, although I was compelled to submit. The second little one died, and soon after the third one came, I was so ill I had to have the doctor, who said there was no disease, but I must go from home and stay as long as possible ... I was so badly treated that when I knew my condition for the fourth time, I took something which nearly ended my existence. It poisoned me.[13]

Interwoven with such accounts of physical and sexual abuse were stories of the misery inflicted through neglect, humiliation, heavy drinking, lack of provision, desertion, and infidelity. Repeatedly, the letters emphasized the inadequacy of the existing laws. A mother of two, separated from her husband and desperate for divorce, could prove 'that he had children by more than one woman, her own sister being one, and that he came home drunk and insulted her, but this did not constitute legal cruelty.' Legal grounds for divorce were only supplied when the midwife was able to prove 'legal cruelty, committed on the first day the wife got up from her confinement.'[14]

Buttressing the bad laws was a value-system which stigmatized divorce and took women's subordination for granted. 'If divorce is considered a sin', Davies reasoned, 'and the patient endurance of degradation and compulsory suffering a virtue, a most serious moral confusion is created. It means that women's self respect and happiness are sacrificed, and adultery on the part of the man is condoned.'[15] The need to contest this inversion was expressed in the strongest terms. 'Is it not more degrading', asked one member, 'for these women to be living in what is, after all, legalised prostitution, than for them to be divorced?'[16] We want 'to get rid of the idea that a man owns his wife just as he does a piece of furniture', wrote another. If there was legal equality then women 'would respect themselves more and really look upon their bodies as their own property, and not so soon give in to the brutal desires of a lazy selfish man.'[17] For the majority of guildswomen, 'the sanctity of marriage' depended upon the quality of the marriage relation not a vow. As one guildswoman, also a churchwoman, put it, 'the only real marriage is when men and women are real comrades. When they are not, then in the sight of God it is not marriage.'[18]

Aside from these moral and philosophical issues, there was a harsh economic reality to be considered: 'the want of any effective and reasonably reliable means of support for married women, felt especially where there are children'.[19] This led many to argue that the marriage ties should be indissoluble 'for the sake of the women themselves and their children'. Davies took the opposite view, however, not simply because she upheld working women's rights, but because as a socialist she believed in the possibility of socio-economic change that would create more supportive structures for married women and children. It was 'painfully obvious', she insisted, that the economic problem would have to be dealt with. Meanwhile, 'our attitude to divorce should not depend upon it'. To allow economic factors to define the relationship in law and in public morality was to tempt women to 'sacrifice their personal dignity and honour' for 'what is little better than prostitution'.[20]

This feminist analysis was deepened by Eleanor Barton, a Sheffield Guild official, whose submission followed that of Davies and brought out how little the 'well to do classes' knew about the experience of working-class wives. Barton insisted that to understand working-class women's circumstances, 'one had to live among them. There is a great amount of suffering which never sees daylight. The women in many cases are martyrs. I think it is really because of the idea of morality. One has the idea if they are married, they have to submit to their husbands.' This operated at all levels of society, she explained, but unlike 'people in a better class of life' working women were trapped: their economic dependence made it hard for them 'to escape from any amount of cruelty.'

By cruelty Barton meant more than mental cruelty or domestic violence. Many women suffered greatly 'by, say, a lustful husband, by bearing children unwillingly. It is not talked about. They feel they are married and because they are married they must submit to this sort of thing.' Like Davies, Barton did not accept that marriage should oblige a woman to surrender the use of her body to her husband. 'I do not', she stated flatly, 'see why marriage should legalise prostitution.' In Sheffield, Guild members were agreed that 'cruelty' should be grounds for divorce. Not only was it harmful to the mother, it was damaging for the children and perpetuated the cycle of abuse: 'it is giving the boy a very bad chance for his own home life ... It does not give the boys any respect for womanhood.' Boys and girls needed to be educated to an understanding of 'the uses of their own body', and an equal moral standard for both sexes should be cultivated.[21]

Barton went on to discuss women who suffered complete breakdowns as a result of post-natal sexual violation. 'There are cases', she explained, 'where women are insane after the birth of each child, and one feels very strongly on this point, that a lot of this evidence is kept underhand and the women suffer, but some feel the doctors might speak out because they know and understand these things. The cases come before them.' Not all the commissioners grasped what she was talking about. Mrs Tennant sought clarification. Did she mean that insanity had been caused by 'what might be defined as the cruelty of their husbands? – Yes.' Did the women 'base that opinion on what the doctors had told them?' Perhaps at this point Mrs Barton pondered the kind of reasoning that led Mrs Tennant to assume that a woman would need a doctor to tell her that her husband had harmed her. The doctors, she tried to explain, 'have this evidence and could give it more conclusively than one like myself.' Was this merely supposition?, continued Mrs Tennant. 'I have had things told me', Barton answered, 'by different women that have given me to understand the doctors do know.'

The chairman, exposing the great distance between his own knowledge and that of the guildswomen, was still confused. What had doctors to do with this? 'What I mean,' Barton attempted to elucidate, 'is that doctors know many things women suffer from by their marriage relations, and that in many cases there have been women who have been sent away completely from their home-life to get a complete rest because of the married relations.' Still missing the point, the chairman remarked that this was rather good advice: 'I do not think you complain of that?', he asked. 'I do complain very largely,' Barton replied in exasperation, struggling to make herself understood without causing offence: 'it is rather a delicate matter to speak on, but personally women are suffering.' When she ground to a halt, the chairman prompted her, and she continued: 'doctors could give very valuable evidence as regards these marriage relations.' 'You mean', responded the chairman, still confounded, 'of the necessity for such advice?' Only with the intervention of his colleagues did it become clear to him that she was proposing that doctors appear before the Commission to give evidence that abuse of the marriage relation was responsible for various kinds of post-natal trauma.[22]

The Guild's submission confronted the Commissioners with some of what Davies termed 'the hidden suffering' of married life, and called for a radical recasting of divorce law. How did this compare with the wide spectrum of opinion considered by the Commission?[23] Explicitly antithetical to the conservative defence of marriage as a pillar of society, it had most in common with the views expressed by other representatives of the women's movement. Here there was a broad consensus on the need, in the words of Miss Homan of the Women's Industrial Council, for 'an equal standard of morality for men and women in the eyes of the law';[24] and for a reduction of costs to make divorce available to the working-class. As Mrs Fawcett argued, it made as much sense to claim that there was no demand for divorce among the poor as it did to say that they did not want race horses or motor cars; there should not be 'virtually one law for the rich and another for the poor.'[25] Dr Ethel Bentham[26] and Mrs Fawcett[27] proposed an extension of grounds to include permanent legal separation and wilful desertion.[28] There was also agreement about the wife's entitlement to a share of her husband's wages, and the desirability of maintenance being paid through the courts; Miss Homan provided evidence of hardship among women workers who had obtained separation orders, yet were not being properly maintained, and proposed that where necessary the courts should take the money directly from the husband's employer.[29] But there were also differences within the feminist camp. While Mrs Fawcett stressed the importance of permanent marriage ties for the family and the state, and referred to 'the harm that is done to home life by married women going out to work',[30] Helena Swanwick believed that marriage should be a civil contract separate from moral and religious law, and that married women should have the opportunity to take paid work to have some money of their own.[31]

The Guild's submission stood out from all of these most obviously because of its 'direct representation of working-class views'.[32] For the empirically minded Commissioners, and the reading public of Edwardian England, this imparted extra weight and credibility to their views. As Dr Bentham pointed out in *The Common Cause*, Guild members typified 'the average of the middle-aged and experienced working women, with all the prejudices, all the conservatism, all the knowledge of life of their class'; and their utterances left no doubt 'that some of the very foundations of society are rotten beneath our feet.'[33]

Another difference between the Guild's conception of the problem and its resolution, and those of moderate reformers, is that it was not limited to a legislative framework. As Davies pointed out, 'Even if unjust laws and public opinion were changed the greater physical weakness, the conditions of maternity, the difficulty of monetary independence, would still put power in the hands of men, and give opportunities for its abuse'.[34] At the same time, the Guild's base in the working-class movement, and its commitment to social and economic transformation, meant that legal reform featured as only one of a number of different strategies to improve the position of working women and the

DIVISION IN THE RANKS?

working-class as a whole. Their views with regard to funding, for example, were not confined to earning potential; as one guildswoman put it, 'I do not see the use of women who have no means applying for a divorce unless the State pays, perhaps then they will begin to ask why it is that a married woman has no money of her own.'[35]

The most radical feature of the Guild's evidence was the explicit refutation of the premise, enshrined in age-old legal and cultural forms, that upon marriage a husband gained possession of his wife's body.[36] This was brought out most sharply in Mrs Barton's evidence, but appeared at numerous points in the detail of individual cases, and underpinned the Guild's advocacy of mutual consent and serious incompatibility as grounds for divorce. Once again, it reflected a capacity to conceive of progress on a broad front and in Davies' phrase to separate out women's 'personal dignity and honour'[37] from both economic necessity and the full force of patriarchal ideology.

The strength of traditional ideas about married women's proper role and, contrariwise, the advanced nature of the Guild's views were highlighted in the religious opposition to the liberal Majority Report published in December 1912. Its sweeping recommendations, which sought to abolish the ways in which divorce law differentiated between rich and poor, and between men and women, and to establish divorce as the legal closure of a relationship already dead, embraced many of the measures supported by the Guild, but did not extend to mutual consent and serious incompatibility as grounds, or to the institution of female court officials.[38] Heading the conservative reaction[39] was a Minority Report, signed, as the Guild noted, by an archbishop and two ecclesiastical lawyers,[40] which claimed that 'the strength, coherence and continuity of the family' were under threat from two counter forces: 'the assertion of individual liberty' and 'the claims of logical socialism'. They took particular exception to the Guild proposals, which were dismissed as advocating 'a facility of divorce hitherto unheard of in any civilized country'.[41] The idea that a woman's unwillingness to bear children should entitle her to a divorce, 'although the husband had committed no offence of any kind', they found fundamentally alien to their conception of marriage as 'a lifelong obligation with all the sacrifices which such an obligation involves'.[42]

As well as staking their critique on a defence of traditional institutions, the Minority group also sought to prove that divorce was wrong because working women did not want it.[43] Even the mandate, in 1910, of 23,501 Co-operative women did not prevent them from seeking to dismiss the Guild's evidence on the grounds that the 131 letters presented 'the extreme opinions of a comparatively few individuals selected by a witness who shares those opinons'.[44] They turned instead to the submissions of the Mothers' Union, piously overlooking the fact that these had been selected by women convinced that marriage vows were indissoluble.[45] In 1910, the Mothers' Union had 278,500 members, women who were, according to Mrs Steinthal, the Ripon diocesan honorary secretary, 'very poor, and they come with shawls and clogs'. They had 'the great instinct of religion in them',[46] and they wanted nothing to do with divorce. Their officers reported them to be afraid of it, believing it to be shameful and immoral, although one officer ventured to suggest that this arose from 'ignorance rather than from moral sentiment'.[47]

Certainly, this aversion was not a reflex of contented married lives. Mrs Steinthal knew mothers who had 'great difficulties with drunken husbands and men who have deserted them, and they say that they feel strongly that they married for better or worse, and that they will stick to their husband.' A Liverpool woman had said that 'she did not know what she had done to be so insulted. Mrs So-and-so had proposed that she should be divorced from her husband. She said: "He may be a brute, but he is my husband." He was a drunkard living in London.'[48] Mrs Hubbard, vice-president of the Union, held that 'to suffer these hardships without attempting to get a remedy' strengthened the national character; the breaking of vows on one side, she insisted, did not release the other from her obligations.[49]

Davies responded to the Minority Report's criticisms in *The Times*, by contrasting Guild democracy with the Mothers' Union's autocratic methods, which denied 'working mothers' any voice in its government.[50] Yet this emphasis on procedure obscures the equally important question of values on which the Guild was not agnostic. Some of 'our branches and members', the General Secretary wrote elsewhere in connection with divorce, 'may shrink from the discussion of this subject', but she trusted they would realize 'the responsibility that is laid upon the Guild as an organisation of married women, to take the lead in a campaign which is concerned with the dignity and respect of married women.'[51] Juxtaposition of the two sets of evidence highlights the Union's lack of interest in the quality of the marriage relationship and the welfare of the mothers, in contrast to the Guild's concern for the dignity and self-respect of working-class wives. The Mothers' Union seemed actively to encourage what Davies referred to as 'the patient endurance of degradation and compulsory suffering',[52] valorizing precisely the kind of womanly self-sacrifice the Guild was intent upon contesting.

From 1910 to 1914 the WCG pursued divorce law reform in earnest. It published accounts of its evidence to the Royal Commission and of the Majority Report; the subject was taken at Sectional Conferences in 1911 and 1913; talks were given at numerous district conferences and branch meetings; and the 1913 Congress passed a resolution in support of the Majority Report.[53] Consequently, within a year of the General Secretary's brush with the pillars of the Establishment represented in the Minority Report, the Guild had drawn fire from another hostile quarter: the Executive Council of the Catholic Federation of the Diocese of Salford, comprising the whole of Lancashire, Yorkshire and Cheshire. Through the assiduous efforts of its paid agent, Mr Burns, whose brief it was to look after Catholic interests in political and labour bodies,[54] the Council had learned not only that the Guild was engaged in 'persistent propaganda of the cause of divorce', but that it received funding from the CU, the CWS, and local Societies. In October 1913, in a letter to the Guild General Secretary, Thos. Canon Sharrock, General Secretary to the Council, claimed that the dividends of Catholic Co-operators were thus subsidizing a cause alien to their faith, and that the 'power and prestige' of Co-operation was being used for alien purposes. 'You will be aware that any person who believes in the principles of Co-operation is eligible for membership of the Co-operative Movement,' the letter warned, 'but you may not be aware that exploitation of legitimate membership for illegitimate purposes will ultimately disrupt the movement.'[55]

In a brief reply, the CC stated that the Guild would continue to deal with the subject, considering it 'one of the most important moral and social reforms which affect Co-operative women'.[56] Having got short shrift from the Guild, the Catholic Federation's next move was to copy the correspondence to the CU United Board (a committee of 14, drawn from the 70 members of the Central Board), with an inquiry as to what action 'the trustee of the prestige of the Co-operative Movement' would take to disassociate the movement from divorce propaganda. The CU General Secretary, Mr Whitehead, tried to head off the problem at a meeting with Mr Burns, assuring him that the CU was not active in the cause of divorce law reform, but was told that unless something was done it was possible that Catholics 'would withdraw from societies in large numbers'.[57]

At the next meeting of the United Board it became apparent that the Catholics were pushing at an open door. There were some objections to being dictated to by the Catholic minority and expressions of sympathy for the Guild's position. Mr Bisset (Aberdeen), for example, reminded those present that the Guild might well argue that 'the movement was formed with the object of improving the moral and social life of the people, and that divorce law reform would be a great help in that direction.' The majority view, however, was that divorce reform was not in accordance with the aims and objects of the movement, and that the Guild should be asked to discontinue its propaganda, although a warning note was sounded when Mr Hainsworth pointed out that if they were not careful it would be 'quite easy to get the backs of the Women's Guild up, and that they wanted to avoid as far as possible.'[58]

Margaret Llewelyn Davies was scathing about this outcome: 'It was so *feeble* of the United Board,' she wrote to Leonard Woolf, 'to give in to the Catholics, who will always try things on. Mr Whitehead tried to alarm me by saying that at a word from the priests, thousands wd. [*sic*] leave the Preston, Liverpool etc. Socs. (I almost wish faith could so triumph over divi.) – but I got him to admit that he didn't see how we could give up.'[59]

The CC's reply to the United Board was indeed robust and uncompromising. The Guild, it pointed out, had long been concerned with 'questions of industrial and social reform affecting its members as married women.' Guildswomen looked to Co-operation not only 'to set up stores where they can obtain their goods and be provided with dividend, but to remove many evils connected with our present laws and customs, and to establish society on a more equal and just basis.' Divorce reform was too important to working women to be abandoned; in any case, for the CC to reverse a Congress decision would be a betrayal of the membership. Finally, the Board members were gently reminded of the Guild's value to the movement: 'The knowledge that fruitful ideas and far-reaching reforms may spring out of anything so prosaic as shop keeping only increases the respect for loyal buying which is the ABC of Guild work.'[60]

The Board's sense of being squeezed between contending Co-operative traditions – of religious neutrality on the one hand, and democratic procedures on the other – was not assuaged by the Dublin venue of the 1914 Co-operative Congress, chosen with the explicit intention of strengthening the movement in Ireland. At its pre-Congress meeting, the full Central Board received Mr Burns and Mr McCreary from the Catholic Federation; divorce, they insisted, was a religious question, the movement should steer well clear of it, and if it did not they would have no alternative but to fight the movement. With the alarming prospect of predominantly Catholic Societies collapsing, as the faithful withdrew and formed their own Societies, and mindful of 'the strong feeling running in Dublin in reference to the matter', Board members vied with each other in protesting their earnest intent not to interfere with the 'liberty and freedom of action' of their Catholic brethren. It was also noted that the proposed divorce reforms were opposed by a great many Anglican church members. When Mrs Gasson, a Guild member and the one woman present, tried to argue that the Guild had not taken divorce as a religious matter, but 'for the uplifting of humanity', her views were dismissed as an example of how 'innocently' the women 'could be drawn into contentious matters'; in fact, 'political matters were interwoven with religious matters. They would find that out in Ireland.'[61]

The terms of the discussion, not to mention its setting, presented the Board with the opportunity to flex its muscles and call the women to order. Despite some eloquent reminders of the Guild's great services to the movement over the years, a hardline consensus emerged that here were the disastrous consequences of 'giving subscriptions to bodies over whom they had no control. If the Board had to pay the piper, they should be able to call the tune.'[62] It was agreed that the £400 grant should be made conditional upon the Guild ceasing its agitation for divorce law reform and not taking up 'work disapproved of by the United Board' in future.'[63]

The lines were now firmly drawn for a major conflict which would turn around conflicting interpretations of the meaning of Co-operation as a social and democratic movement. 'You will see', Davies wrote to Leonard Woolf, 'that we are in a nice hole as regards Divorce etc.' She was confident that the CC would 'not hear of being dictated to' yet saw difficulties ahead. 'It isn't only divorce they (the Board) object to. They have disliked our taking up Suffrage – and indeed all political work.' There were local educational committees that had refused to have 'Maternity' included in Guild programmes, and while the Guild had good friends among the Societies there were many who would support the Board as a matter of course.[64]

The Board's decision was formally communicated to the Guild as it prepared for its own Congress at the end of June 1914. At its meeting on 15 June, the CC heard Mr Burns and Mr McCreary again put their case, and then received a deputation from the Central Board, but without reaching an agreement.[65] As Congress convened, a lengthy CC statement appeared in *Co-operative News*, which carefully focused on self-government as the key issue. Although 'the divorce question has been made the reason for this action, the real object and effect of the new conditions are to control the whole initiative and destroy the independence of the Guild'. There was much at stake here. Not the least of the injustices entailed by this move was the damage that it would inflict upon the position of women in the movement. Women and men contributed to the funds of the CU, but 'unfortunately the constitution of the Union makes it most difficult for women to be represented on official bodies.' The Guild itself, for example, had no official representation in the CU. In effect, then, this proposal meant that an organization of some 32,000 women should be asked 'to submit its policy to the United Board, composed at the present time entirely of men.'

A brief audit of the Guild's achievements highlighted the benefits to date of self-government. It had gained national influence in representing married women. 'No other body stands and speaks for them as the Guild does', and before its advent 'their sufferings and grievances remained hidden'. Yet many aspects of its Citizenship work had been opposed by Societies and would not have been pursued had the Guild not controlled its own policy. In its Co-operative work, too, there were Guild campaigns, such as the minimum wage, now twice endorsed by Co-operative Congress, which initially enjoyed 'little official support'. As an educational and propagandist body, the Guild depended upon the 'freedom to open out new paths', and appealed to the Societies for continued confidence in the value of their work and to the Guild membership for support: 'Our freedom has in the past allowed us to fight for our co-operative ideals, and for a higher status for married women, and to create an effective demand for justice and equal fellowhip. We cannot doubt that you will reject the terms offered, and whatever crippling of our work may be entailed, will resolve that we, in our own democratic organisation should decide on our own policy and activity. We know that this freedom is the very life-blood of our Guild.'[66]

The CC was not to be disappointed. At the Birmingham Congress, delegates queued to speak to an emergency resolution rejecting the terms laid down by the Board, proving that far from having its freedom curbed, the Guild had become more vociferous in its support for divorce law reform and learnt a lesson about the practical value of self-government. The women were outraged at the men's interference. Mrs Daymond (St Budeaux) felt that the Board had taken 'a very backward step', but the Guild was 'not going to be led into the trap. They were determined not to sacrifice principles for money. (Applause.) She knew what the proposed reforms meant for downtrodden women, and she could not help but raise her voice in protest of [sic] the action taken by the Co-operative Union.' She 'regretted that there were such men in the co-operative movement but she hoped that they would repent of their ways and apologise. (Laughter and loud applause.)' Mrs Baldwin (Clapton Park) exclaimed at 'the ignorance of the Union. Did they think that they were the only ones who knew what was good for the women. Then they forgot that the women could think for themselves. (Applause.)'. Guildswomen, Mrs Beattie (Birkenhead) explained, 'they wanted to work with the men side

143

by side, not as subordinates with restrictions, for they possessed the powers and abilities of adult women. (Hear, hear, and applause.) They were open to criticism; but they did not take any action without having first carefully considered the question. (Hear, hear.) ... This subject of Divorce Law they had been considering for the past four years; but for how many years had women been suffering?' When the vote was taken, 'a great sea of red cards' appeared, and loud and prolonged cheering broke out when the resolution was declared carried with no dissentients and only a few abstentions.[67]

Lest there be any doubt about the Guild's commitment to divorce law reform, a CC resolution was submitted calling for a Government Bill to implement the Majority Report's recommendations, with the addition of mutual consent and the appointment of female court assessors. Moving the resolution, Mrs Barton (CC) owned that their most contentious recommendation was mutual consent, but she pointed out that 'if two people decided that they could not live together after a two years' separation, the chances for happiness at the end of that time were less than ever.' In the discussion many examples were supplied of the misery caused by broken marriages; the resolution was carried with 54 dissentients.[68]

Attended by 864 delegates,[69] and the last before the declaration of war in August 1914, the Birmingham Congress provided a remarkable demonstration of the Guild's vigour and coherence. More than two decades of organization and education had generated a high level of self-confidence among these guilds-women; their determination to fight their own battles over the matters that affected them most closely, and their contempt for the assumption that the women of the movement would allow male officials to take control of their destiny, was very pronounced. For Davies the Congress was the crowning moment of the Guild's history: 'We reached our highest point at B'ham.', she wrote to Woolf:

> Tuesday morning was a most remarkable demonstration. I had no idea the strength and unity of feeling wd. be so great. And that the determination to keep our independence should be connected with Divorce was all the more remarkable. There was never any doubt in the women's minds about the

way the Independence vote would go – nor had they any doubts during the Divorce debate. Someone said the Guild had found its soul, it has certainly found its feet. I feel the women have now "arrived" – & they will never go back.[70]

The Guild had made its mark, but the dispute with the Central Board was far from being settled. The CC met with the Central Board in September to discuss the Congress resolution; a motion rescinding the Dublin decision was defeated by 47 to 12 and the Board agreed that the Guild grant for the year would be paid providing they dropped the work on divorce, and that the wider question of the conditions attached to CU funding should be considered by the full Co-operative Congress in 1915. The CC's reply stated that although the outbreak of war seemingly presented an opportunity for compromise, by making 'all public action in support of Divorce Law Reform impossible', it felt that this would not be an honourable settlement, nor one consistent with their democratically agreed determination to maintain control over their own policy.[71]

At the end of the year, the North-Western Sectional Board published a paper by Mr Goodenough, a member of the Central Board, which implied further threats to the Guild's position. Stressing that he had no objection to divorce law reform as such, only 'to its advocacy on co-operative platforms',[72] Goodenough's main purpose was to show that there were no grounds, constitutional or otherwise, for the Guild's claim to autonomy. Ignoring the terms of the Dublin resolution, he stated that as the CU Central Board had always determined the policy of the whole movement, and exercised that power through a process of consultation, it was unreasonable for any part of the movement to defy the Board. He also claimed that if local funding was taken into account, the Guild probably received in total about £2,000 per annum from the movement. This prompted the Guild CC to put its own case to the movement, and it began to urge its partisans to submit a supportive resolution to the forthcoming 1915 Co-operative Congress.

The next round of the conflict was fought out at the Leicester Co-operative Congress in May 1915. Before Congress opened, Margaret Llewelyn Davies and Eleanor Barton met the Central Board with a proposal to break the deadlock: a joint conference

More resistance from inside the Co-op [handwritten marginal note]

145

should be held each year between the Board and the Guild to review the Guild's work, and the Guild would undertake not to spend any of the CU grant on subjects not approved by the Board, using its own income from subscriptions instead. Davies then made an eloquent case for the Guild's right to autonomy and to support divorce law reform. Despite the movement's dependence upon women's 'basket power', the Guild had no official representation at Congress, or on the Board: why, then, should it be bound by it? The 'Guild was built up by its own members, who were married women as well as co-operators, and who represented a class which never before had had organisation or power to express needs and reforms.' There was no question of renouncing divorce law reform, which was a great social issue: to treat it as a religious matter was 'an interference with civil liberty'. The objections arose from a 'narrow sectarian body', uttering 'empty threats' about disruption in the movement; if it was allowed to triumph, the movement would be exposed to other such attacks, and would have undermined its reputation 'as a great social regenerating force.' The Board's decision, Mrs Barton suggested, had been too hasty, and had they not been 'meeting in a great Catholic city like Dublin', it would not have been taken.[73]

After the Guild deputation had withdrawn, it became apparent that for the majority of the Board the crux of the matter was that the women were still being disobedient. 'The official men of the Bd.', Davies later wrote to Woolf, 'cant [sic] stand our acting independently. It is just the same feeling as between husband and wife.' They believed that 'there must be a controlling head in a democracy ... The idea of rank and file independence, and experimenting in democracy, makes no appeal ... They would like us well inside the movt. – a position really fatal to us of course.'[74] During the Board's meeting, Mr Redfearn (North-Western Section) said that to give the Guild its £400 would be 'the thin edge of the wedge ... When the Guild had got it, they would snap their fingers at the Central Board.' Mr Goodenough (North-Western Section) 'had seen this problem coming for years', and was 'thankful that it was one on which they could be unanimous.' Divorce had no place in the movement. Miss Davies said it was 'a social problem; another person would say it was a religous question, or a sex question; but he would say it was a boundaries

146

Support from males (some anyway)

More support

question.' Mr Johnston (North-Western Section) was of the opinion that they had been unwise to listen to the Catholic Federation: divorce was already legal but 'operated to the disadvantage of the poorer classes of the community.' It was an entirely legitimate concern for the Guild. Nevertheless, the Guild's proposal was defeated by 33 to 16, and the Board looked to Congress to affirm its right to withhold funding from 'any organisation which, in its opinion, is pursuing a policy detrimental to the best interests of the co-operative movement.'[75]

Before Congress were three resolutions on funding: that of the Central Board, affirming its executive powers; one from several Societies on behalf of the Guild, endorsing the principle of self-government; and one from the Eccles and Longridge Societies on behalf of the Salford Catholic Federation, condemning the Guild's divorce work as alien to Co-operative principles. The last was the fruit of the Federation's serious efforts to manufacture opposition to the Guild. 'Week by week', stated the WCG *Annual Report*, 'the Catholic press has published long statements, speeches and directions by the Secretary of the SCF, bishops and others. Leaflets have been distributed at church doors, and priests have given instructions to Guildswomen and Co-operators.' Societies had been asked to refuse grants to local Guilds and to submit a resolution to the Co-op Congress.[76] It was gratifying for the Guild, therefore, to note that the resolution was practically ignored, 'only two or three cards being held up in its support'.[77]

Few delegates admitted to moral or religious objections to divorce as such; the substantive issue was whether or not it pertained to the movement. As Mr Hayhurst (CWS) argued, 'they should keep the movement clear of all politics and religion. They were working for co-operation; and surely in the name of reason there were a thousand and one economic subjects in civil life which could be taken hold of without introducing politics or religion into the movement.'[78] Mr Maddison (Blackpool Union Printers) confessed that 'personally, he would probably agree with the attitude of the guild on the subject of divorce; but it was an outside question.' It was also, he claimed, 'a business question ... It had to do with the selling of tea and sugar and treacle and the rest of it. Co-operators were social reformers by trade, and they must be aware that in their great communities in Lancashire they had a great number of loyal co-operators to whom this was an offence.'[79]

As well as conflicting conceptions of Co-operation, there were also differing ideas about democracy. Mr Greening (Agricultural and Horticultural Association) argued that as part of the movement, the Guild should 'accept the decisions of the representative co-operative body as to what was and what was not to be publicly advocated in the name and with the influence of co-operation.'[80]

The Guild's formal position – a reiteration of its right to self-government, taken as an amendment to the Central Board's resolution had significant support from delegates, many of whom had already been alerted to the issue by Guild work in the Societies.[81] Mr Wood (Coventry) thought that the United Board had made a mistake, and that Congress should repudiate the outside interference. 'The Women's Guild – which was an organisation of 32,000 members – had decided in democratic assembly what their policy should be. What more could they decide? It was a woman's question, and women should be the ones to decide whether it was right or wrong.'[82] Mr J. Penny (Planet Mutual Insurance Sheffield) insisted that the 'co-operative movement did not stand merely for selling sugar and treacle; it was to uphold democratic principles, and divorce law reform was simply to establish equality between man and woman. That was a fundamental co-operative principle.'[83]

Perhaps the strongest contribution to the debate came from one of the guildswomen present on behalf of their Societies. Mrs Wimhurst (Woolwich) argued that for the women Co-operation could not be severed from citizenship – 'Social reform consisted of things that merged together; it could not be chopped up into sections.' Pressing hard on the question of sex inequality within the movement, she stressed that all the women wanted was the same degree of self-determination the men claimed for themselves. A previous speaker had 'said that the salvation of the workers depended upon the workers taking their destiny in their own hands. Would he refuse to the women the same right of salvation? She believed that the women should work out their own salvation, and if they did not agree with them, the men should leave them alone.' She was offended by the tone of certain speakers. 'The seconder talked to them as though they were pet rabbits ... In all sweet reasonableness the lion and the lamb were asked to lie down together; without discussing which was the lion and which the lamb'. Of course, she added, taking a swipe at the Catholics, they might have sorted out their differences had it not been for 'the interference of the wolf.'[84]

In the end, the Guild was not strong enough to carry a majority against the weight of the Central Board; its resolution was defeated by 1,430 to 796. Yet as the CC pointed out, 'to have stirred Congress in the way that it was stirred, and to have concentrated the interest of delegates on a subject involving matters of principle is a tribute to the force of the Guild, and a reward to all those who have worked so well for our resolution in their local societies.'[85] The Board, for its part, had produced no evidence of the Guild's divorce work causing disruption; nor had it inspired confidence in its capacity to judge what might be detrimental to the movement. What it had done was to confirm the Guild's perception, based on experience, 'that a body practically composed of men, does not understand or give due consideration to the views of women, and that therefore it is most undesirable that the Guild's freedom of action should be limited by such a body.'[86]

The Board's ultimatum had given rise to a potent mixture of grievance, on the one hand, and a sense of collective agency, on the other, which crystallized the Guild's understanding of its own identity and purpose. Unbowed, delegates at the Guild's own Congress the following month reaffirmed 'the vital importance of Self-government', and instructed the CC to refuse any grant whose terms 'deprived the Guild of the full control of its own policy.'[87]

Given the opposition of significant numbers of guildswomen to the 1914–18 war, there is perhaps some irony in the fact that the war brought changes which served both to soften the blow of a 40 per cent cut in the Guild's income, and to shift the balance of power in the funding dispute to the Guild's advantage. The 'national crisis' immediately suspended certain of the Guild's propaganda work and opportunities for launching major campaigns, and this enforced curtailment in its activity made it somewhat easier to cope with a reduced income. At the same time, the Government's treatment of Co-operators in wartime dislodged the movement from political neutrality, a shift which opened up a valuable new area of Co-operative activity for guildswomen as they gained the vote: organizing women in support of the Co-operative Party.

A variety of methods was used to make up for the lost £400 without compromising the Guild's independence: in 1915, the CC turned down the offer of £100 from an executive member of the Divorce Law Reform Union who admired their fight for self-government and their 'protest against clerical interference with their work'.[88] The General Secretary took on the literature debt with a £100 loan,[89] and a Self-Government Fund reaped over £250 in 1914 and £325 in 1915; the CWS upped its annual contribution from £75 to £150; the 1916 Guild Congress voted to double the subscription to the Central Fund from 2d to 4d per member; in 1917 a special appeal to the Societies raised over £180. Despite these measures, the annual income dipped from £1,021 in 1913 to a low of £858 in 1916, and economies had to be made through a reduction in clerical staff, office expenses, and assistance to the sections and districts.[90] The 1917 *Annual Report* painted a bleak picture of the difficulties faced by the Guild: membership down, from 32,182 in 1914 to 27,060 in 1917; branches suspended; towns darkened against air raids; meeting halls lost to the military; war-work making demands on women; and grief for those killed and injured in the fighting. In the national office work had been hampered not only by the spending cuts, but also by staff illness.[91]

Yet circumstances created by the war were also conspiring to the Guild's obvious advantage. Offended by the state's apparent discrimination against the movement, especially the imposition of an Excess Profits Tax in place of the traditional tax exemption,[92] Co-operators voted in 1917 for direct Parliamentary representation. Almost simultaneously, the enfranchisement of women over 30 created a new role for the Guild. Guildswomen, Davies commented in 1918, 'will find that they have suddenly become much more important, and that their views and actions will receive far greater consideration.'[93] Keen to secure the Guild's energies in building up the women's vote, and despite the reappearance of divorce law reform on the Guild agenda that year,[94] the Central Board agreed to terms which did not violate the principle of self-determination – indeed, which were virtually identical with those proposed by the Guild in 1914. In 1918 the grant was reinstated. Celebrating 'the happy termination of the four "lean" years', and affirming its readiness to assist every part of the movement, the Guild *Annual Report* none the less re-stated the firmness of its attitude 'as regards both self-determination and greater equality'.[95]

The restoration of funding was a great relief, boosting income to £1,594 in 1918 and meeting a long list of areas deserving more money, which included grants to sections and districts, expenses for CC and sectional council members, a free speaker to branches on women's political work, and a pay rise for the office cleaner.[96] With the armistice, the vote, and new members flooding into the organization, it seemed as if the Guild had 'never shown signs of greater vitality'.[97] Equally strong was its determination to retain its separate identity and to resist the trend against single-sex organizations that was sweeping through the labour movement, causing not only the dissolution of the WLL, reconstituted as the LPWS in 1918, but also the absorption of the WTUL by the TUC, and the NFWW by the NUGW, in both cases virtually without trace.[98] As the 1920 *Annual Report* firmly stated, Congress that year passed a resolution which approved joint work with the Men's Guild (formed in 1911) but 'strongly opposes any proposal to merge the Women's Guild in a Mixed Guild.'[99]

Organizationally, the Guild was secure. But despite the promising signs, it was a long way from being able to replicate the full range of its pre-war activities. The war had arrested the growing momentum of the Guild's citizenship work. Campaigns that did not dovetail into the war effort in the same way as maternity had been suspended; and the war had interrupted the major project launched in 1913 to stimulate special education in the Guild by holding schools for 'Guides', who would conduct rank-and-file training. The scheme was inaugurated in October 1913,[100] and the Co-operative Education Committee provided teachers for Guides Courses held in different parts of the country in 1913 and in 1914. In 1915, however, the Co-operative Education Committee complained that the subjects were not sufficiently 'academic', and the CC agreed 'that we must make our own arrangements for training our Guides.'[101] Guild education was not abandoned, and the practice was established of distributing 'Notes for Speakers' on selected subjects each year. However, the specific project of Guide training did not reappear with the same clarity.

The priority in the aftermath of the war was not only to repair the damage of the previous four years, but to cope with the Guild's largest ever influx of new members: some 20,000 from 1919 to 1922. Growth on this scale, coming after a period of depletion, imposed huge organizational strains on the national office. The departure, at the beginning of 1922, of Davies, now aged 60, along with Lilian Harris, signalled the beginning of a period of administrative difficulties which dragged on until Eleanor Barton became General Secretary in 1926. These circumstances left little scope for major campaigning initiatives of the kind that had characterized the Guild from 1900 to 1914.

Apart from these purely organizational disruptions, however, the war years had brought structural alterations to the political landscape which destroyed the autonomy that had been a pre-condition of the Guild's pre-war activity. This had opened up to feminist analysis the situation of married women in the working-class family, and was remarkable not simply because it generated a more radical account of the rights and wrongs of married women but because that account was informed by the growth, and enjoyed the support, of a rank-and-file organization of working women. The Guild's most significant interventions – for maternity care and for divorce law reform – had both led it to assert that married women should have particular kinds of rights – a degree of economic independence, freedom from unwanted pregnancies – which Labour and Co-operative leaders perceived as a threat to their own sectional interests. In the 1910s, by virtue of its leadership and its organizational autonomy the Guild was sufficiently detached from these pressures to defy them, and to pursue the logic of its analysis.

In the post-war period, however, the political space in which this radical agenda had flourished disappeared. Enfranchisement, women's incorporation into the Co-operative and Labour parties, and the emergence of Guild officials ambitious for party-political careers, steadily undermined the former commitment to married women's rights, and the wider connections with socialist and feminist ideas that had sustained it. Simultaneously, the loose alliances of the pre-war period between labour and socialist groupings hardened into rigid distinctions between reformist and revolutionary politics. Increasingly committed to the disciplines of parliamentarism, Guild leaders followed priorities set by the Labour Party, rather than by their membership; as they did so, they tacitly laid to rest the critical analysis of sexual relations in the private sphere, alongside the willingness to recognize the gendered character of the working-class, which had been such outstanding hallmarks of the earlier, pioneering phase of its history.

Notes

1. See L. Stone, *Road to Divorce: England 1530–1987* (Oxford University Press, 1990).
2. WCG, Central Committee Minutes, 5 and 6 May; 28 May; 2 June; 4 June; 8 and 9 September 1910.
3. Ibid.
4. 'Miss M. Llewelyn Davies', *Minutes of Evidence taken before the Royal Commission on Divorce and Matrimonial Causes*, 1912, III (Cd. 6481) PP 1912–13, XX, p. 150.
5. *The Nation*, 23 July 1910, Gertrude Tuckwell Collection.
6. 'Miss Davies,' *Minutes of Evidence*, p. 152.
7. Ibid., p. 149.
8. Ibid., p. 150.
9. WCG, 'The Women's Co-operative Guild, 1895–1916: A Review of Twenty-One Years' Work', *Annual Congress Handbook*, London, 1916, p. 11.
10. 'Miss Davies', *Minutes of Evidence*, pp. 150–1.
11. Ibid., p.156.
12. Ibid., p. 167.
13. Ibid., p. 166.
14. Ibid., pp. 162–3.
15. Ibid., p. 162.
16. Ibid., p. 154.
17. Ibid., p. 151.
18. Ibid., p.151.
19. Ibid., p. 151.
20. Ibid., pp. 161–2.
21. 'Mrs. Barton', *Minutes of Evidence*, III, p. 171.
22. Ibid. pp. 172–3.
23. The Commission invited submissions from any individuals or

bodies with useful information and spent several months collecting three volumes of information and opinions, and one of appendices. *Minutes of Evidence taken before the Royal Commission on Divorce and Matrimonial Causes*, 1912, I (Cd. 6479) PP 1912–13 XVIII; II (Cd. 6480) PP 1912–13 XIX; III (Cd. 6481) PP 1912–13, XX. *Appendices to the Minutes of Evidence and Report of the Royal Commission on Divorce and Matrimonial Causes*, 1912 (Cd. 6482), PP 1912–13, XXI.

24. 'Miss Ruth Homan', *Minutes of Evidence*, III, p. 173.

25. 'Mrs Fawcett', *Minutes of Evidence*, II, p. 372; see also David Rubinstein, *A Different World for Women: the Life of Millicent Garrett Fawcett* (New York: Harvester Wheatsheaf, 1991, pp. 208–9).

26. Representing the Fabian Society, Dr Bentham expressed the view that 'marriage should be able to be dissolved when it has ceased to serve its purpose'; the WLL, of which she was a prominent member, had not had time to get a mandate from all branches but she reported that opinion was generally in favour of equalization and cheapening, 'Dr Ethel Bentham', *Minutes of Evidence*, III, p. 30 and p. 37.

27. 'Mrs Fawcett', *Minutes of Evidence*, II, pp. 371–2.

28. Overall, these recommendations constituted the moderate reform position and seem to contradict the assertion that 'neither feminists nor non-feminists were generally in favour of liberalisation of the divorce laws.' J. Lewis, *Women in England 1870–1950 Sexual Divisions and Social Change* (Brighton: Wheatsheaf, 1984).

29. 'Miss Ruth Homan', *Minutes of Evidence*, III, p. 173.

30. 'Mrs Fawcett', *Minutes of Evidence*, II, p. 373.

31. 'Mrs Helena Maria Lucy Swanwick', *Minutes of Evidence*, II, p. 459. Dr Bentham also specified the need for a civil contract, 'Dr Ethel Bentham', *Minutes of Evidence*, III, p. 33.

32. 'Report of Women's Guild', *Co-operative Congress Report (CCR)*, 1913, p. 240; WCG, *Annual Report*, 1909–1910, p. 16. As such it received considerable attention from the Commissioners, the press, and the public.

33. *The Common Cause*, II, no. 91, 5 January 1911, p. 637 (thanks to Sybil Oldfield for this reference).

34. 'Miss Davies,' *Minutes of Evidence*, p. 161.

35. Ibid., p. 154.

36. See C. Pateman, *The Sexual Contract* (Cambridge: Polity, 1988); Anne Phillips, *Engendering Democracy* (Cambridge: Polity, 1991).

37. Ibid., pp. 161–2.

38. Equal treatment of men and women, grounds to include in addition to cruelty and adultery, incurable insanity after five years, habitual

drunkenness, imprisonment under a commuted death sentence, desertion for three years, *Report of the Royal Commission on Divorce and Matrimonial Causes*, 1912 (Cd. 6478), PP. XVIII, p. 113. Stone, op. cit., p. 393.

39. The controversy it engendered delayed legislation: a limited bill eventually appeared late in 1914; progress was then interrupted by the war; the sexual double standard was abolished in 1923 and its full scope not enacted until 1969. See Stone, op. cit., ch. XIII; J. Weeks, *Sex, Politics and Society: the Regulation of Sexuality since 1800* (Harlow: Longman, 1989, ch. 13).

40. *Co-operative News*, 19 April 1913, p. 499. The signatories were His Grace the Lord Archbishop of York, Sir William R. Anson, BART, MP, Sir Lewis T. Dibdin, DCL.

41. 'Minority Report,' *Report of the Royal Commission on Divorce and Matrimonial Causes*, 1912, (Cd. 6478), PP 1912–13 XVIII, p. 177.

42. Ibid., p.188.

43. Despite the points made by Mrs Fawcett, Miss Swanwick, the Guild and others, Lawrence Stone follows this judgement. Without giving any sources, he states: 'As for the wives of the working class, they remained as suspicious of divorce as they were of the vote.' Stone, op. cit., p. 392.

44. 'Minority Report', p. 177. In response, Davies stated that at the outset she had not known the opinions of most of the women that had been approached, and that in her submission she had faithfully represented the views of those who opposed divorce, *The Times*, 14 November 1912, 13e.

45. One Guild member, a churchwoman and a communicant, wrote that she had resigned from the Union after 15 years 'because I do not hold with the line they are taking over this divorce. I am told they are getting up a petition, and that people are signing it just to please the ladies, although as a matter of fact they approve of divorce', 'Evidence of Miss Davies', op. cit., p. 151.

46. 'Mrs E. Steinthal', *Minutes of Evidence*, II (Cd. 6481) PP 1912–13, XX, p. 196.

47. Ibid., quoting Mrs Coller of Moss Side.

48. Ibid.

49. 'Hon. Mrs E. Hubbard', *Minutes of Evidence*, II, p. 195.

50. *The Times*, 14 November 1912, 13e.

51. *Co-operative News*, 26 April 1913, p. 529.

52. 'Miss Davies', *Minutes of Evidence*, p. 162.

53. WCG, *Working Women and Divorce: an account of the evidence given on behalf of the WCG before the RC on Divorce* (London: David Nott, 1911); recommended reading for all Co-operative women, *Co-operative News*, 5 August 1911, p. 1012; WCG, Spring

Sectional Conferences, *Divorce Law Reform: The Majority Report of the Divorce Commission*, Manchester, 1913; WCG, *Annual Report*, 1913–14, pp. 27–8. The Guild supported the Majority Report while continuing to press for desertion after two years, mutual consent after a two-year separation, and for female assessors and assistant registrars in divorce courts.

54. MLD to L. Woolf, n.d., Monks House Papers (MHP), University of Sussex.
55. General Secretary, Catholic Federation Diocese of Salford, to General Secretary, WCG, 22 October 1913, MHP.
56. CC Minutes, 13 and 14 January 1914; WCG, *Annual Report*, 1913–14, p. 27.
57. *Co-operative News*, 28 March 1914, p. 398.
58. Ibid.
59. MLD to L. Woolf, Sunday n.d., MHP.
60. WCG, *Annual Report*, 1913–14, p. 27.
61. 'Meeting of the Central Board', CCR, 1914, pp. 12–14.
62. Ibid., pp. 15–16.
63. *Co-operative News*, 20 June 1914, p. 807.
64. MLD to L. Woolf, Friday, n.d., MHP.
65. CC Minutes, 15 June 1914.
66. *Co-operative News*, 20 June 1914, pp. 807–8.
67. *Co-operative News*, 20 June 1914, p. 808; WCG, *Annual Report*, 1914–15, p. 4.
68. *Co-operative News*, 27 June 1914, p. 14.
69. WCG, *Annual Report*, 1914–15, p. 5.
70. MLD to L. Woolf, n.d., MHP.
71. WCG Central Committee reply to Mr Whitehead, CU General Secretary, 27 October 1914, WCG, *Annual Report*, 1914–15, p. 5. A Bill based on a compromise agreement between the Majority and Minority Reports had been introduced in the 1913/14 session by Mr France (the Guild issued a memorandum to all MPs, WCG, *Annual Report*, 1913–14, p. 28); this was blocked by opponents, and then the war interrupted any possibility of legislation for almost a decade.
72. C. Goodenough, *The Central Board and the Grant to the Women's Co-operative Guild*, Manchester, 1914, p. 4.
73. CCR, 1915, pp. 20–3.
74. MLD to L. Woolf, Sunday evening, n.d., MHP.
75. CCR, 1915, pp. 26–7.
76. WCG, *Annual Report*, 1914–15, p. 7.
77. WCG, Annual Congress, 1915, *The Self-Government of the Guild* (London: Co-operative Printing Society, 1915, p. 2).
78. CCR, 1915, p. 527.

79. Ibid., p. 526.
80. Ibid.
81. WCG, *Self Government*, p. 1.
82. *CCR*, 1915, p. 522.
83. Ibid., p. 524.
84. Ibid., p. 523.
85. WCG, *Self Government*, p. 2.
86. *CCR*, 1915, p. 3.
87. WCG, *Annual Report*, 1915–16, p. 19.
88. CC Minutes, 14 June 1915.
89. CC Minutes, 19 and 20 October 1914.
90. 'Statements of Accounts, Reports of Women's Guild', *CCR*, 1914–19.
91. WCG, *Annual Report*, 1916–17, p. 1.
92. See Chapter 1, note 54.
93. M. Llewelyn Davies, *The Vote at Last! More Power to Co-operation*, Co-op Union Ltd., Political Pamphlet No. 2, London 1918, p. 1.
94. Wartime couplings and separations had intensified the need for divorce law reform, and the CC had issued a leaflet explaining the situation to branches: WCG, *Annual Report*, 1917–18, p. 11; note of requests from branches for information on divorce, CC Minutes, 11 and 12 March 1918.
95. WCG, *Annual Report*, 1918–19, p. 2.
96. CC Minutes, 17 and 18 October 1918.
97. 'Report of Women's Guild', *CCR*, 1920, p. 271. 11,000 women joined in the year to May 1920.
98. In 1920, the TUC took over the work and role of the WTUL, and the militant NFWW became a 'District' of the National Union of General Workers, which was then so effectively silenced that by 1930 'the NUGW did not send one woman delegate to the TUC conference.' S. Boston, *Women Workers and the Trade Unions* (London: Lawrence and Wishurst, 1987, p. 150). See also N.C. Soldon, *Women in British Trade Unions 1874–1976* (Dublin: Gill and Macmillan, 1978, ch. 5).
99. WCG, *Annual Report*, 1920–1, p. 19; the formation of the National Guild of Co-operators in 1926 linked up a number of Mixed Guilds already in existence but neither the Men's Guild nor the Mixed Guilds achieved the same strength and independence as the WCG.
100. *Co-operative News*, 20 September 1913, p. 1282; 'Report of Women's Guild', *CCR*, 1914, p. 253.
101. CC Minutes, 1 November 1915; 'Report of Women's Guild', *CCR*, 1916, p. 350.

Chapter Six

Labour

The first concern of the new Labour Party that emerged at the end of the First World War was to prove its credentials as the parliamentary representative of an organized but well-disciplined working class. From the perspective of its industrial and political leaderships, there were a number of obstacles to this desirable state of moderation. Most obviously, grass-roots militancy threatened to disrupt the reformist agenda. In addition, however, there was a radical working-class women's movement to contend with, organized in their own unions, suffrage groupings, the WCG, and, increasingly, in the Labour Party itself. In the immediate post-war period, many of these women were absorbed into the industrial and political labour movement,[1] bringing with them strong expectations that the party would take up issues of gender as well as class. During the 1920s, Labour became the main focus for these working-class feminist aspirations, as rank-and-file women pressed for their demands to be adopted as official policy.

Yet as the 'gender struggles'[2] of the 1920s were to demonstrate, a mass female membership was no guarantee that the party would take up issues of importance to those women. Certainly, there was no place for matters deemed electorally sensitive, such as birth control, or a threat to trade-union interests, such as family allowances. What did take shape was a welfare agenda, largely determined by senior Labour women, which sought to improve the social conditions of the working-class family.[3] Of course, working-class mothers had much to gain from better housing, health and maternity care. But there was to be no recognition of the sexual oppression of working-class women, and the defeats of the 1920s signalled the end of feminist initiatives in the party for many decades.[4]

The nature of the WCG's involvement in this history is obscured by an apparent detachment from Labour politics that stemmed both from its position in the Co-operative movement and from its traditions of autonomy. Yet beneath the surface of organizational continuities, after the retirement of Margaret Llewelyn Davies in 1922 the Guild was effectively captured by a leadership faction whose first loyalty was to the Labour and Co-operative Parties, and which rapidly succumbed to Labour Party orthodoxies. This influential group embodied the most decisive force in the organization as a whole, and its unity and sense of purpose gave it an obvious advantage over the fragmented dissonant voices raised in defence of the broad democratic and feminist traditions of the Guild. As one Co-operator pointed out in 1924: 'If the women who are individual members of the Labour Party dominate the Central Executive Committee, or any branch of the Women's Guild, that only proves they are the stronger section, who know what they want, and are determined to carry out their ideas of progress.'[5]

This shift set in train a reconfiguration of the Guild's aims and objectives. Instead of being grounded in the experience and needs of the membership, policy now became a reflex of the official Labour Party stance. This change took place partly because it was willed by a new generation of Guild leaders, especially the next influential General Secretary, Eleanor Barton, but partly also as a result of deeper structural transformations in the conditions of its existence. Yet for reasons internal to the Guild's history – in particular, the absence of explicit political debate in its proceedings – the slide towards Labour is more apparent in its policy omissions than its policy discussions. From the early 1920s, although not formally registered as such, it was the Guild's new relationship with party politics, specifically with senior Labour women, that determined the issues with which it would, and most significantly, would not, become seriously involved.

The main factor undermining the conditions which had previously facilitated the organization's autonomy was the emergence in the Guild of an entirely different attitude to, and structural relationship with, parliamentary politics. Before the war, the

Guild's head office had developed sophisticated lobbying techniques that enabled it to bring pressure to bear on the legislative process, and to ensure that its views gained a public hearing. As well as reflecting Davies' political skill in utilizing opportunities engendered by the Liberal Party's reform programme from 1906, these interventions exploited the Guild's unique position as a mass organization of working women against a general background of working-class militancy. The Guild was thus able to bend the ear of government without submitting to party discipline, or allowing its conception of politics to be defined by the Westminster–Whitehall nexus.

Almost at a stroke, the female franchise, the collapse of the Liberal Party, the rise of the Labour Party, and the formation of a Co-operative Party rendered this approach obsolete, creating a political environment in which it would be far more difficult for the Guild to maintain its free-standing position and contribute to policy debates. All the political parties were now obliged both to develop policy that would go some way towards addressing women's concerns, and to take the organization of women more seriously, but basic considerations of ideology and class solidarity ruled out any possibility of the Guild seeking to influence Conservative governments, and dictated that it would, at the very least, support the Co-operative–Labour alliance in elections. Meanwhile, for institutional reasons, its relationship with the socialist Left, in particular the newly formed Communist Party,[6] would be limited. In the absence of a firm determination to maintain a critical distance from parliamentary politics, the Guild now had to look to actual or potential Labour governments as a means of achieving reforms.

Yet this strategy was bound, sooner or later, to place the Guild at a disadvantage given the growing strength of Labour's own women's organization. In 1918, as the party's new Constitution was drawn up, the Women's Labour League was dissolved, and Labour Party Women's Sections (LPWS) established under a formidable chief woman officer, Marion Phillips.[7] Single, and from a Fabian-oriented academic background, Phillips had already proved her worth as secretary of the WLL. Beatrice Webb described her as 'redoubtable', 'shrewd and capable'. Katherine Bruce Glasier was struck by her intelligence, 'amazing energy and powerful lead', and the way that 'she identifies the Women's Labour League with herself and toils for it untiringly', but also found her egotistical, and 'as hard and cold as glass.'[8] In the Labour Party generally she was known for her efficiency and organizing ability, 'her fearless and often very sharp wit on public platforms', and an autocratic bearing.[9]

The LPWS soon dwarfed the WCG: in 1923 the executive claimed a total of 120,000, and a year later over 150,000.[10] 'In many cases,' Phillips reported in 1926 when official returns showed 1,656 women's sections and a membership approaching 250,000, 'the bulk of the Party in small towns and villages is women, and often the attendance at Labour Party meetings shows a majority of women.'[11] The LPWS thus gained the prestige formerly enjoyed by the Guild as the only broad-based organization of working women. Yet it did not use that position to develop an independent voice. The priority was to build a mass female membership within the official parameters of Labour policy and to curb rank-and-file militancy. The constitution 'relegated women members to a literal no-man's-land',[12] while leaders like Phillips worked to promote uncontentious social policies – health, housing, maternity care – and to bar sexually sensitive subjects from the political arena.[13]

Not only was the WCG steadily overshadowed by the LPWS in the political sphere. Alongside the rest of the working-class women's movement, it was brought under an informal party discipline through its involvement in the Standing Joint Committee of Industrial Women's Organisation (SJC).[14] In 1918 Phillips, the SJC secretary, secured its acceptance as Labour's Women's Advisory Committee to the National Executive Committee (NEC).[15] In a remarkable 'coup of organizing ability', Phillips had created and gained partial control of a body 'with no grass-roots organization save that imposed from above'.[16] Despite the initial veneer of a democratic forum in which representatives of the various working-class women's organizations could debate and agree policy, the privileged position of the SJC's Labour members – four of whom held seats on the NEC[17] – was indisputable. Margaret Llewelyn Davies' retirement at the end of 1921 and the premature death of Mary Macarthur in January 1922, removed the two most powerful non-Labour Party members of the SJC, leaving Phillips an unchallengeable 'first among equals'. The SJC steadily assumed 'responsibility for all questions relating to women in the working classes',[18] acting as a kind of supreme court which, in the light of Labour priorities, made final rulings about what should and should not be adopted as policy by its constituent organizations, ensuring that what remained of the working-class women's movement[19] was firmly bolted to the Labour Party.

The SJC's influence in the Guild is evident, for example, in a resolution, carried by a large majority at the 1926 Congress, in which a Hampstead delegate urged that the Guild CC should approach the SJC to bring forward a statutory scheme for family allowances.[20] No action followed. But in this and other matters, the SJC's indeterminate constitutional status meant that there were no formal mechanisms by which it could be held accountable to the members of its component organizations.

These new organizational structures were such that for the Guild to have preserved its independence and influence in public debate on women's issues would have required a major reappraisal of its relationship with the Labour Party, the Labour women, and the SJC. The maintenance of its autonomy would have involved a number of initiatives to adjust the Guild's core values to new circumstances. Its progressive Co-operative traditions – in particular, the conception of non-parliamentary routes to social transformation, and its commitment to democratic practices – might conceivably have been adapted to facilitate the evolution of a position of critical support for the Co-operative and Labour Parties, which need not have excluded the possibility of alliances with other, especially women's, groupings, or indeed with socialists in and outside the Labour Party, but would have retained its capacity to recruit and politicize women with no prior experience of party politics.

Yet far from being adequately equipped to reflect on these matters and evolve such an alternative strategy, from 1922 to 1925 the Guild leadership was fully occupied with internal problems following Davies' retirement. It has been suggested that by the end of Davies' period in office, the CC wanted to check the General Secretary's powers, and assert its own executive role.[21] Certainly, its first choice[22] for a successor was a woman whose qualities resembled those of a civil servant, rather than a politician. Honora Enfield (1882–1935), single, middle-class, and Oxford educated, was strong on administrative experience, gained working for the NFWW from 1913–17, and then as Davies' personal assistant,[23] but weak on leadership skills: 'shy and self-effacing', she was a poor platform speaker and found conferences a trial.[24] There is no reason to suppose that Enfield's political sympathies differed significantly from those of her predecessor, but she certainly lacked the energy and initiative to translate policy into action, to orchestrate new developments, or even to steer the Guild through this testing transitional period.

Enfield faced substantial organizational problems. Davies' departure coincided with unprecedented membership growth, from about 30,000 in 1919 to over 50,000 in 1922, which made great demands on the head office. As Davies commented, 'routine work becomes mountainous and, more and more, help is indispensable; while to go ahead, discover and prepare the paths for reaching new heights, a freshness and energy which cannot exist with overwork, are essential.'[25] There were also new financial pressures. While Davies and Harris had given their services gratis, their successors, Enfield and the new Assistant Secretary, Eleanor Barton, received salaries of £400 and £300 per annum, respectively – overheads which ate into the head office's limited budget at a time when prices were rising even faster than income from membership growth.[26] A CC minute in September 1923 illustrates both the strains on the office and the tight controls which the CC was imposing upon the General Secretary. Enfield reported that there was 'widespread demand' for closer contact between the centre and branches, and that an additional half-time clerk would be needed to free herself and Mrs Barton for more visits: the CC, however, voted 6–1 to defer this in view of costs.[27]

The situation was not helped by the fact that Enfield herself was overcommitted. The International Co-operative Women's Guild, formed from the 1921 International Co-operative Congress in Basle, was being run from the English Guild office and receiving 'the services of their general secretary, together with all other accessories in connection with the office.'[28] In March 1924 Enfield confessed that this international work was 'so mixed up with Guild work that it was impossible at times to define one from the other.'[29]

The chaos worsened that summer when sick leave almost brought the office to a standstill. In June 1924, with Miss Yuill, the clerical assistant, and Miss Enfield off sick, the CC noted that Miss Harris had kindly taken on the work of tabling Congress amendments, and assisting the Standing Orders Committee.[30] By October, Miss Enfield was back at work, but the office was still in disarray, and the CC agreed that 'it was not in the best interests of either the English or the International Guild for the same person to act as secretary to both longer than could be avoided'.[31] Finally, in September 1925, Enfield announced that she was resigning from the WCG to prioritize international work and to relieve the strain on her health.[32]

In these circumstances, it is hardly surprising to find that the Guild lacked the wherewithal to engineer a new independent role for itself even as its former seniority and status were being eroded by the growing importance of the LPWS. Briefly, in 1923, the CC registered concerns about the Guild's position in relation to the Labour women.[33] Yet in the absence of an inventive leadership, committed to a political alternative, and initially, at least, from convenience as much as conviction, the CC began to defer to decisions issuing from the SJC, tacitly accepting a more marginal position in the new power structures of working women's politics.

The contours of the Guild's *sotto voce* retreat from its former independence may be traced in two key policy debates of the early 1920s: on motherhood or family endowment, and birth control. The first of these demands, which had been given impetus by Eleanor Rathbone's establishment of the Family Endowment Committee in 1917,[34] was especially close to the Guild's concerns. As Davies pointed out in 1919, in an article for a book edited by Marion Phillips entitled *Women and Labour*, the demand for cash payments, paid directly to the wife in recognition of the social value of her work, was a logical extension of the Guild's maternity work. While the existing system of maternity benefit was 'totally inadequate', she stressed that it constituted an 'epoch-making reform', because through it the state acknowledged 'the claims of motherhood', and the right of married women to some income of their own. Wartime Separation Allowances had further demonstrated the value of regular cash payments to the wife,[35] and should now be extended in the form of tax-funded 'National

165

Endowment'. Such provision promised significant gains to the working class in general, and to women in particular. It would radically change the national distribution of wealth and, by removing the fear of family starvation, would strengthen labour's position in any industrial struggle. It would also reduce women's economic dependency. In a comment resonant with the knowledge gained from the divorce inquiry, Davies noted that an independent income would give 'working women a possibility of escape from degrading conditions of life, for they have been far more at the mercy of bad marriage relations than rich women, through having no money of their own.'[36]

The 1919 Guild Congress passed a resolution in support of a state scheme of endowment, and set up a WCG Committee on the Economic Position of the Mother. Its report, accepted by the CC in May 1920, identified two problems, one relating to gender, the other to class: firstly, married women's economic dependence deprived her of 'her rightful status in the home, her freedom, and individuality, and too often her health'; secondly, the structural gap between wages and the cost of raising children condemned many working-class families to poverty. Women's low wage levels and the burden of domestic labour made it undesirable for the problem to be solved by the wife going out to work; while men's wages were not adequate for the allocation of a fixed proportion to the wife. Accordingly, the Guild proposed a universal 'State Bonus', a cash allowance for every child and dependent adult (including 'the childless wife, or widow') and mothers of grown-up children, funded by a fixed percentage of all earnings. This redistribution of the national income would enable women who so chose to remain at home with their children, and in the longer term undermine the concept of the 'family wage' as the key justification of the disparity between men's and women's pay levels.[37]

The key point for the Guild was that motherhood endowment was a means of guaranteeing an income for married women regardless of their position in the labour market, while at the same time tackling the structural inequality between male and female earnings. The Labour view, however, as on the question of maternity benefit before the war, was dominated by a trade-union perspective which saw cash payments as a liability *vis-à-vis* wage negotiations, and urged assistance in kind. In the early joint

Labour–TUC Committee on Motherhood and Child Endowment, Mrs Hood, a Labour member of the Committee and also a prominent guildswoman, fought hard for cash payments. But the proceedings were dominated by its secretary, Marion Phillips,[38] and accordingly, in line with the Labour leadership's sense of the feasible, the Committee's 1922 Interim Report declared for endowment in kind not cash.[39]

The Guild CC strongly opposed this view at its meeting in March 1923, and looked to the forthcoming Labour women's conference as an opportunity to challenge the position. It agreed that, by way of preparation, arguments in support of cash payments should be rehearsed in *Co-operative News* and drawn to the attention of guildswomen who would be delegates at the conference.[40] Almost in the same breath, however, CC members expressed concern about the Guild's representation at the conference. The Labour women's conference had started life in 1918 as a general forum for women in the labour movement. However, since 1920 it had been held under the auspices of the Labour Party and the SJC. In her opening address as chairman that year, Mary Macarthur emphasized the value of a national conference which brought together the different working-class women's organizations.[41] Yet by 1923, as Guild members on the SJC had been made aware, the conference was effectively a Labour Party women's conference at which other organizations had only token representation.

Nevertheless, as the 1923 Conference approached, the Guild's feminist objections to endowment in kind were elaborated in letters, reports and articles in the 'Women's Pages'. The Labour–TUC Interim Report's great failing, argued one piece, was that it dealt only with the physical well-being of children and neglected the 'psychological requirements of the mother'. Married women, it claimed, were steadily developing 'a desire for economic independence', just as 'the demand for equal pay for equal work has grown more insistent and determined on the part of employed women.' Cash payments had been proposed 'to work a revolution in a country where women and children have been represented to working men as dependents ... not as human beings who have a right to live, and where the subconscious prejudice against wives having direct control over money to spend as they think fit still lingers in the minds of husbands.' The report's proposals uncritically reproduced this 'bread-winner mentality'.[42]

The Labour report was further criticized for only taking into account the effect of endowment payments upon 'trade union bargaining and negotiating', while ignoring the growing demand among women that 'their children shall not be dependent upon one breadwinner'.[43] Services in kind were a form of 'dole', protested Mrs Hood; the mother needed cash so that she could 'feed and clothe her children at home.'[44] 'The working-class mother', wrote Mrs Ferguson, 'has her own ideas of home life and home responsibilities, and has never shirked facing them; and I am sure she would prefer to know how much money she can depend on rather than have to ask for the milk, boots, etc., as the need arose.'[45]

In the event, however, hopes for a debate and a vote at the 1923 Labour women's conference proved vain: the report was presented by Marion Phillips,[46] and no opportunity was given for discussion,[47] or expression of the 'point of view of the feminist who desires the economic independence of the married woman'.[48] The report was referred, unamended, to the Labour Party Conference, at which it was duly adopted and a resolution passed calling on the Parliamentary Labour Party to work for 'a system of payment in kind, as any money allowance would be rendered insufficient by the rise in prices which follows any rise in wages or allowances, as experienced by housewives during the war.'[49] Yet Labour's short-lived 1924 Government was not in a position to implement this, or any other, social reform, and the matter duly faded from the agenda until it was raised as part of the ILP's 'Socialism in Our Time' initiative in the second half of the 1920s.

The Guild's defeat in the 1923 round of discussions on Motherhood Endowment must have brought home to its leadership that with regard to Labour Party policy it had very limited scope for advancing proposals that differed from those of the senior Labour women. Advocacy of the feminist case for family endowment was, in fact, its first and last attempt to oppose the Labour women. If we turn to the record of the Guild's involvement with the question of birth control – another pivotal issue for working women in the 1920s – it is clear that between 1923 and 1924, far from objecting to Labour's official line, the

Guild CC was almost gratefully falling back on the SJC as a means of keeping its own house in order.

In contrast to Motherhood Endowment, which had been introduced, as was normally the case, by the head office, the Guild's involvement with birth control stemmed from the rank and file. As the pre-war literature on divorce and maternity indicates, many members were already taking steps to limit family size, or approved of such practices.[50] As the birth control movement gained momentum after 1918, Guild branches began to invite activists such as Marie Stopes, Jennie Baker and Stella Brown to speak at meetings.[51] The leadership's initial response was positive: in September 1922, taking note of these meetings, the CC considered 'taking up the question of Birth Control', as a special subject for study and practical action throughout the organization. Had this proposal been given effect, the WCG would have become an important focus for working-class women's support for birth control. Yet from the outset, there were signs that the leadership was wary of the issue, mindful of both its controversial nature and the danger of precipitating a repeat of the conflict over divorce law reform. The discussion touched on possible 'complications' with the Co-operative Union, and it was agreed that before reaching a decision, more information should be obtained by inviting Marie Stopes[52] to the next London CC meeting.[53]

Pending this interview, the matter of birth control took on a political as well as a moral dimension when, in December 1922, Nurse Daniels, an Edmonton health visitor, was dismissed by the public health authority for giving women attending a maternity clinic the address of the Marie Stopes clinic. The decision was upheld by the Ministry of Health as a general ruling, and its reversal became the focus for a left-wing campaign to broaden working-class women's access to contraception.[54]

Marie Stopes, who, for the record, refused to support Nurse Daniels,[55] meanwhile lost the first round of her libel action against the Catholic convert, Dr Sutherland, assisted by the Church, for insinuating that she was subjecting the poor to harmful experiments.[56] The next month, in March 1923, she addressed the CC 'on her work for birth control and the aims and methods she advocated', answering their questions. This would presumably have covered the work of her first clinic, opened in Holloway in 1921, the use of the check pessary, sheaths and other contraceptive methods which she recommended, and her perceptions of working women's need for such information.[57] As a result of the interview, the CC decided to supply branches with information about her work: the Guild office would purchase copies of *Married Love* (1918), and *Wise Parenthood* (1919), and branch requests for speakers would be passed on to the appropriate quarters. Yet there was still no determination actively to promote the subject. Once again, the question was deferred, this time to 'test the opinion' of Congress.[58]

The delegates at Congress in June 1923 were unequivocal about where they stood in the dispute posed by the Daniels case. Mrs Johnston (Sale, Manchester) moved that in the interests of women's health, the Ministry and local health authorities should recognize the advisability 'of information in regard to Birth Control being given at all maternity and child welfare centres in the country.' Seconding, Mrs Harling (Battersea) argued that this was a matter of class as well as sex. Knowledge of the 'great Law of Nature' had 'been in the hands of the wealthier and cultured classes for quite a long time and they lived normal, healthy and happy lives; but at the same time they limited their families according to the number they desired and were prepared to maintain and educate.' Why should such knowledge be denied to working women? Only one speaker opposed – Mrs O'Kane (Eccles), a Catholic, who upheld 'self-control not birth control' – and the resolution was passed by a large majority. The WCG thus became the first women's organization, *and* the first working-class organization, formally to support birth control, the vote promptly being hailed as an important landmark in the movement's development.[59]

If the CC needed proof that there was rank-and-file support for a Guild campaign on birth control, then the 1923 Congress vote should have sufficed; if it needed any reminder about the sensitivity of the issue, this too was forthcoming in the shape of a letter of complaint from the Guild's old adversary – Mr Burns of the Manchester and Salford Catholic Federation. His letter arrived soon after Congress,[60] and was read to the CC at its September meeting. Yet here the sense of history repeating itself ended. In contrast to the militant response on divorce law reform in 1914, it was agreed to let the letter 'lie on the table'. The birth control resolution was then discussed. Branches wanting to take further action should be put in touch with speakers and advised to pursue the matter with their local authorities. There was to be no national lead: the CC resolved 'not to make this a special subject but to await the report of the SJC as to other action.'[61]

What might appear to be one more deferral was in fact a closure, for it is hard to believe that the Guild CC would have regarded the conclusions of the forthcoming report as an open question. The sub-committee had been set up from the 1923 Labour women's conference to avoid taking a resolution on birth control;[62] and it is unlikely that Guild SJC members would have been unaware that senior Labour women wanted to keep birth control off the party agenda. This determination was strengthened a few months later when, following its comparative success in the 1923 election, Labour formed its first government in January 1924, and John Wheatley, a Catholic, was appointed Minister of Health. Facing the eager anticipation of a militant rank and file, the Labour women's leadership made their position clear. 'We do plead', ran an editorial in *The Labour Woman* in March 1924, 'that this subject of the relations of husband and wife should not be treated as a political issue at all.'[63]

On a deputation to the Labour Minister of Health on 9 May 1924, organized by a core of activists who formed the Workers' Birth Control Group, was a young Guild member, Mabel Cumins. Wheatley was presented with a petition bearing 6,000 signatures (including 20 Labour MPs), calling for a reversal of the policy on maternity clinics. He replied that it would require parliamentary approval. 'I heard afterwards', Mabel Cumins recalled, 'when we came back and discussed it, that he was a Roman Catholic, so what chance did we have!'[64] In June 1924 Wheatley issued a circular which explicitly prohibited any mention of birth control in the maternity clinics – a ruling which was upheld until 1930.[65]

At the 1924 Labour women's conference, Marion Phillips did her utmost to block the resolution on birth control. 'Sex', she famously announced to Dora Russell, 'should not be dragged into politics, you will split the Party from top to bottom.' The chief woman officer existed, Russell decided, 'not so much to support the demands of the women, as to keep them in order from the point of view of the male politicians.'[66] At the women's conference Phillips failed: following a debate in which the only opposition came from a mother of 11,[67] delegates demanded by 1,000 votes to 8 that local authorities be empowered to give birth control information when requested.[68] One of the main speakers in the debate, Rose Davies (Aberdare), a Labour Party member and an active guildswoman, marshalled 'some strong facts about the preventable suffering and deaths of mothers and children', pleading that the question of birth control, like that of maternity care, was not 'a "woman's question" only, but one of general importance to all.'[69]

Coming as it did a year after the majority vote at the 1923 Guild Congress, this overwhelming vote left no room for doubt about the views of organized working-class women on this question. The announcement given in the next edition of *The Labour Woman* sent an equally clear message about the priorities of the leadership. The SJC, it announced, was unable to recommend that birth control advice be given out at maternity clinics, 'in view of the conflicting views of medical experts and others'.[70]

The Guild CC was thus relieved of any responsibility *vis-à-vis* birth control. To some extent, its willingness to be bound by the SJC was a matter of expediency: while not opposed to birth control being discussed in the Guild, the CC was anxious not to risk a dispute with the Catholic Federation and/or the Co-operative Union, especially given the financial strains and staffing problems in the national office. Yet this was also a political choice. A national initiative over maternity clinics would have problematized its relationship with the Labour women on the SJC, and its attitude to the Labour government. The CC had found a face-saving way out of a difficulty, but by the same token had tacitly admitted that the days of Guild autonomy on questions of importance to working women were over. Its retreat from the birth control issue implicitly signalled the leadership's acceptance of its new role as the junior partner of the Labour women. After 1923, the Guild leadership took no significant initiative on family endowment, birth control, or any other issue of concern to working women that did not enjoy the prior approval of the Labour Party.

In an organization which lacked any solid experience of political debate, an increasingly Labour-oriented leadership had been able to gain control of the machinery of policy-making in the Guild without inciting concerted opposition. The next and, given the organization's democratic traditions, more difficult step would be to attempt to impose party-political uniformity on the Guild, by introducing measures to regulate the political affiliations of officials. These measures, and the conflict which they generated, will be examined in Chapter 7.

Despite the influx of militant rank-and-file women,[71] including many Guild members, looking to advance the cause of their sex, the rapid growth of the LPWS did not bring a commensurate share of influence in the party. Structurally blocked as they were by more powerful interests in the Labour Party, the women's sections could not assume the Guild's former role in providing radical, autonomous representation for working-class women; the central debates on women's issues in the 1920s demonstrate that policy remained under the control of socially conservative, trade-union dominated interests within the party.

The struggle to win Labour Party support for the birth control position, orchestrated by the Workers' Birth Control Group,[72] continued for three years. In 1925 the NEC refused a conference debate on the subject since it was supposedly not one 'which should be made a political party issue'.[73] This verdict was challenged the following year. 'Let any of them,' Dora Russell told delegates, 'imagine a section of the Party bringing a proposal to Conference which they considered vital to their life and health and being told they could not discuss it ... would it not make them wild? Well the women were wild'. If the delegates' places were taken 'by their wives and sisters', Dorothy Jewson informed a conference with only 70 women present, 'there would be no doubt about their support.' Despite Ramsay Macdonald's claims that birth control was 'a question of Neo-Malthusianism', conference voted by a slim majority (1,656,000 to 1,602,000) to refer back to the executive's ruling that it was not a party-political issue.[74]

It was a pyrrhic victory. Labour was back in opposition, anxieties about the Catholic vote were rife, and, in Dora Russell's view, 'the surrender of the General Strike had badly shaken the nerve of the Party'. (For Russell, it is worth noting, 1926 was the year that any revolutionary hopes for Labour died.)[75] In 1927 the birth control position was reversed as a result of energetic mobilization of the block vote, following Mrs Harrison Bell's scathing attack on the idea that working women might have interests distinct from working men. Exhibiting the qualifications that had earned her one of the four seats reserved for women on the NEC, she stressed that she deprecated 'any Party interfering in the intimate relationships between husbands and wives, fathers and mothers and children.' As a final poisoned dart, she added that 'she could say, if she liked, that here was another evidence of Communist activity, but she would forbear.'[76] In 1928, by a margin of only three, the Labour women's conference accepted the NEC's position, and henceforth the birth control movement lacked the official support of the working women's organizations.

The defeat over birth control made it plain that the party was not going to engage in issues of sexual oppression; in effect, the domestic sphere was ruled out of bounds and remained so for almost half a century. It also demonstrated that, whatever the membership figures, women had very little influence in the party. The constitution had been carefully designed to mobilize activists for electoral purposes, while silencing them in policy-making.[77] Decisions taken at the Labour women's conference had still to survive the trade-union block vote at the main conference; even if passed, in practice they were not binding on the PLP. The four NEC seats reserved for women were filled by candidates chosen by Conference, not by the female membership, and their qualifications for office were invariably those of moderation and restraint, as exemplified by Marion Phillips' impeccable grasp of the party's bounds as regards women's issues.[78]

If the conflict over birth control demonstrated Labour's resistance to 'sex questions', perceived (for moral or cultural reasons) to be vote losers, the struggle over family allowances from 1926 to 1930 emphasized the weight of the TUC in policy-making. At the 1926 Party Conference, the ILP pressed for some consideration of family allowances as part of a Living Wage programme, formulated under its 'Socialism in Our Time' policy initiative. By a two-to-one majority Conference voted for an inquiry, and in July 1927 the TUC–Labour Party 'Joint Committee on the Living Wage' was instituted, with six representatives from each side. From the outset the proposal met with strong opposition from TUC leaders, who were determined that the question of wages should not be taken out of trade-union hands, and that cash allowances should not be allowed to undermine their position in collective bargaining. The committee's brief was almost immediately limited to the question of whether family support should take the form of a money allowance or services in kind. As far as the Labour leadership was concerned, majority support for cash payments from the Party, and even from a significant section of the unions (including the impoverished Miners Federation), was less important than the imprimatur of leading trade unionists, and for three years the TUC blocked any firm recommendation.

As Arthur Henderson (TUC secretary), explained at the 1928 Birmingham Labour Conference, 'the matter was somewhat complicated, and doubt was expressed as to how far trade unions would accept the principle'. Ernest Bevin (TGWU) 'warned the conference that it must not be assumed that the principle was accepted by the trade unions.'[79] In 1929 it was reported to Conference that the trade-union side was most reluctant to make up its mind, and there was no definite pronouncement.[80] Although the weight of speeches ran in favour of family allowances, and even though (as James Maxton (ILP) pointed out), the issue had been before them for three years, Henderson indicated that labour unity was more important than any single reform, no matter how popular. Once again conference accepted a delay, pending the TUC's verdict.[81]

Finally abandoning the quest for unanimity, in February 1930 the Joint Committee issued a majority report of nine in favour of cash payments, and a minority report of three for services in kind.[82] At the 1930 TUC conference, speech after speech condemned the 'cash only' scheme, because 'it would make reliance on the trade-union weapons less necessary, and would render these weapons less efficacious.'[83] Services in kind, C.T. Cramp of the NUR told delegates, would be more productive than 'scattering' money into individual homes, since the working-class mother would not necessarily budget effectively. Furthermore, cash payments would diminish a workers' motivation to join a union, and thereby 'sap the foundations' of the movement.[84]

Labour Conference duly defeated a move to refer back the TUC decision in support of services in kind by 1,740,000 to 495,000,[85] terminating the attempt to win labour movement sponsorship of family allowances until the 1940s.

The Guild's growing attachment to Labour Party orthodoxies was cemented by Enfield's successor, Eleanor Barton, who became General Secretary at the end of 1925. Barton's role in the Guild illustrates the fact that the Labour Party's major impact on the working-class women's movement was not simply the product of changing structures – external factors which limited the Guild's scope for intervention – but also a result of the affinities and ambitions of leading guildswomen.

Enfield's period in office had served to prove that the Guild organization needed effective and purposeful full-time leadership of a kind that the CC – voluntary officials meeting about six times a year – simply could not provide. The chaos in the head office, and the lack of a strong sense of direction are apparent in the lack of distinctive interventions of any kind by the Guild during these years. There were complaints from members of a decline in energy and initiative from the centre; the Guild was 'not as active as it used to be, and campaigns were begun and never finished'.[86]

The experiment in weak leadership was not repeated. The vacuum at the heart of the Guild was now filled by a leader who was strong to the point of intransigence, and whose methods and values were very similar to those of her Labour counterparts. Even the most respectful accounts suggest that Eleanor Barton was a domineering woman. The Guild centenary history makes reference to her strong personality and her reputation as 'a very efficient but strict General Secretary', whose considerable 'administrative and judicial experience made her a formidable opponent in committee discussion'. Kathleen Kempton, who joined the Guild in 1935, thought that she could be 'rather dictatorial',[87] while Sheffield guildswomen, half a century later, described her as a 'strict autocrat'.[88]

In one respect, Eleanor Barton was a testament to the success of the Guild project: a working-class woman who had worked her way up from the rank and file. Nellie Stockton was born in Manchester in 1872.[89] 'I started early as a rebel,' she told guildswomen at her retirement in 1937, 'on the platform at an open-air meeting with Keir Hardie when I was eighteen years old.'[90] In 1894 she married Alfred Barton, a self-educated librarian, son of a Bedfordshire foundry labourer's son, and a socialist.[91] In 1897 the couple moved to Sheffield, where they raised a son and a daughter; Alfred worked in commerce, as an insurance agent, and as a full-time secretary for the ILP. Both were active in the local labour movement – Alfred as a trade unionist and socialist, and Eleanor from 1901 as a guildswoman.

Eleanor Barton climbed steadily up the Guild committee structure: secretary of Hillsborough Guild in Sheffield for a total of 17 years, she served on the district committee, and the Yorkshire Sectional Council; on the CC from 1912–14, and again in 1920. She was national president in 1914; and a member of the Citizenship Sub-Committee from 1912–14. In 1921 she was a candidate for the post of General Secretary, and as runner-up in the membership ballot, was appointed Assistant Secretary, and then proved herself indispensable during Honora Enfield's illness in 1924: in October the CC's 'appreciation of the work of the Assistant Secretary during the General Secretary's absence' was minuted.[92] Following Enfield's resignation, Barton won the vital first-place recommendation from the CC, and was duly elected General Secretary, taking office at the beginning of 1925.[93]

In contrast to women like Marion Phillips, whose avoidance of contentious gender politics was as apparent in the WLL as in the LPWS, Barton's early years in the Guild furnished her with an acute sensitivity to the sexual oppression of working-class women. This is most pronounced in her evidence to the Divorce Commission in 1910, when she insisted that women should have the right to divorce rather than be subjected to unwanted sexual demands.[94] Her effort to inform the commissioners about post-natal rape, involving as it did a struggle to find a vocabulary to discuss sexual abuse in a setting which lacked the necessary legal or cultural conceptual framework, is particularly striking. In her account, 'cruelty' had to serve for penetration against medical advice or the wishes of the woman; 'suffering', for severe depression and a range of injuries, including lesions and infections. Faced with Royal Commissioners who were insulated by their social status, and their sense of propriety, from any consideration of such matters, Barton turned to medical science for an expert but clinical treatment of the subject. Doctors, she claimed, 'have this evidence and could give it more conclusively than one like myself.'[95]

In the 1920s, however, Barton abandoned these strongly held feminist convictions, and to understand this shift we need to consider her career in Co-operative–Labour politics in the 1920s. Since this involves taking into account her personal as well as her public aspirations, we should note her remark to the Commission that a doctor could give more conclusive evidence than 'one like myself'. These three words signal the struggle of a working-class woman to overcome the gulf between the Guildroom and Westminster, acutely conscious of her lack of education and expertise before well-bred, self-assured members of a Royal Commission; Davies would never have uttered such words. 'One like myself' implicitly articulates a consciousness of class that might sustain militancy, but it also intimates a hunger for self-improvement. Like many others who had entered the socialist movement at the turn of the century, labour politics after the war became for Eleanor Barton a means of individual as well as collective advancement. Among other compromises, the price of that political career included turning her back on the sexual politics that had served as her apprenticeship, while simultaneously graduating from the ILP socialist influences of her early career to a right-wing Labourism.

By the time Barton became General Secretary, her base in the Guild had provided the springboard for a role in the Co-operative Party, and it was this that determined the political agenda which she brought to the post. In 1918 she took a seat on the Executive of the newly formed Sheffield Political Council (its very first meeting was held in the Guildroom), won a nomination for the municipal elections, endorsed by the Trades and Labour Council, and got herself on the Co-operative list of parliamentary candidates.[96] She served as a Co-operative–Labour councillor from 1919–22, and became one of the first woman JPs in the country. She next set her sights on Westminster, fighting hard but unsuccessfully to secure a parliamentary seat at Kings Norton (Birmingham), in 1922 and 1923, and at Nottingham East in 1929, her last attempt.[97] Standing as a Co-operative–Labour candidate put pressure on Barton to use her Guild office to prove her commitment. A report she gave to senior guildswomen on the 1923 Kings Norton campaign, for example, caused Mrs Ferguson, an experienced official of the 'old guard', to say that she was troubled by the question of 'how far the Labour Party should be allowed to dominate the Guild.'[98]

In marked contrast to Davies' priorities, Barton's main objective during the 1920s was as far as possible to dovetail Guild developments with those which promoted her chances as a Co-operative–Labour candidate. This cut two ways. In the Guild, as we shall see in Chapter 7, she instigated a move to prohibit the selection of Guild officials who did not support Co-operative politics. In the Co-operative Party she sought to use her role in the Guild to underline her worth to the party. Thus, at the first Co-operative Party Conference in 1925, Barton is to be found expressing concern about rival parties entering the Guilds.[99] In the same month, at Guild district conferences, she criticized 'narrow-minded' branches that were not active on behalf of the Co-operative Party, and predicted the implementation of a political rule to compel such involvement;[100] later that year, she introduced 'Politics in the Guild Room' as a special subject.[101] At the 1926 Party Conference, Mrs Barton referred to the 'valuable work' of the Women's Guild, and several of her fellow delegates paid tribute to the example that had been set by good work in the Guild.[102]

Like the majority of Co-operative Party activists, but unlike the majority of Co-operators, Barton was also a Labour Party supporter, who would have regarded it as 'the established instrument of working-class unity in the political field.'[103] This outlook was strengthened by her personal ambition to win a seat, which entailed securing nominations as a Co-operative–Labour candidate. Of course, Barton was not the only guildswoman committed to Co-operative–Labour politics but she was the most prominent and the most powerful. She provided a lead for the many guildswomen who were active in the Co-operative and/or Labour Party, some of whom were also ambitious for office.[104] As Mrs Bird (Guild President) told the 1927 All Councils meeting, the Guild 'had thrown in its lot with the Co-operative Party'.[105] What she meant was that the dominant section of the leadership under Eleanor Barton now conceived of the Guild as a kind of Co-operative Party women's section. As we shall see in the next chapter, this aspiration went against the grain of strongly held

Guild and Co-operative traditions, which had to be challenged (or even dismantled) to secure the kinds of control necessary to impose such political homogeneity.

The point to note here is that from 1926 onwards the main priority of the Guild leadership was to maximize Guild support for the Co-operative Party. In two respects this explains the Guild's increasingly low-key and extremely moderate approach to questions of gender. For a start, the focus on parliamentary politics inevitably marginalized women's issues; furthermore, Barton would have been too mindful of the need to maintain Co-operative–Labour support for her candidature to adopt any policy that was politically sensitive. Like other women seeking to enter Labour politics she had to demonstrate herself to be unquestionably loyal to the movement.[106] Like the Labour Party chief woman officer, as Guild General Secretary she needed to steer the organization clear of controversial 'sex issues'.

Accordingly, in the 1920s, Barton took a pragmatic view of the needs of working women. Her acute awareness of their vulnerability within marriage, which would surely have led her to support birth control and family allowances, vanished as though through amnesia, as she steered the Guild towards support for the less contentious proposals of the late 1920s. Her paper, *The National Care of Motherhood*, discussed at Sectional Conferences in 1928,[107] was written with a careful eye on mainstream opinion in the Labour Party, emphasizing the need for basic improvements in working-class living conditions. 'Medical science and the best Maternity services', it argued, 'will be of no avail unless the mother also has Nature's requirements – enough good food, warm clothing, cleanliness, a certain degee of comfort in her home, and rest.'[108] All well and good, no doubt, yet many women, inside and outside the Guild, were continuing to argue that unwanted pregnancies and economic dependency also had considerable bearing on the health of the mother.

At the 1926 Congress, a resolution calling for a change in the government's ruling on birth control information and maternity clinics was submitted, but not discussed.[109] Debating the Hampstead motion calling for the SJC to press for family allowances, a delegate from Ripon, 'where the men earned less than 35s a week' as agricultural workers, stated that 'their members wanted the guild to press for birth control information and a living wage'.[110] In a discussion on the 'Care of Maternity' at a Manchester district conference in 1927, Mrs Derbyshire (Gorton) 'thought the workers had a right to knowledge concerning birth control for often they were unable to support their families'.[111] At the 1928 Congress, Mrs Betts (Crouch End) moved a radical amendment to a CC resolution on maternity care: 'in view of the terrible maternal death rate in this country scientific contraceptive knowledge should be made available for all mothers and young wives at all maternity centres and clinics when asked for, as ... unscientific attempts at contraception are responsible for a great number of maternal deaths.' It was pointed out that many mothers 'were not in a fit state to have a child, yet were bearing one every year, and the suffering through abortion was a danger to life.' The amendment was passed 'amidst enthusiasm',[112] but no further action was taken.

Despite such rank-and-file opinion, Barton was careful to avoid these politically sensitive aspects of maternity, and to treat the issue in ways that conformed to the senior Labour women's programme of better housing, wages, and health care for the workers. She thus collapsed the specific needs of women into a general concern for the welfare of the working-class family. The same tendency is apparent in the vision of the ideal Co-operative community she sketched out in a 1929 Co-operative Party pamphlet, *Woman in the Home, the Store and the State*:

Where the health and welfare of the people is the first law.

Where old age is tended and honoured.

Where childhood is cherished and made lovely.

Where young people are trained to useful and capable social service in those things for which they are best fitted.

Where men have employment at reasonable human wages, and

Where the woman can survey her family and her home, and be happy that the State in which she lives is a home of homes, holding out the hand of affection and friendship to her homes in all parts of the world.[113]

Relegated to the very bottom of the list, it is striking that the adult woman is promised no more in this utopia than marriage and motherhood. She will have the satisfaction of seeing others – children, young people, men, the elderly – enjoy a full and rewarding life, largely, one assumes, as a result of her services. Furthermore, it is made clear that her entry into the state, as a citizen, would be through marriage and motherhood, not by virtue of her rights as an individual. In effect, Eleanor Barton was endorsing women's place in the home by advocating an extension of its boundaries:

> Now that women have full political power it rests with them to see that the affairs of the nation are adjusted and carried on with that same earnestness and desire for the good of all as is to be found in the vast majority of cottage homes in this country ... What women have to realise is that the State is nothing but a larger home, and that its problems, duties, and responsibilities should be considered in the same spirit of mutual helpfulness as in the home.[114]

Under Barton's dispensation, social reform was increasingly presented by the Guild as a means of supporting, rather than contesting, women's domestic identity. Speaking on 'Housing and Motherhood' at a district day school in December 1930, for example, Mrs Roe (Sectional Council) argued that if 'houses for the poor were built at reasonable rents, with labour-saving devices, mothers of the working-class could perform their natural functions without the danger to life and risk of after effects to-day endured.'[115]

The 1931 Guild All Councils (the annual gathering of Sectional Councils) discussed 'Mothers of the Future'. By way of introduction, Mrs Priestley (Yorkshire Section) considered the position of married women in Britain, touching on the difficulties which prevented working-class wives from playing a full role in public life. Ideally, she thought, they should have the choice either 'to follow a career or to stay at home.' Yet while sex was no longer a barrier to the professions or voting rights, 'economic conditions' still held them back. How, she asked, were they to gain the economic independence necessary for their own well-being and that of their children, and be 'freed from the double burden of housework and wage earning?'

The ensuing discussion reveals the dead weight of Labourism pressing on the organization. 'What had become of the State Bonus?', asked one Guild official. It had been abandoned, the General Secretary answered revealingly, because 'the Labour Party of that day considered it impracticable'. Mrs Matthews (Lancashire Section) further explained that CC speakers had promoted the scheme, 'but the trade unions and the Labour Party had rejected it.' 'Even to-day,' commented Mrs Beavan (Lancashire Section), 'trade unions are against family allowances, alleging the scheme is against the workers, and means lower wages'.

A number of those present believed that they should keep pressing for family allowances and any other measure that would assist married women. Yet there was also strong sympathy for the union position. 'The point of view of the trade unions should not be ignored', stressed Mrs Prosser (Western Section). 'Lower wages would make matters worse.' Mrs Rowes (Midland Section) held that 'unemployment and insecurity of wages were at the root of the trouble', a view shared by the General Secretary. Mrs Ganley (South Eastern Section) was not at all convinced that family allowances would help the situation in the homes; she wanted to see more women on public committees. 'But women', she said, 'did not care. In many cases they did not understand and, mainly, they were apathetic.'[116]

The Guild's new policy in relation to family welfare, 'Milk for Schoolchildren',[117] indicated that whatever the spread of opinion at All Councils, the Guild now shared the official Labour Party commitment to assistance in kind, not cash. In her presidential address to the 1931 Congress, Mrs Mellis stressed that guildswomen 'had long recognised that an ill-nourished child cannot advantageously benefit by education. Let us therefore see to it that we build healthy bodies, as physical and mental conditions react on each other.'[118] Delegates duly passed a resolution calling on the Board of Education to supply school milk, believing that regular milk was essential to the health of schoolchildren'.[119] In contrast, a 1937 resolution from the Leyton and Barking Guilds in London's East End, calling for a state scheme for the endowment of motherhood, was referred back because, as Mrs Billan (CC) explained, 'the committee agreed with the TUC that at the present time it was better to press for increased social services rather than for a State scheme such as that proposed'.[120]

Congress again defeated a call for family allowances in 1941. Opposing the motion, Mrs Brown (Willesden Green) described the measure as 'a great threat to organised labour'. Mrs Barton (now ex-General Secretary) stated that the Guild had already considered and rejected family allowances; what they should be doing, she argued in language now saturated with the 'bread-winner mentality', was making sure that 'every citizen should as a right be able to build a home for his wife and children.'[121] The following year, however, the Guild was upstaged when the Labour Party NEC, the General Council of the TUC, and the Co-operative Congress all approved a Government White Paper setting out a scheme of non-contributory cash benefits on the birth of the second child.[122] The Guild was now free to retrieve its earlier position of support for such a scheme, and in due course to play a part in the fight to make the benefit the property of the wife.[123] Its 1943 'Notes for Speakers' on the Beveridge Report made reference to Guild discussions of allowances in 1917, but glossed over its differences with Labour in the early 1920s, stating only that it had refrained from pressing the issue because the trade unions had held that such payments would reduce their bargaining power in wage discussions.[124]

Certainly from the late 1920s, especially in the defensive and demoralized atmosphere following the General Strike, the dominant view on women's issues among Guild officials consisted in a close identification with the sectional interests of labour, betraying a strong tendency to view the working class as homogeneous, and united in its quest for parliamentary power. Solidarity with that project had by now become so important as to require the Guild's acceptance of party discipline, tailoring its policies to suit the mainstream, rather than arguing for positions which reflected the specific needs (not to mention the views) of its members. Absent from this perspective was any awareness of the inequality between working-class men and women that had been such a marked characteristic of the Guild's earlier citizenship campaigns.

In less than a decade, the WCG had travelled a long way from its singleminded commitment to an autonomous politics of working women. The factors behind this shift are complex and interwoven. The structural changes in working-class politics in turn pulled working-class women's organizations away from organized feminism, and therewith, closer to the mainstream of the Labour movement. Here, senior and ambitious activists, who wholeheartedly believed in the indispensability of parliamentary power, for the first time had the opportunity to be recognized in the mainstream party – to stand alongside the men as candidates for office, and in local and national elections. The price of this acceptance was to be 'reasonable' or 'realistic' about women's issues. Thus, despite a sterling record as advocates of the cause of working women, women like Eleanor Barton were ready and willing to be convinced that there was more to be gained from gradual social reform, than from pressing the case for working-class feminist policies.

Notes

1. In 1920, the TUC took over the work and role of the WTUL, and the NFWW became a 'District' of the National Union of General Workers, see N.C. Soldon, *Women in British Trade Unions 1874–1976* (Dublin: Gill and Macmillan, 1978, ch. 5).
2. P. Graves, *Labour Women in British Working-Class Politics 1918–1939* (Cambridge University Press, 1994, ch. 3).
3. P. Thane, 'Visions of gender in the making of the British welfare state: the case of women in the British Labour Party and social policy, 1906–1945', in G. Bock & P. Thane (eds), *Maternity and Gender Policies: Women and the Rise of the European Welfare States, 1880–1950s* (London: Routledge, 1991); P. Thane, 'Women in the British Labour Party and the Construction of State Welfare', in S. Koven & S. Michel (eds), *Mothers of a New World: Maternalist Politics and the Origins of Welfare States* (London: Routledge, 1993).
4. As Hinton comments, neither 'trade-union strategies or political demands appropriate to the needs of the female half of the working class' emerged, J. Hinton, *Labour and Socialism A History of the British Labour Movement 1867–1974* (Brighton: Wheatsheaf, 1983, p. 130).
5. *Co-operative News*, 17 April 1924, p. 12.
6. See Chapter 1, note 50.
7. The daughter of an Australian Jewish lawyer, Phillips (1881–1932) took a BA in history and philosophy from Melbourne University, completed a D.Sc.(Economics) at the London School of Economics (LSE), and from 1906 to 1910, supervised by Beatrice Webb, worked as a Poor Law Commission researcher. She joined the Fabian Society and the ILP in 1907, the WLL in 1908; and worked for the

NUWSS and the WTUL in 1910 and 1911. She was chief woman officer until her death in 1932; in 1929 she was elected MP for Sunderland but lost the seat in 1931. J.M. Bellamy & J. Saville (eds), *Dictionary of Labour Biography* (DLB), V (London: Macmillan, 1979).

8. C. Collette, *For Labour and for Women The Women's Labour League 1906–1918* (Manchester University Press, 1989, pp. 133 and 134).

9. *DLB*, V, p. 177.

10. Growth rates which outstripped male recruitment, R. McKibbin, *The Evolution of the Labour Party 1910–1924* (Oxford: Clarendon Press, 1974, p. 141).

11. Labour Party, *Annual Report*, 1926, p. 7.

12. Graves, op. cit., p. 109.

13. *DLB*, V, p. 175.

14. Formed in 1916 to co-ordinate war-time representation of working women on national and local government bodies; composed of senior officials from the WLL, the WTUL, the WCG, and the Railway Women's Guild (women connected with members of the Amalgamated Society of Railway Servants).

15. McKibbin, op. cit., p. 215.

16. Collette, op. cit., pp. 170–1.

17. NEC Minutes, 23 April 1924, British Labour Party Archives, Series One, Part One 1900–1926; Graves, op. cit., p. 109.

18. *DLB*, V, p. 174.

19. See Chapter 5, note 98. Holloway concludes that the postwar mergers virtually silenced the women's trade unions, G.Holloway, 'A Common Cause? Class Dynamics in the Industrial Women's Movement, 1888–1918', Sussex University D.Phil. thesis, 1995, ch. 6.

20. *Co-operative News*, 19 June 1926, p. 7.

21. J. Gaffin & D. Thoms, *Caring and Sharing: The Centenary History of the Co-operative Women's Guild* (Manchester: Co-operative Union, 1983, p. 91).

22. The CC advertised the post in *Co-operative News* and *Woman's Outlook*, and from the responses unanimously recommended Miss Enfield. Branch returns: Miss Enfield 696 first preferences; Mrs Barton 40. WCG, Central Committee Minutes, 22 and 23 September 1921; 2 November 1921; 14 and 15 December 1921.

23. Proximity to the leader continued to determine the succession: Eleanor Barton (General Secretary, 1925–37) was Enfield's Assistant Secretary; Rose Simpson (General Secretary, 1937–40) was Barton's niece; Cecily Cook (General Secretary 1940–53) had been Barton's secretary.

24. Tribute to Honora Enfield compiled at her death in 1935, bound

and typescript MS and cuttings, 'Co-operative Archive', Bishopsgate Reference Library.

25. *Co-operative News*, 5 January 1924, p. 12.
26. CC Minutes, 22 and 23 September 1921. The office clerk earnt £3:8s a week, and the cashier £247 p.a.
27. CC Minutes, 19 and 20 September 1923.
28. *Co-operative News*, 6 September 1924, p. 13 (initially the International Co-operative Women's Committee, see Gaffin & Thoms, op. cit., pp. 113–5).
29. Speaking at the Leeds Executive Guild, *Co-operative News*, 15 March 1924, p. 13.
30. CC Minutes, 16 June 1924.
31. CC Minutes, 8 and 9 October 1924. It was also noted that 'Miss Yuill's arm did not allow her to do even her previous amount of typing', a new clerk, Miss Cox, was only learning shorthand; the decision, three months earlier, to appoint a temporary clerk had still not been implemented.
32. CC Minutes, 22 and 23 September 1925; *Co-operative News*, 10 October 1925, p. 13.
33. CC Minutes, 14 and 15 March 1923.
34. In association with suffragists, ILP and Labour Party members and other radical reformers; from 1924, the Family Endowment Society. See Eleanor Rathbone, *The Disinherited Family* (1924), introduction by S. Fleming, 'Eleanor Rathbone Spokeswoman for a Movement' (Bristol: Falling Wall Press, 1986, p. 70); J. Macnicol, *The Movement for Family Allowances, 1918–45* (London: Heinemann, 1980).
35. M. Llewelyn Davies, 'The Claims of Mothers and Children', in M. Phillips (ed.), *Women and the Labour Party* (London: Headley Bros., 1918, p. 33).
36. Ibid., p. 38.
37. *Co-operative News*, 12 June 1920, p. 12; made up of Mrs Barton (Sheffield), Mrs Hood (Enfield), Mrs Davies (Aberdare), Mrs Ferguson (Darlington), Mrs Matthews (Eccles); their report was adopted by the CC in May 1920, *Co-operative News*, 5 June 1920, p. 13.
38. Labour Party, *Annual Report*, 1922, p. 42.
39. Graves, op. cit., pp. 101–2.
40. CC Minutes, 14 and 15 March 1923.
41. *Co-operative News*, 1 May 1920, p. 12.
42. *Co-operative News*, 28 April 1923, p. 12 (article).
43. *Co-operative News*, 14 April 1923, p. 12 (editorial).
44. *Co-operative News*, 14 April 1923, p. 12 (speaking at a Guild meeting in Leamington).

45. *Co-operative News*, 21 April 1923, p. 12.
46. Labour Party, *Annual Report*, 1923, p. 38.
47. *Co-operative News*, 26 May 1923, p. 18.
48. *Co-operative News*, 19 May 1923, p. 12.
49. Labour Party, *Annual Report*, 1923, p. 247.
50. An article in the women's pages in 1911, on the high incidence of abortion, claimed that many women were refusing to have children because the sacrifices were too great, *Co-operative News*, 18 March 1911, p. 366. See also Davies on family limitation, MLD, 'Introduction', in M. Llewelyn Davies (ed.), *Maternity Letters from Working Women* (1915) (London: Virago, 1978, p. 13), quoted in Chapter 4, note 98.
51. CC Minutes, 27 and 28 September 1922; *Birth Control News*, December 1922, I, no. 8, p. 4; April 1923, I, no. 12, p. 4; June 1923, II, no. 2, p. 4; S. Rowbotham, *A New World for Women: Stella Browne Socialist Feminist* (London: Pluto, 1977, p. 51). Jennie Baker was a WCG member.
52. Stopes was the most prominent advocate of birth control of the time, 'shrilling out her message and plunging her barbed truth into the minds of many hitherto docile matrons.' Rathbone, op. cit., p. 379.
53. CC Minutes, 27 and 28 September 1922.
54. J. Liddington, *The Life and Times of a Respectable Rebel: Selina Cooper 1864–1946* (London: Virago, 1984, p. 324); Graves, op. cit., p. 85.
55. Ruth Hall, *Marie Stopes: A Biography* (London: Deutsch, 1977, p. 210).
56. Sutherland did not name Stopes but 'a doctor of German philosophy' who had opened a birth control clinic in a London slum. When the case came to court in February 1923 she received widespread public support but did not convince the jury of the harmlessness of the contraceptive methods she advocated; five months later she won an appeal but in November 1924 the Law Lords ruled against her. Sutherland's defence was underwritten by the Catholic Church. See Hall, op. cit., ch. 13; *Birth Control News*, March 1923, I, no. 2, p. 1. Stopes' interest in working women was heavily influenced by eugenics: '"Are these puny-faced, gaunt, blotchy, ill-balanced, feeble, ungainly, withered children the young of an imperial race?"', Marie Stopes, 'Mrs Jones does her worst', *Daily Mail*, 13 June 1919, quoted in Hall, op. cit., p. 173.
57. See, for example, Marie Stopes, *A Letter to Working Mothers On How to Have Healthy Children and Avoid Weakening Pregnancies*, Published by the Author (Leatherhead: Elmer, 1919).
58. CC Minutes, 14 and 15 March 1923.

59. *Co-operative News*, 16 June 1923, pp. 14-15; *Birth Control News*, July 1923, II, no. 3, p. 4; Rowbotham, op. cit., p. 51.
60. CC Minutes, 16 July 1923.
61. CC Minutes, 19 and 20 September 1923.
62. R.A. Soloway, *Birth Control and the Population Question in England 1877–1930* (London: University of North Carolina Press, 1982, p. 284).
63. *The Labour Woman*, XII/2, 1 March 1924, p. 34.
64. Interview with Mabel Cumins, Brighton, February 1982.
65. In 1930, with Cabinet approval, the Minister of Health (memorandum, 153/MCW) permitted Maternal and Child Welfare Centres to give contraceptive advice to married women for whom further pregnancies carried a health risk. The decision was not discussed in Parliament, or given wider publicity until leaked by Stopes. J. Weeks, *Sex Politics and Society: the Regulation of Sexuality since 1800*, second edition (Harlow: Longman, 1989, p. 193).
66. D. Russell, *The Tamarisk Tree* (London: Virago, 1977, p. 172).
67. *Co-operative News*, 24 May 1924, p. 12.
68. Russell, op. cit., p. 173.
69. *Co-operative News*, 24 May 1924, p. 12.
70. *The Labour Woman*, XII/6, 1 June 1924, p. 85.
71. Selina Cooper, for example, Liddington, op. cit., p. 295.
72. The Workers' Birth Control Group was formed by socialists, in part to break the association with eugenics, Russell, op. cit., p. 173.
73. Labour Party, *Annual Report*, 1925, p. 365.
74. Labour Party, *Annual Report*, 1926, pp. 201; 230–1; 207.
75. Russell, op. cit., p. 188.
76. Labour Party, *Annual Report*, 1927, p. 192.
77. See G. Elliott, *Labourism and the English Genius: The Strange Death of Labour England?* (London: Verso, 1983, p. 32).
78. Liddington, op. cit., p. 294-5.
79. *Co-operative News*, 6 October 1928, p. 12.
80. *Co-operative News*, 7 September 1929, p. 12.
81. *Co-operative News*, 12 October 1929, p. 12; Graves, op. cit., p. 106.
82. Macnicol, op. cit., p. 147.
83. *Co-operative News*, 20 September 1930, p. 12.
84. *Report of Proceedings, 62nd Annual TUC*, 1930, pp. 51 and 213.
85. Labour Party, *Annual Report*, 1930, pp. 52 and 213; Macnicol, op. cit., p. 149.
86. *Co-operative News*, 5 June 1926, p. 17; 11 October 1924, p.12; 27 September 1924, p. 8.
87. Gaffin & Thoms, op. cit., pp. 91–2; Kathleen Kempton became General Secretary in 1963.

88. Conversation with Cathy Burke, then carrying out research on the WCG in Sheffield, 10 May 1987.
89. Eleanor Barton, *DLB*, I, 1972.
90. *Co-operative News*, 12 June 1937, p. 12.
91. Alfred Barton (1868–1933) taught himself philosophy, history, classical history and several languages. When he moved to Manchester in 1890, to work as a clerk and then in Rylands Library, he was a member of the Socialist League. In Sheffield he played a prominent role in the Trades Council, and in municipal politics; he was active in the ILP, and then the British Socialist party, joined the Communist party for a month in 1920, and then committed himself to the Labour Party. One local Guildswoman remembered him being dumped in a horse trough during the run up to a council election 'because he was talking about socialism. Working men just picked him up and put him in. They said he was talking rubbish.' (Interview with Hilda May Crompton by Kitty Fitzgerald, *The Leveller*, December/January 1982/3, no. 90, p. 12.) He served as a councillor from 1913–20, and after 1926 but failed to secure a parliamentary seat despite winning 20.4% of the poll in 1918; in 1929, by now noted for his moderation, he became an Alderman. *DLB*, V, 1982.
92. CC Minutes, 18 and 19 October 1924.
93. CC Minutes, 14 November 1925.
94. *Minutes of Evidence taken before the Royal Commission on Divorce and Matrimonial Causes, Minutes of Evidence* (1912), III (Cd. 6481) PP 1912–13, XX, p. 171.
95. Ibid., pp. 172–3; see also Chapter 5.
96. Co-operative Political Council, Minutes, 5 January 1918; 16 February 1918; 4 May 1918; Minute Book, 1918–1921, Political Council, Co-operative Party Records, Sheffield Local Studies Library.
97. In 1930 she failed to regain the Nottingham nomination, *Co-operative News*, 1 February 1930, p. 12. See McKibbin, op. cit., pp. 183–91, for Labour–Co-operative tensions in the constituencies.
98. *Co-operative News*, 16 February 1924, p. 12.
99. *Co-operative News*, 7 February 1925, pp. 4–5.
100. *Co-operative News*, 28 February 1925, pp. 12–13.
101. *Co-operative News*, 10 October 1925, p. 13.
102. *Co-operative News*, 6 February 1926, p. 4.
103. G.D.H. Cole, *A Century of Co-operation* (London: Allen & Unwin for the Co-operative Union, 1944, p. 324).
104. Three became MPs in 1945: Mrs Mabel Ridealgh (Ilford North); Mrs Caroline Ganley (Battersea South); Mrs Edith Wills (Duddeston); see Chapter 8.

105. *Co-operative News*, 5 February 1927, p. 16.
106. Martin Pugh, *Women and the Women's Movement in Britain 1914–1959* (London: Macmillan, 1993, p. 166).
107. *Co-operative News*, 12 May 1928, p. 12; 19 May 1928, p. 13.
108. Eleanor Barton, *The National Care of Motherhood* (London: WCG 1928, p. 4).
109. WCG, *Annual Report*, 1926–7, p. 20.
110. *Co-operative News*, 19 June 1926, p. 7.
111. *Co-operative News*, 14 May 1927, p. 12.
112. *Co-operative News*, 16 June 1928, p. 8.
113. Eleanor Barton JP, *Woman – in the Home, the Store and the State* (Manchester: Co-operative Union Ltd. for the Co-operative Party, n.d., 1929), pp. 6–7.
114. Ibid., pp. 2–3.
115. *Co-operative News*, 27 December 1930, p. 13.
116. *Co-operative News*, 31 January 1931, p. 12.
117. *Co-operative News*, 1 November 1930, p. 13; 15 November 1930, p. 13.
118. *Co-operative News*, 13 June 1931, p. 5.
119. *Daily Herald*, 11 June 1931, Fawcett Library.
120. *Daily Herald*, 4 June 1937, Fawcett Library; *Co-operative News*, 12 June 1937, p. 14.
121. *Co-operative News*, 28 June 1941, p. 13.
122. *Co-operative News*, 16 May 1942, p. 10; 30 May 1942, p. 4.
123. *Co-operative News*, 19 May 1945, p. 12.
124. 'Beveridge Plan for Social Security', WCG Notes for Speakers, 1943, typed MS, Hull University.

Chapter Seven

Rules

The new relationship with Labour–Co-operative politics impacted on the democratic structure of the Guild to an even greater extent than on the content of its policy, and in ways that harmed not only its radical identity but also its organizational vigour. As support for the Labour and Co-operative Parties became dominant, senior guildswomen entered into conflict with that section of the membership whose politics reflected the ideological diversity of the wider trading movement. Unable or unwilling to exclude or expel these women, the CC set out to discipline them by means of rule changes that shifted the balance of power in the organization from the periphery to the centre. In an attempt to create a loyal and politically reliable layer of officials, the freedom of branches to choose their own officials and delegates was overriden by the requirement that in order to qualify for such positions, members must support the Co-operative Party (later amended to include Labour), and have no connection with private trade. Despite these precautions, in the 1930s the leadership became increasingly paranoid about rival organizations, and Communist infiltration in particular. In 1936, the 'political rule' was supplemented with a long list of party and organizational affiliations which specifically disqualified members from Guild office.

These measures went against the grain of the Guild's history and culture, provoking unprecedented levels of criticism and dissent. The leadership became increasingly autocratic, no longer seeking to build a consensus, but rather to manage the 'democratic' process so as to secure its own objectives. The organization's communication lines hardened into one-way conduits transmitting directions from above, while blocking representations from below, and the Guild frequently appeared as an organization divided against itself. The damaging consequences of these constitutional changes are most apparent in the evolution of the Guild's peace policy through the 1930s. The dominant bloc among the leadership was both individually committed to absolute pacifism and determined that it should be the official Guild policy. This became increasingly contentious as the international situation deteriorated. Yet the authoritarian forms of governance in place blocked every attempt at amendment. Pacifism now defined every aspect of the Guild's activities, and when war broke out this uncompromising position caused a mass exodus of members from which the organization never recovered.

The first obstacle facing those whose ambition was to deliver the Guild membership as a kind of block vote was the Co-operative tradition of political neutrality, which in practice meant a tolerance of political diversity. Despite the fact that the decision to seek direct Co-operative parliamentary representation had won majority support at a Co-operative special conference in October 1917,[1] the movement as a whole remained ambivalent about the initiative. Between 1918 and 1924, the number of Societies affiliated to the new party actually fell, from 563 to 393, and a decade later 56 per cent were still unaffiliated.[2] Many active Co-operators retained allegiances to the Liberals, a few to the Conservatives, and some to the idea that Co-operation was about trade, not politics. Others supported the Co-operative Party but objected to a formal alliance with Labour, although in the absence of either a distinctive political platform, or adequate constituency organization, the election of Co-operative candidates was dependent upon such local agreements, and in practice the majority of politically active Co-operators were also involved in the Labour Party.[3]

Inevitably, given that it recruited from the trading membership, the same spectrum of opinion ran through the Guild. 'We have all parties represented', Eleanor Barton had admitted to the Divorce Commission in 1910, 'both Liberals, Conservatives, and the Labour Party. Of course, we do not introduce party politics.'[4] At that time, Guild activity revolved around women's issues, and did not involve fixed party-political allegiances. By the end of the war, however, such detachment from party politics had become difficult to sustain. The 1918 Guild Congress welcomed the enfranchisement of women, urged all Co-operative women to join the Co-operative Party, and called for a Co-operative–Labour alliance to secure 'a People's Government' at the next general election. Political education – literature, day schools, and special speakers – became a major aspect of Guild work. Meanwhile, guildswomen were recruited to work for both the ten Co-operative candidates in the 1918 election and 'those Labour candidates who supported co-operation'.[5]

The Guild thus aligned itself with those Co-operators who had no confidence in the Liberals or the Conservatives to represent 'their' interests, whether defined narrowly as 'Co-operative' or, more broadly, as working-class. The initial emphasis on educational activity indicates a sensitivity to the uneven level of political consciousness in the Guild, and to a constitution which did not require any branch to follow Congress policy. Steadily, however, the quantitative logic of the ballot box overtook this approach. The Guild's autonomy was eclipsed by a vision of it as a kind of Co-operative Party women's section, and the leadership became steadily more prescriptive about party politics.

Before the 1922 general election a CC circular warned that while the capitalist parties had many names – 'Conservative, Coalition, Independent, Liberal, Anti-Waste' – only the Co-operative and Labour Parties represented the workers and deserved guildswomen's votes.[6] For a variety of reasons, many guildswomen took exception to this directive, some as Liberals or even Conservatives, others as traditional Co-operators. One self-styled Labour Party supporter, for example, described the circular as 'narrow, intolerant and dictatorial'; the CC, she added, should remember the Co-operative motto: 'In things essential, unity; in things doubtful, liberty; in all things, charity.'[7]

Co-operative–Labour supporters among the leadership, however, saw no reason to be charitable to political opponents, even if they were guildswomen. Yet they were frustrated. Under the constitution there was no compulsion on branches to follow any particular policy. Despite frequent reminders that 'every loyal guild branch' should be working for the Co-operative Party in accord with Congress decisions,[8] some branches insisted on their right to be non-partisan. Even worse, there were troubling reports of Guilds being exploited by rival parties, and senior guildswomen began to complain that branch autonomy was being exploited to nourish rival political parties. At the 1923 All Councils meeting, there were complaints that in Yorkshire 'lots of branches had subjects which were not useful, and political women were getting into the branches to oppose the Co-operative Party.'[9] The formation of the first Labour Government in 1924 further strengthened the determination to exclude rival parties.

Rapid membership growth, combined with the drift away from working-class feminism, had outstripped the Head Office's capacity for focused and effective educational work of the kind practiced before the war. The leadership turned, instead, to more coercive methods, concentrating not on the rank and file, but on officials and delegates. Discussing 'Politics in Guild Branches' at All Councils in 1925, Mrs Bain (CC) claimed that behind the talk of political neutrality members 'were taking sides with the capitalistic parties'. She wanted the Guild's position precisely defined, so that only those prepared to support it could gain office.[10] At Congress that year, a CC resolution called on all branches 'to make the question of co-operative politics an essential part of their guild programme', and looked 'to the honour of all guild officials' to uphold their national policy. The resolution was passed 'by an overwhelming majority'. But an amendment to the effect that all branches should work for Labour as well as Co-operative politics, since 'Labour and Co-operative interests were identical', was defeated when a vote of 224 to 268 demonstrated that for almost half the delegates support for the Co-operative Party did not extend to Labour.[11]

Despite CC appeals to 'honour', at branch level there was resistance to politics of any kind; and the right to 'local autonomy' was invoked to ignore Congress policy. Given that these recalcitrant elements posed the threat of political embarrassment, the leadership sought rule changes to secure conformity. This harder line emerged in a series of speeches by Eleanor Barton, the only guildswoman to have been adopted as a parliamentary candidate. While still Assistant Secretary, she complained, at district conferences early in 1925, of the 'narrow-mindedness' of Guilds which refused to discuss party politics, and predicted that 'the time was coming' when Liberals and Conservatives would be barred from holding office in the Guild. In Lancashire delegates objected to this. Members were not asked about their politics when they joined, and if 'women were taught to think for themselves the Guild would be doing a good job.' When one delegate stated that such a ban would be 'domination not co-operation', Eleanor Barton snapped back: 'What else is it but domination when branches take an opposing view to that laid down by the Guild parliament?'[12]

When Barton became General Secretary, qualifications for the selection of officials were introduced for the first time in the Guild's history. The aim was to create a politically homogeneous bureaucracy. As Mrs Matthews explained at All Councils, 'there was no desire whatever to interfere with the membership of the guild, but it was necessary to control those controlling guild policy.'[13] The first step was to target Co-operation's economic, rather than its political, competitors – adjudged, correctly as it turned out, to be a more acceptable way of securing the principle of general conditions of eligibility for office. All Councils recommended, and Congress subsequently approved by the requisite two-thirds majority, that the model branch rules be revised to disqualify private traders, or the wives of private traders, from standing for office.[14] The 1926 Congress also voted to include support for the Co-operative Party in the aims of the Guild. In 1928, ten years after the Guild first expressed support for the Co-operative Party, and following Barton's adoption as Co-operative–Labour candidate for Nottingham East,[15] the CC won Congress approval for a further amendment of the model branch rules, stipulating that 'all Guild officials should work for and support the Co-operative Party'.[16]

These innovations provoked prolonged and heated debate. One criticism of the ban on private traders was that it defined women purely in terms of their husband's occupations, compounding women's lack of economic independence by curtailing their democratic rights in the organization. The Guild 'was not an organisation of employees' wives', stated one correspondent to the 'Women's Pages', 'but a body of women who were free to work out their own destinies apart from their husbands.'[17] Another member pointed out that as only a tiny percentage of Co-operators were employed in the movement, the exclusion of all those with husbands working for a private company could result in 'a wholesale resignation of guild officials'.[18]

A major objection to the political rule was that it ignored local conditions. Many of the Societies which funded Guild branches did not actively support the Co-operative Party; indeed, in many areas there was no Co-operative Party organization in existence. Moreover, as Mrs Wimhurst, an ex-President, pointed out in 1928, of the 1,200 Guild branches, only 319 were affiliated to the Co-operative Party; 'were the others to be debarred from joining in the work of the guild?'[19]

The main problem for the CC was the adherence of many branches to 'local autonomy': model branch rules had always been voluntary, hence they were not bound to follow the new regulations. Senior officials at All Councils continued to bemoan this disobedience. In 1927 Mrs Hammett (South-Western Section) reported that Guild circulars were not generally discussed, 'clubs were being carried on in their branches which ought not to be; and many branches said they could not have addresses because they were arranging for bazaars'.[20] A year later, Mrs Hewitson's (CC) judgement was that the 'rules are still too elastic', and that the whole concept of optional rules should be abolished. Congress decisions should be binding on all branches, and local autonomy should only apply to such matters as the time and place of meetings.[21] Finally, in 1929, noting that the 'difficulties with regard to guild rules seem to have gone on and multiplied', the CC proposed that the model branch rules be revised, and instituted as compulsory general rules. In addition to a standard minimum subscription, these would include the requirements that while all women were welcome to join the Guild, only those prepared to support the aims of the Co-operative Party, and unconnected with private trade, would be eligible to hold office, or serve as Conference and Congress delegates.[22]

This measure came before Congress only weeks before the general election in which Eleanor Barton stood as the Co-operative–Labour candidate for Nottingham East. It was made clear to delegates that 'the Guild had to protect itself and the Movement from the attacks of the private traders and of anti-Co-operative politicians.'[23] All the rule changes were voted through in an atmosphere charged with the importance of the General Secretary's campaign.

Strong criticisms of the rule changes soon revealed considerable divergence between loyalty to Mrs Barton and loyalty to the Guild's traditions. One outspoken attack came from the influential Mrs Tomlinson, editor of the 'Women's Pages'. A Guild member for four decades, she was well versed in its constitution and democratic ideals. Fighting fire with fire, her verdict was that as the rule changes had gone through without any formal modification of the General Rules, they were unconstitutional, and 'for the VOLUNTARY acceptance of branches'. Their effect, she pointed out, would be to 'override the local autonomy of branches, and to do away with the power of self-government which the guild has always held to be such a precious possession.'[24]

The CC made no public response to Mrs Tomlinson's remarks. However, its members were clearly stung by her remarks, and privately requested a meeting at which they protested that Guild policy was being attacked in the *News*, with the opposing side receiving unfair coverage. Mrs Tomlinson replied that she always did her best to give both sides of a discussion as this was of greatest interest to readers.[25] The correspondence and reports of meetings in the 'Women's Pages' continued to reflect the opposition to the rule changes, revealing the divisions in the Guild over the question.

'We talk a lot about democracy,' wrote one guildswoman, of the political rule, 'but, if applied, this will be autocracy. I am perfectly sure some branches will ignore this new rule.'[26] Officials were soon registering irritation that in many parts of the country, 'little or no notice' was being taken of the Congress resolution.[27] An exasperated Mrs Mellor, President of Huddersfield District Committee, wrote that those who could not accept the rules 'should drop out. True, we do not like losing old members, but there must be uniformity in a large organisation.'[28]

Speaking at meetings in different parts of the country, senior guildswomen had to deal directly with members' objections. Their standard response was to disclaim any responsibility for the changes. In the Northern Section it was put to Eleanor Barton that the political rule savoured of 'coercion rather than persuasion', and that many branches objected to this. 'There is no coercion', she replied, 'simply a rule stating they were to support the aims of the Co-operative Party.'[29] In Lancashire, Mrs Moorby, the national Vice-President, when told that members 'refused to adhere to the new CC rules', hastily pointed out that Congress, not the CC was responsible. When a delegate from Monkton Guild reported that her branch had simply crossed out the political rule, she was told that it must be reinstated as 'no branch has the right to do this'.[30]

The General Secretary faced a barrage of criticism at the South Western Section Conference in November. She insisted that there was 'no intention of forcing anything on Guilds'; and denied that the CC was responsible for the changes. One delegate demanded to know what would happen if a branch refused to conform: 'would that branch come out of the movement?' Treading cautiously, Mrs Barton asked if the branch would leave 'if the issue had to be decided on politics?' 'Yes', was the emphatic response.[31] A few weeks later, the North East Devon District Conference resolved by a large majority that 'those guilds unable to accept the new rules cease affiliation with the central body.'[32] Apparently, there were limits to the CC's power to impose its will on the Guild.

Meanwhile the general election had come and gone, and although a Labour Government had been elected, Mrs Barton had not; and neither had she been nominated to stand again.[33] There was less pressure to be seen to be doing everything possible to get the vote out, and more to mend some of the gaping holes that were appearing in the fabric of the organization. Despite the threats that had been issued, when the CC discussed the problem of branches refusing to adopt the new rules in January 1930, it was agreed that disaffiliation was undesirable. The majority of branches seemed to be 'falling into line', but further educational and propaganda work was badly needed. The CC must go on explaining that 'Congress, and not the CC' had passed the rules, reminding branches that they were free to submit further amendments to Congress.[34] Whatever the CC professed, however, such branches were increasingly unlikely to be successful. The new power to control who became delegates ensured that a growing majority at Congress would share the leadership's political priorities.

Nevertheless, to be on the safe side, at its next meeting the CC decreed that rule alterations were not to be allowed at the 1930 Congress; all such resolutions would therefore be out of order.[35]

The leadership's readiness to manipulate and hide behind the constitution, rather than to address issues directly, is apparent in its handling of a dispute between 1928 and 1930 about the status of the General Secretary. In 1928 a Congress resolution from Alston Guild proposed that, since the Guild needed a full-time, paid, and permanent General Secretary, if she, or any other paid official, became an MP, she should resign. This appeared on the order paper as a rule change, and was passed with the necessary two-thirds majority – 681 to 209 – reflecting widespread resentment of salaried posts in the Guild.[36] Eleanor Barton and the CC, however, believed that having a General Secretary in Parliament would enhance the Guild's prestige, and that practical problems could be overcome by pooling the two salaries to pay for extra clerical staff. Senior Co-operative Party members backed this on the grounds that prospective MPs would not stand if they risked losing their salaried positions. Fortunately for the CC, it hit upon an escape clause: the contentious resolution had been worded not as an 'instruction', but as a 'recommendation'. This left the final decision with the CC; the Congress vote was therefore ignored and the item excluded from the revised rules.[37]

The practical significance of this matter receded along with Mrs Barton's hopes of a seat at Westminster. But the underlying principle did not, and throughout 1929 and 1930 the issue became the focus for resentment at the leadership's overbearing methods, even for accusations that they were acting as a 'dictatorship'.[38] CC members were unwilling to deal with their opponents directly: Mrs Barton reported to the CC that this was 'too personal a matter for her to reply to', but she did obtain legal advice which supported the judgement that as a recommendation, the resolution did not have to entail a rule change.[39]

In the light of this dispute, the CC's 1930 decision to disqualify all Congress resolutions dealing with rule changes is revealed as a self-serving move to prevent potentially critical interventions. The rationale for the dismissal of the 1928 Alston resolution was not to be ventilated, and Congress was certainly not to be given the chance to vote on a properly worded motion. Alston's request that the issue be raised again at Congress was not answered;[40] a Birmingham Guilds resolution criticizing the CC was ruled out of order, and another letter from Alston Guild protesting this ruling was left 'to lie on the table'.[41] At a Midlands sectional conference just before Congress, the CC member informed delegates that 'no good purpose would be served' by a discussion of the matter, and a delegate was ruled 'out of order' when she attempted to raise it.[42] At Congress the General Secretary simply announced that the CC's ruling on the 1928 resolution had been endorsed by the Co-operative Union solicitor; no opportunity was given for questions or discussion.[43]

Long-standing members might well have registered the CC's use of an external legal opinion to overturn a decision of this 'self-governing working women's organization' as emblematic of the wholesale transfer of power from the membership to the leadership that had occurred. Certainly, the tensions generated by the handling of the Alston resolution would have been one reason why the 1930 Congress, the largest to date with over 1,200 present,[44] was, for one seasoned delegate, a disappointment: 'private grievances and grudges' abounded; 'old and tried members are suspected, and are growing in their turn suspicious'. As well as having a bad atmosphere, the Congress achieved little by way of setting an agenda for the year's work. 'Most of the resolutions were hackneyed and foregone, and those which needed careful discussion and study were voted on hurriedly. Isn't it the job of an Annual Congress rather to review the work of the past year and shape the policy of the coming year than to turn itself into a resolution-passing machine?' Overall, she felt, the proceedings indicated that 'a different spirit is invading our movement', and that the old feeling of 'comradeship and true co-operation' was lacking.[45]

The constitutional changes of the late 1920s formalized a new Guild order. The rank and file had lost the right to control not only the policies to which they subscribed, but also which officials they could elect. Implicit in the new regulations was an emergent hierarchy of official and non-official ranks, with greater status accruing to the bureaucracy, and large numbers of ordinary members relegated to a more or less inert role. By 1930, although reluctant to go to the extreme of disaffiliation, the General

Secretary and the CC were able to suppress or contain any initiative to which they were opposed. Yet as their hold on the organization tightened, they became less secure about its coherence. The attack on local autonomy, the strict regulation of official and delegate status, the abandonment of policies grounded in the needs and interests of the members – these seemed to act as solvents on the glue that had previously held leaders and led together. As this relationship became less organic and more legalistic, there was a proliferation of official anxiety about 'outside bodies'. In the 1930s the CC became increasingly convinced that there were parasites inside the host body of the Guild, and predators getting fat at its expense. Two different kinds of danger presented themselves: firstly, new competition for members from the growth of the self-styled 'non-political' women's organizations (especially the Townswomen's Guilds (TG)); and secondly the internal challenge posed by guildswomen in other political parties (especially the Communists).

The TG, often seen as the urban equivalent of the Women's Institutes (WI) which originated in the First World War, were formed in 1928 from a rump of the suffrage societies.[46] From as early as 1930, the CC believed that it needed 'a membership campaign to counteract the influence of the Town Guilds',[47] and in 1932 CC members gave talks on 'The Guild in Relation to Other Organisations' which stressed that members should prioritize the Guild rather than the Townswomen's Guilds, or the WI.[48] Although the Guild continued to grow steadily to a peak of over 88,000 in 1938, the leadership was haunted by the idea that these younger organizations were poaching from branches.[49]

The threat of the TG and the WI, however, was insignificant in comparison to official Guild anxieties about the creeping menace of Communism. In the 1920s, the focus of Guild concerns about rival parties had been the Conservatives, not the Left. While the Labour Party voted to exclude Communists in 1925, two years later the CC was still ruling that the status of a Communist member 'was a matter for the branch to decide upon'.[50] Yet as the leadership followed the dominant trends in the labour movement, its political centre of gravity shifted to the right. One explanation for the introduction of the political rule in 1929, for example, was that 'Communists turned out of the Labour women's sections began coming into the co-operative guilds.'[51] Between 1929 and 1933, as the Communist Party (CP) eschewed work with reformist organizations, Guild leaders followed the Labour Party in giving a wide berth to any initiatives associated with the Communists. The WCG had 'no official contact' with the National Unemployed Workers' Movement, although many Guild members gave practical assistance to the Hunger Marchers;[52] and despite branch appeals for a national campaign against the Means Test, the CC refused on the grounds that 'the Guild's work is not so specialized', suggesting that branches take action locally.[53]

For the CC, any taint of Communism immediately cancelled the need to weigh the significance of the issue at stake. The most significant thing noted by the CC about Hitler's constitutional coup was that the Guild 'must be alive to counteract the use which was made by Communists of (such) incidents'; a branch proposing help for the victims of German fascism was instructed to go through the channels of the organized labour movement.[54] Official mistrust of rank-and-file initiative was also evident in December 1932, when the troublesome Alston branch pressed for action against proposed 'economies' in education spending. Fewer teachers, larger classes, closure of small rural schools – enough, claimed the branch, to 'set on fire a blaze of protest sufficient to cause the whole proposals to be reduced to ashes.' Yet when a 'humble member from a vigilant branch' attempted to have the matter discussed through an emergency resolution at the Midland Sectional Conference, she was refused because the item was 'not on the agenda'. 'I venture to submit', wrote F. Mary Whatley, the branch President, that 'there is not another organisation whose Standing Orders cannot be suspended in case of emergency to permit immediate action when necessary.'[55]

Communist women became gradually more visible in the Guild following the united front line that emerged from Moscow after the German debacle. In January 1935 the CC was incensed by a leaflet, dutifully sent to them by the Golders Green Guild Secretary, publicizing a meeting under the auspices of the Communist Party, with Mrs Marjorie Pollitt[56] billed as representing the Guild.[57] Concern about Communist entryism now became the most pressing element of a general phobia about 'other bodies' exploiting the Guild for their own purposes. The

CC deemed it necessary to define even more precisely who could, and who could not, rise to positions of influence in the organization, this time without even the semblance of consultation.

In January 1936, the year before her retirement, Eleanor Barton issued a circular. The size and importance of the Guild, she explained, meant that 'outside people who wish to build up an organisation for some particular purpose', were trying 'to gain their strength from us'. They needed 'certain principles for guidance in regard to those organisations with which we do not work and the members of which are, therefore, not eligible to take office'. The political rule had been revised at the 1935 Congress to state that only members who supported the Co-operative Party, or a party with which it operated an electoral alliance, were eligible for office.[58] This meant, according to Barton, that Conservatives, Liberals, Communists, and Fascists were disqualified, as were guildswomen who held office in Townswomen's Guilds, Women's Institutes, British Legion Branches, the National Council of Women, and Women Citizen's Associations.

A settling of old and new scores was involved here. In one election, a member of the National Council of Women had opposed the Co-operative–Labour candidate as an Independent.[59] For many years, Barton had been infuriated by Conservative-dominated Guilds in Yorkshire and Plymouth. The CC was by now convinced that the Townswomen's Guilds were being built up 'largely at the expense' of the Guild,[60] were 'cutting across' its work, and in many cases 'serving the interests of private trade', while the British Legion's opposition to the Guild's peace work was also 'causing difficulties'.[61]

The principal enemy within, however, was the Left. Barton warned that the list was not exhaustive. There might well be other groups attempting to use the Guild's name and strength 'for some pupose other than Co-operation', and branches were urged to guard against infiltration so that the whole burden of the work did not fall upon the CC. Only a month later, the CC received an enquiry about the position of ILP women, and hastened to confirm that as the ILP was 'definitely in line with the Communists' it too was disqualified.[62]

Not all members were prepared to co-operate with this decree, however. The circular contravened the Guild's broad-church traditions, as well as the politics of left-wing activists still in the Guild, and provoked a storm of controversy. Letters for, and against, the measure appeared in the 'Women's Pages' for several weeks. 'No subject has been so thoroughly discussed in these pages for many years', commented the editor when she finally closed the correspondence at the end of March.[63] The question was also raised at conferences and meetings in various parts of the country. In these debates, underlying the claims and counterclaims about the significance of the Circular were very different ideas about what the Guild stood for, and what constituted its greatest strengths.

At the 1936 All Councils meeting, Mrs Kendall (CC) appealed for loyalty employing a discourse characteristic of the view from above. The Guild, she insisted, grandly, if inaccurately, was a 'living testimony to the life and work of our leaders ... a legacy that we must safeguard and cherish.' Its future depended on fresh blood, new recruits and new branches. But new members could 'get up and "tell a story" and secure a following'; there were 'people in office, even in the chair, who at election time were seen to be working against the Co-operative Party.' The CC had to keep 'a watchful eye', and branches must follow CC rulings and Congress decisions to guarantee uniformity. The Guild was growing so rapidly, she added, that it could afford to 'cut out' branches that refused to obey the rules.[64]

Sharing its basic premises, the mainstream Labour women in the Guild supported the CC. They harboured a condescending view of ordinary members as gullible dupes. Mabel Langford, for example, argued that the Circular was necessary because the political rule had been broken by Guilds which acted as 'Primrose Leagues' or 'Communist Groups', when officials led astray 'the rank-and-file membership, some of whom are either uninterested or unaware of what is happening.'[65] For these women loyalty to the Guild was indivisible from loyalty to the Co-operative and Labour parties. Annie E. Corrie pointed out that the Co-operative Party had a working agreement with the Labour Party, and that the latter had found it necessary 'to disaffiliate (or exclude) the Communist Party because of their disruptive methods.' Many Communists had worked with the ILP against Labour candidates in the general election, and although the Communist Party had since applied for re-admission, the Labour Party had refused 'on very good grounds.' Guildswomen must, she concluded, 'be loyal to our Co-operative Party.'[66]

Yet as opponents were swift to point out, this position inclined more towards Labour than to the Co-operative Party, because it ignored the fact that Communists were free to join Co-operative Societies and the Co-operative Party.[67] Florence R. Toon, an experienced Guild official and member of her local Co-operative Party executive, was fully conversant with its programme but could see 'nothing in it to bar Communists. Neither do they, for they sign our constitution and are some of our best workers.'[68] The working agreement with Labour, pointed out Mrs Spector (Holloway Guild), did not prevent members of so-called 'disruptive' bodies from being elected as Co-operative Party officials. 'Why then', she asked, should the Women's Guild, which supported the Co-operative Party, feel 'called upon to operate a policy which the Co-operative Party itself has not considered necessary?'[69] The CC's loyalty, it seemed, lay more with the Labour than the Co-operative Party.

The CC was also criticized for undermining the Guild's broad democratic traditions and its former confidence in the membership. Mrs Sybil White (Hounslow) dismissed the new measures as 'obviously undemocratic' in restricting members' voting powers: 'the choice of officials can safely be left to the good sense of the guildswomen. They can be trusted to decide for themselves whether the work of Communists, either inside or outside the guild, is harming the co-operative movement.'[70] Mabel Cumins, West Norwood Guild secretary in the 1930s, saw the Communists as 'a ginger group always in a minority.' If 'we had, say, six Communists, which I've never known, we'd put things to the vote ... and they'd still be in a minority and that would be that.' Brixton Guild, as she recalled, had a Communist official – 'I think she was secretary' – but the branch 'didn't sack her, they took no notice of it (the political rule). She was a good secretary – perhaps she was the only one there who belonged to the Communist Party and if she put something forward and it wasn't guild policy we'd go against it.'[71] Flo G. Jones (Barry) pointed out that as well as infringing the 'democratic rights of guild members', the Circular would 'bring a spirit of separation into the guilds which can only end in guild disintegration.'[72]

Mrs May Ainley (Manchester) was likewise concerned about the damage the Circular would inflict upon their 'fine, wide democracy'. Guild pioneers 'did not consider it necessary to hold an inquisition on the political and social affiliation of its members, such as this circular suggests.' Since their inception, 'the guilds have been regarded as the working-class women's most active and democratic movement.' They had taken part in 'all the progressive women's campaigns for better working conditions (e.g. for the minimum wage) and for more social welfare facilities. Are we going to see this fine tradition broken? This is what the circular will do if it is operated. It will shut out from our ranks the most energetic, progressive, and broad-minded women, and in doing so will narrow down and weaken the whole guild movement.'[73]

Other Guild activists shared the fear that the most loyal and energetic members would be driven out. Mrs Spector pointed out that in her Guild the best Co-operative workers, both in 'propaganda and purchases', were the so-called militants whose influence the CC wished to curtail.[74] The Guild's great achievements, wrote Mrs Tanner (Streatham), had 'not been won by a policy of discrimination against members holding unorthodox or unofficial views.' Exhibiting precisely the left-wing tendencies the CC was anxious to exclude, she argued that when 'every effort is needed to resist the dangers of Fascism and war', it would be tragic were the Guild to be diverted by the 'internal sectarian quarrels' that would result 'if active members who happen also to belong to organisations of which the CC disapprove are barred from office.'[75] Underlining the Guild leadership's compliance with reactionary tendencies in the labour movement, Ilma Robson (Barrrow in Furness), a member for 20 years, wrote of guildswomen's condemnation of the TUC 'black circulars'.[76] 'We never thought for one moment', she remonstrated, that 'the CC would do the same thing, just when numerous local Labour parties and trade union branches are calling on their executives to accept affiliation to the Communist Party.'[77]

Such appeals fell on deaf ears. Speaking in Southampton, in April 1936, Eleanor Barton insisted that the Guild was threatened from all sides: by Conservatives, by the Townswomen's Guilds and most insidiously, by the Communists who were out 'to wreck the co-operative political work. The same thing was happening in the Labour movement.' The Communists accused them of not being ' "progressive" enough, but the truth was that the Communists were out to use them. They had a perfect right to belong to their own organisation, but no right to enter the guilds and take office for the purpose of spreading Communist propaganda. Those who took positions in the guild should subscribe to the rules and to the general policy of the co-operative movement.' They would not 'be dictated to by those who belonged to an outside organisation.' Why should the rest of the organization accept Communist officials who had been elected by certain Guilds? The time might come, she threatened, 'when guilds who refused to follow the policy of the elected leaders would have to be disbanded ... She thought they had a big fight ahead of them.'[78]

At a Cheshire and West Lancashire District meeting in May, Mrs Thorley, a senior official, found 'resentment and confusion' over the Circular, and 'much argument about excluding the Communist element'. She was obliged to admit that its contents had not actually been passed by Congress, but insisted on the CC's right to list organizations which contravened Guild policy.[79] Her stern reply to questions about dissenting branches was that the Guild was 'big enough and strong enough now to do without such branches, and she would lop them off.'[80] This 'was not generally accepted' by the meeting; as one woman stated, 'there were many militant women in the guild, all good leaders and organisers, who belonged to no party and whom the guild could ill afford to lose.'[81]

Mrs Mackay (national President) told a Gloucester District meeting in May that they 'must not grumble' about the rules, 'for they themselves had made them'.[82] At Keswick District conference in June, the General Secretary argued that because the Guild was so 'large and important', an occasional 'spring cleaning' was required. Democracy did not mean that 'every member and every branch' should do as they pleased. That would be 'chaos'. Rules, she stressed, 'were not imposed by any dictator, nor by the CC, nor the secretaries. They were framed in the annual Congress, the Parliament of the movement.' The CC had not invented anything: it had simply applied Congress policy.[83]

In private, however, the CC was busy fixing the Congress agenda to prevent an open debate about the Circular. A number of oppositional resolutions had been submitted, in addition to letters requesting that the matter be placed before Congress. The CC's main anxiety was that all the dissenting elements would unite against it. In some areas Communists were the problem, in others Conservatives; in the Midlands it was other women's organizations – the TG, WI and the National Council of Women. 'Unless the position was most carefully watched we might get a number of bodies whose interests were completely opposed to one another lining up on this particular issue.'[84]

The General Secretary had been confronted with just such a worst-case scenario at the Leeds Women's Guild Executive Committee in March 1936, when she had again defended the Circular on the grounds that numerous organizations were intent on capturing the Guild. Opposition took the form of an unlikely alliance between the redoubtable Miss Gration, a well-known Conservative and leading Co-operator, who referred to the Circular as a form of 'dictatorship', and Mrs Sandforth (Bradford District), a Communist and Co-operator who 'had never preached Communism in the guild. She thought there should be local autonomy where branches finding officials not true co-operators could dispense with them without a general rule being made.' Delegates wanted to go on with the discussion, but Mrs Barton was 'obliged to leave for a train'.[85]

An alliance of this kind was less likely at Congress, where delegates were supposed to have been more rigorously vetted. However, the CC was taking no chances. At its meeting in April, it was agreed 'that the matter was one dealing with rules and therefore no resolution could be placed on Congress Agenda by a branch.' The CC had been elected to be responsible for Guild administration, so there was no need for them to refer this matter to Congress. A statement would be made on behalf of the CC, to clarify the situation, and 'there should be no discussion allowed'.[86] Neither was the Circular discussed at the next three-yearly rules Congress in 1938, at which 16 resolutions on the political rule were whittled down to three by the Standing Orders Committee. The first two – that members 'use their own discretion when electing officals', or that the rule be deleted – were both defeated;

the third, successful amendment required that, instead of support
for the aims of the Co-operative Party, the rule should specify a
readiness to work for Co-operative and Labour candidates at
municipal and parliamentary elections.[87]

As subsequent events were to prove, this formulation was open
to differing interpretations. Following reports from district and
sectional officers that Clayton & Bradford Guild had a
Communist secretary, the CC again turned to the CU solicitor,
who decided that the Circular should stand as an extension to the
political rule. Although no formal decision had been reached on
the penalty for disobedience, the CC had already made it plain
that such branches could be 'lopped off'; Clayton & Bradford was
threatened with disaffiliation on 31 March 1939 if the offending
secretary was not removed, and she promptly resigned.[88] In a
letter of protest, branch officials argued that the election of the
Communist secretary had been entirely legitimate: 'We read the
rules. We knew, from personal experience, that she had a good
record of work for the Labour and Co-operative movement and
that all her work was in support of our aims.' The 1936 'by-law'
regarding Communists had not been incorporated into the rules as
part of the 1938 Congress revisions, so by what right had the CC
forced the exclusion of this ideal officer?[89] It was regrettable,
agreed M. Watson, a member of Bradford Road Guild, that the
political rule had been used 'to force the resignation of a loyal and
efficient guild secretary.'[90]

Yet virulent anti-Communism was now stalking the Guild, as a
letter from Mrs J.T. Nutt of Liverpool makes plain.
Impressionable guildswomen, she maintained, did not understand
'the danger of the penetration of the Communist Party into our
movement. It is part of a plan to gain control of the whole co-
operative movement, which is a wonderful prize when you
consider its wealth and propaganda capabilities, and its value to
an organization as poor as the Communist Party.' Even more
dangerous than known Communists, she warned, were covert
ones:

> You will find that a certain resolution will be moved about the
> same time, in all the guilds and political parties in your area.
> They support the same things, use the same arguments, for
> they have received their orders from the local headquarters.

They have no opinion of their own, and are just a regimental vote. Have you ever studied and wondered why a certain person suddenly comes into the limelight and in next to no time is holding all kinds of official positions in your society while genuine hard workers wait years. Again all part of the plan.[91]

'Witch-hunting' became an increasingly time-consuming part of the work of the CC and regional officials. In 1939, by 23 votes to 3, Hampstead Garden Suburb Guild elected a guildswoman who was a Communist and a Labour Party activist as their Congess delegate. But the CC would not accept her credentials and refused to meet a branch deputation to justify its ruling.[92] During the proceedings, a Holborn delegate asked 'if it made for the unity' referred to in the *Annual Report*, 'to bar Communists from being delegates', and demanded to know why the CC refused to explain its actions. Mrs Williams (national President) replied that 'the CC regarded delegates to Congress as officials of the branch for the time being, and therefore applied the test of Rule 5 to them as to other officials. In view of this there was nothing to be gained from receiving a deputation.'[93]

Many left-wing guildswomen were firmly dealt with by zealous regional officials.[94] Hilda May Crompton, a pioneer member of Alfreton Guild, joined the Communist Party in 1928: 'the time came when there was a ban on Communist Party members in the Guild. We weren't allowed to go to any meetings at all, we could just be a member of the Guild. Anyway I kept it on for about three years, but I was out of touch you see, couldn't meet anyone.'[95] Bessy Wilde, a Sheffield Communist, remembered with some resentment how all the 'live wires' like herself were excluded from official and delegate status.[96] Another Communist guildswoman from the Western Section got through the net and attended the 1938 Congress as a delegate; she had also been elected to the District Committee and was due to attend her first meeting the following week. But following the Rules revision, the District secretary pounced on her: 'she couldn't wait. I can see her now, coming up that aisle in that big hall ... and she said, "You won't need to come to the next meeting, because you're no longer eligible." ' That, she added, was the kind of leadership 'that killed the Guild movement.'[97]

Mrs Cumins, the West Norwood secretary, also believed that the political rule did great damage to the Guild. 'It was never generally accepted, every year they'd put in a resolution against it'. There was, she recalled, 'a lot of unpleasantness', and even women without any fixed position resented being told what to do: 'A lot of people left over that ... People thought "Oh no, we shan't be bothered with them." And of course the bright active ones – they lost interest. They didn't like the idea of proscribing. ... it upset things all round that rule did ... If I hadn't thought a lot about the Co-operative movement, as I did, I would have left over all that.'[98]

As well as transforming the Guild's politics, the changes that intervened between the wars created a situation in which the leadership lost its capacity to respond effectively to changing circumstances, the power that it wielded through the constitution apparently obviating any need for sensitive interpretation or evaluation of the likely consequences of a particular course of action. This myopia, and its damaging effects, are most apparent in the internal conflict over the Guild's pacifist policy in the late 1930s.

The Guild's involvement in the peace movement that sprang up after 1918 originated in a predominantly socialist opposition to imperialist war which, for many guildswomen, was understood to be grounds for – indeed, inseparable from – pacifism.[99] Steadily, however, the international tensions of the 1930s fractured what began as a broad-based movement, exposing the wide spectrum of ideological and ethical positions which it contained. The response of a number of leading guildswomen, Eleanor Barton in particular,[100] was to promote their own deeply-held pacifist convictions through the WCG, even to the point of opposing the official Labour Party position. While they succeeded in establishing pacifism as Guild policy, the political and practical consequences of this action caused major internal conflict, and ultimately inflicted permanent damage on the organization. For in their efforts to secure their own absolutist position, the leadership sacrificed the viability of the organization – its capacity to maintain its membership – to what they perceived to be a 'test of faith'.

The emergence of uncompromising pacifism from the range of demands, for disarmament and a strong League of Nations, advanced by the Guild – in common with the wider peace movement of the 1920s – was signalled by a resolution at the 1928 Guild Congress. As well as urging the Co-operative movement to use all possible means 'to prevent and stop Imperialist war', it called upon Co-operative women 'in all nations to pledge themselves to take no part whatever in the pursual of any future war'.[101] This line was strengthened in 1933 by the CC's introduction of the Guild White Poppy, a non-militaristic symbol for Armistice Day, and a Peace Pledge Card which explicitly committed signatories 'to refrain absolutely from militarist or war-promoting activities in any shape or form.' 'I solemnly declare', it read, 'my firm conviction that world problems can best be settled by reason rather than by force, and I therefore declare that under no circumstances whatever will I take part in, or help towards, the propagation of war.'[102]

From the outset senior officials expressed reservations about this move. At All Councils in 1933, it was pointed out that in some areas, the husbands, daughters and sons of guildswomen were employed in the arms industries: what were they expected to do? In the event of war, moreover, the pledge would close down important areas of influence for guildswomen. The General Secretary's response, however, indicated that the issue had already ceased to be a matter for rational discussion. Ignoring the specific difficulties raised, she urged the officers present 'to have courage and go forward'. The Guild 'had always been a pioneer and this was a work to be done.'[103] At Congress later that year, Barton was similarly dismissive of complaints that supplies of the white poppy had been ordered before Congress had approved the proposal. Ignoring the question of accountability, she taunted delegates by suggesting that they 'would not have the courage' to wear a white poppy. Rather than quarrelling over a symbol, she went on, they should 'remember the underlying principle'; this was 'a pioneer act, showing guildswomen stood for peace in its purest ideals.'[104]

These remarks firmly set the tone for the Guild's peace policy, and by 1936 loyal membership was being defined not by Co-operative work but by an individual act of conscience. The *Annual Report* affirmed that the Guild stood 'firmly behind the pacifist declarations which it has made from time to time by means of Congress Resolutions';[105] at the Northern Section Annual School in October, Barton called for the Guild 'to be completely pacifist'.[106] The 1938 Congress pledged the organization 'to work for the Guild Peace policy, which is the absolutist pacifist policy, and refuses to take part in war or preparation for war between the workers of the world.'[107]

The dominant group in the Guild, then, identified with the pacifist position upheld by Lansbury in the Labour Party. This aspired to unify socialism and pacifism by characterizing all militarism as imperialist and advocating individual conscientious objection as the way to prevent war. In the 1930s, however, this synthesis came unstuck, as international developments undermined the socialist case for pacifism. Pacifism offered no means of distinguishing between aggressors and victims or, for that matter, between liberal-democratic and fascist regimes and proposed only abstention as a means of frustrating war.[108] By 1936, with the Abyssinian crisis, the Spanish Civil War, and the militarization of the Rhineland, pacifists occupied an increasingly marginal position on the Left and in the Labour Party, and implicitly faced a choice between political engagement or ethical commitment.[109]

These developments were mirrored in Guild discussions. 'What is our Policy on sanctions?', wrote Florence Ranson in July 1936, complaining that at a South Eastern Sectional Conference the speaker's only answer had been: 'We believe in what George Lansbury believes.' Ranson's own opinion – that sanctions were inconsistent with Guild policy, because they implied a willingness and a capacity to use force – was endorsed by Barton, who expressed surprise that the confusion had arisen. Guild pacifists generally viewed the international situation as a test of their faith, and continued to urge members individually to renounce war. 'This is a pledge which every true guildswoman should be eager to make',[110] announced a 'Women's Pages' leader, 'Pacifists' Courage in Dark World', about the recently formed Peace Pledge Union.

Yet beneath this swelling propaganda, there was a substantial and growing body of Guild opposition to pacifism, as members who were involved in Labour Party and other policy discussions on the Left began pressing for such debates within the Guild. A week after Barton's disavowal of sanctions, it was reported that in June the Huddersfield Guild had sent a resolution to the Prime Minister, the Foreign Secretary, and their local MP condemning the National Government's agreement in the withdrawal of economic sanctions as a betrayal of Abyssinia which would damage the League of Nations.[111] Other guildswomen demanded a definitely non-pacifist position on Spain. In September, for example, the Kentish Town Guild passed a resolution calling for arms to the Republic and denouncing Non-Intervention as 'a definite assistance to Fascist victory.'[112]

The Guild pacifists in turn began to accuse the Labour Party of being ready to compromise with the Conservatives on rearmament, and agitated for the Co-operative Party to take a 'really determined stand on the peace question.'[113] At the Co-operative Party Conference in April 1937, Barton sought to secure this outcome: 'Women are the realists today,' she claimed. 'We recognise that the peace of the world has got to be preserved, and to preserve that peace we must suffer for peace, as we have suffered in the past for war. The women wanted the co-operative movement to give a lead for peace, even if it meant sacrifice.' Her appeal did not prevent conference calling for arms for Spain, and 'a policy of collective security' which would enable the League of Nations to act effectively against aggressor nations.[114]

Even as the labour movement formally gave its support to collective security and rearmament,[115] the Guild leadership strengthened its links with the peace movement and asserted that its primary role was as a peace organization. Anti-war feeling in the Guild was undoubtedly very strong. The 1936–7 *Annual Report* claimed that 1,029 of the 1,713 branches had sold white poppies, and that guildswomen had collected 30,000 Peace Pledge Union signatures (not necessarily all from within the organization).[116] The 174 guildswomen who attended the Pacifist Convention in September 1937 constituted the largest group from a single organization.[117] Yet the pacifist hard core seems to have been a minority of the whole membership, and probably a dwindling, albeit powerful, one. In May 1939, for example, only 48 Guild branches of a total of more than 1,800 were represented at a demonstration organized by the No Conscription League. Nevertheless, the contingent was led by the national President, Mrs Williams, and the new General Secretary, Rose Simpson,[118] carrying the torch passed by her aunt, Eleanor Barton.[119]

The leadership's commitment to pacifism meant that the full weight of the constitution could be used to protect the policy against proliferating attempts to bring it into line with the mainstream of the working-class movement. At the North Manchester District Conference in November 1937, in a talk called 'Thoughts on Peace', Mrs Winn (Sectional Council) told delegates that the 'absolute pacifist policy must be upheld.' The discussion revealed 'division of opinion', with questions on how to implement League of Nations policy and the course of action to be taken if, as in Spain, it was necessary 'to choose between democracy and Fascism.' The speaker's answers were not compelling. Mrs Winn insisted that 'the guild would hold to its policy of non-violence if Spanish conditions arose here', and reminded delegates that whatever their differences, guildswomen should 'uphold the ruling of congress' and 'loyally accept its decisions.'[120]

Ellen Jarman from Manchester claimed in a letter to the 'Women's Pages' that an individual ballot of the membership would reveal majority support for 'a peace policy on co-operative lines' that did not ordain passivity in the face of 'cruel aggression'. 'I have searched my soul these last few years', she wrote, 'and I know that I am not an absolute pacifist.'[121] Rose Simpson replied somewhat evasively that if guildswomen could not all be pacifists, they could at least find a common platform to pursue peace while 'agreeing to differ'.[122]

In response to the *Reynolds News* initiative for a United Peace Alliance in 1938,[123] Rose Simpson warned that the forthcoming Congress would 'be a test of the guild's pacifist faith', and declared that the CC would stand by absolute pacifism'. If 'guildswomen know their own minds', she continued, 'they will not be in doubt at Congress. Neither will there be confusion in discussion.' The Alliance she described as a 'half-way house', emphasizing that 'those who hold the pacifist faith, which is akin to the Quaker light, will vote and stand firmly for the present guild constitution, which is absolutely against war.'[124]

The pivotal item on the 1938 Congress agenda was the peace policy. A CC resolution pledged the Guild to 'the absolutist pacifist policy', and to refuse 'to take part in war or preparation for war between the workers of the world'.[125] An opposing resolution called, 'in view of the acute international situation', for the suspension of the pacifist policy and the adoption of the Co-operative Party's policy of collective security. Although printed as a separate resolution, this was taken as an amendment to the CC resolution. Its supporters argued the limitations of pacifism: 'there were "two mad dogs" running riot over Europe who would not be restrained by pacifism'; Fascism meant 'concentration camps and no chance to fight back'; delegates should consider the prospect of having 'to defend your position as members of the working class, fighting for what it has taken you 200 years to gain.' Yet the discussion was cut short by a decision to vote before lunch. Summing up, Mrs Pavitt (ex-President) claimed that all the opposing arguments demonstrated 'the effect Government propaganda was having. The remedy was to vote for the Government's removal and to stand firm to absolute pacifism.'[126]

The CC's position prevailed when the amendment was lost in a card vote. But the numbers – 897 to 623 – demonstrated that the Guild was seriously divided on the issue. As Margaret Greenall (Bristol) pointed out, the fact that hundreds of delegates voted against the policy indicated that 'guildswomen are beginning to realise that it is one thing to have an ideal, and another thing to put it into practice.' In her view the resolution, and the tendency to discuss pacifism in isolation from international politics, reflected 'muddled and misinformed thinking'.[127] Mrs Nancarrow (Newcastle) was another guildswoman convinced that in circumstances such as those of China or Spain, 'it would be impossible for me to remain passive'. What was the value of pacifism, she asked, if Co-operation was wiped out? 'The individual member may derive satisfaction through maintaining such an attitude, but she has not benefitted the movement.'[128]

The political confusion underlying the official position was evident in Rose Simpson's response to the Munich Agreement of September 1938.[129] Although she acknowledged that there were those who believed that Britain's bond to 'a small democratic State' meant that war would have been the right course of action, she hailed the outcome of the four-powers conference as a victory for the pacifist camp – proof that 'the method of reason and negotiation ... can avoid war!' Affirming that pacifism was 'essentially based on individual conscience', she then pointed out that the international situation dictated a choice not between war and peace, but between war and fascism. Implicitly maintaining that war was the greater evil, she then struggled to articulate a position that would indicate some distance between the WCG and Chamberlain's Government. Ignoring the Labour–Co-operative commitment to collective security, she concluded with a vague call for 'our democratic principles based on co-operation,' to be entrenched 'into the very structure and framework of society and the State.'[130]

A number of guildswomen disagreed with her verdict. 'But what did the League of Four accomplish?', asked Doris Tuckfield; 'a brave little democratic nation was crucified and delivered up to the most brutal dictatorship ever known in history. Co-operators, both Czech and German, will face death, mutilation, and concentration camps, and the great Czech and German co-operative movement is in ruins. Such was Mr Chamberlain's achievement at Munich.' Hitler had now gained the resources to start a large-scale war to pursue his next act of aggression: 'Chamberlain gave them to him … The absolutist pacifist policy says in effect "no resistance to Fascist aggression." But this is also what Chamberlain says, and the Fascists everywhere!'[131]

Alice Maybee (Cosham) argued that opposition to imperialist war did not preclude the need to fight Fascism. Pacifist methods had betrayed Czechoslovakia, and would lead to an alliance with Fascism and against democracy unless they had 'the courage to face world conditions as they are, and not as we think they are.' Guildswomen needed to consider the implications of absolute pacifism: in Maybee's view, at least 60 per cent of them 'don't realise what it means or what is at stake.'[132]

As well as implying a foreign policy that was indistinguishable from Chamberlain's, pacifism was also having the practical consequence of excluding the Guild from preparations for civil defence and social work in wartime. At meetings with the Minister of Health, Walter Elliott,[133] and with the Home Secretary, Sir Samuel Hoare, and Lady Reading,[134] senior Guild officials were formally invited to participate in contingency planning for evacuation and the establishment of a Women's Voluntary Service (WVS). It was envisaged that women's groups such as the WCG would co-operate in the selection of representatives to work with the local authorities in preparing schemes for each area. This was precisely the kind of representation of working women that the

219

Guild had encouraged in the First World War. Now, however, the CC's response was that the pacifist policy of the Guild 'would not allow us to take part.'[135] This was roundly attacked by Mrs Johnston Elliott at a well-reported conference of the South Suburban Education Committee in February 1939. The pacifist policy, she declared, had 'landed the Guild in the greatest muddle of its history.' In particular, the refusal to participate in the evacuation schemes was 'a grave tactical blunder.' There were rival women's organizations that would 'jump at the chance of securing control of a new local authority, and the Guild refusal to accept responsibility was a policy of social suicide which she hoped would be reversed without delay.'[136]

Once again, the 1939 Congress revealed not only deep divisions among delegates over pacifism, but also hidden hands directing the proceedings. As one delegate subsequently charged, 'there were certain forces at work which were determined to squash any anti-pacifist resolutions or amendments by any means, fair or otherwise.'[137] A Communist-inspired resolution on Air Raid Precautions (ARP) represented the growing pressure on Government to 'protect the people' from the likely consequences of aerial bombardment.[138] Its supporters pointed to recent events in Spain, the inadequacy of existing arrangements, and demanded that workers should have decent shelters and adequate evacuation arrangements.[139] The discussion was interrupted by lunch, then by a speech from the Minister of Agriculture. Congress finally returned to the ARP debate with a passionate speech from Mrs Matt Lewis, one of the Guild's staunchest pacifists, and a defeat for the motion. Subsequently, irate delegates claimed that the break, and the Minister's appearance, gave 'delegates more time to forget the case put up' in favour of the resolution, especially as all the arguments against were 'reserved until last.'[140] Even the result was disputed, amid complaints that a card vote would have been more reliable than a show of hands; the numbers were so close that one newspaper reported that the resolution had been carried.[141]

Resolutions affirming the Guild's policy of refusing to co-operate in 'a war on other nations', and opposing conscription, were passed.[142] Yet various contributions from delegates made it plain that the organization was in no condition to hold the line on these high-minded principles. One speaker reported that the CC decision to boycott ARP 'was causing endless division in branches'. As a woman who had lost every male relative in the last war, and who had a son of 17, she dreaded war, and well understood the 'splendid ideals of pure pacifism', but surely, she remonstrated, 'we could not refuse to put a gas mask on our own and other people's children, or on terrified working people.' Even more revealingly, a pacifist declared that she wanted to reassure her son, a conscientious objector, that he had the 'power of 87,000 guildswomen behind him.' She was anxious, however, that not all members were wholehearted pacifists and urged every one present 'to go home and convert her fellow members'.[143]

Three months later, the British Government declared war on Germany following the invasion of Poland. By the following summer, a national mobilization was under way which increasingly emphasized the defence not of the Empire, but of liberal-democratic values, and the promise of egalitarian social reconstruction. Women of all ages were required for war work, and were subject to immense pressures to give their all. The consequences for the Guild organization of the uncompromising pacifist stand steadily became apparent. It had refused any official role in relief work, and the CC had ruled that involvement in the war effort 'should be a voluntary decision for individual members.'[144] As the *Annual Report* stated in 1939, if guildswomen 'serve on regional committees and National Service committees and ARP work, they do so as individuals and not as representatives of the Women's Guild.'[145] The main pattern of voluntary work was fixed very rapidly: 'one had to join the WVS to take part in humanitarian work in rest centres, canteens, communal kitchens.' But the Guild 'was not recognized by local authorities', complained Councillor Mrs G. E. Lloyd at the Northamptonshire District Conference early in 1942. Their members were told that they 'must work through the WVS. At the outbreak of the war the guild had been advised nationally not to take office in organisations unless the work keyed in with Guild policy, and now guildswomen found themselves shut out'.[146]

In the first two years of the war, 44 per cent of the membership – some 38,000 women – disappeared from the Guild; of those who remained, it was claimed that an estimated 90 per cent were 'furtively or openly engaged in some sort of war work.'[147]

221

Meanwhile, the WVS, and rivals such as the TG, experienced 'mushroom growth',[148] confounding attempts to explain falling numbers by reference to wartime disruption.[149] Yet the leadership was unrepentant. Evincing the kind of attitude that was speeding the Guild's decline as a national organization of any significance, and which had already terminated its claim to be a 'democracy of working women', Cecily Cook, the General Secretary, spoke contemptuously of those members who had failed the test of faith. If it was the case that members had left because of the peace policy, she wrote in 1942, then 'it is well that the organisation should have purged itself of dead wood.'[150] Attempts to reform the peace policy continued to be blocked. A resolution calling for the pacifist rule to be rescinded was dismissed by the 1942 Standing Orders Committee 'on the ground that there was no such rule operating', only a policy.[151] Several resolutions on the peace policy were again rejected in 1943, and the CC agreed that 'the course of the war was set and it was too late in the day for the Guild to alter its policy.'[152]

In a long and reasoned letter that appeared in the 'Women's Pages' in May 1943, Dora Taylor (Manchester) argued that although official speakers proclaimed the Guild a pacifist organization, this was 'not accepted by a very large number of guildswomen, and very deeply resented by the main body of the guilds.' She, for one, strongly disagreed with the claim. The Guild's 'formation, its original rules and objects, and the financial and other support given by the co-operative societies which are its basis, assume that the guild is for the purpose of "educating the co-operative woman in the principles and practice of co-operation and in expressing the same through citizenship." The pacifist and her views should be welcome but we ask not to be *compelled* to march under her banner.'[153]

Dora Taylor was, of course, correct in her observations about the character of the Guild, and her remarks serve to highlight the extent to which this Co-operative auxiliary body had been captured by a pacifist sect[154] as part of its slide into ever greater sclerosis. Absolute pacifism was not the progeny of the Guild's engagement with Co-operative–Labour politics; to the contrary, in the inter-war period it was the one policy that the WCG pursued (post-Lansbury) in defiance of the official line. For many of the

Guild's most dedicated and prominent pacifists (including Margaret Llewelyn Davies and Lilian Harris), this commitment was visceral, and any suggestion that it might be reconsidered in the light of Fascist aggression implied a betrayal of principles that had been tempered by the mass slaughter of the First World War. Yet while there is no doubt of Eleanor Barton's long-standing pacifist convictions, it is also clear that in the early 1930s she focused the Guild on the subject with the same single-mindedness with which she had promoted Labour–Co-operative politics in the late 1920s, suggesting, perhaps, a quest for an alternative political role following her disappointing failure to win a parliamentary seat. It is also worth noting that despite its independence over pacifism, the Guild leadership retained right-wing Labour positions on other matters; in particular, its antipathy to Communists – and the Left in general – would have strengthened its resolve not to engage with political debates that might have produced a more flexible set of responses to the international crisis of the late 1930s.

Yet while adherence to absolute pacifism was not dictated by the Guild's loyalty to Labour–Co-operative politics, the methods by which it was established as 'official policy' were the same forms of internal control that had been devised to impose party discipline. The constitutional changes that were introduced to commit the whole organization to parliamentarism enabled the pacifists in the leadership to dedicate the Guild to the cause to which they gave their first allegiance, without ever being obliged to explain or justify their action. This development was indicative of the way in which the political choices of the 1920s, and the accompanying centralization of power, had eroded the Guild leadership's capacity, or willingness, to respond to the concerns of members, to engage imaginatively with social and political developments, or even to make sound judgements about the kinds of interventions that would develop, rather than paralyze the Guild's effectiveness as a broad-based organization. From the late 1920s, internal conflict over the questions of branch autonomy, the political rule, and the pacifist policy, had been the symptoms of this malaise; at the beginning of the war, however, the haemorrhaging of members emphatically demonstrated that the leadership was so far removed from the concerns of Co-operative women that it could no longer maintain the organization's viability.

Notes

1. Variously attributed to harsh treatment in wartime, and rising working-class militancy, see Chapter 1, note 54.
2. But representing only 36 per cent of the membership of the movement, G.D.H. Cole, *A Century of Co-operation* (London: Allen & Unwin for the Co-operative Union, 1944, p. 320); A.M. Carr Saunders, P. Sargant Florence, R. Peers, *Consumer's Co-operation in Great Britain: An Examination of the British Co-operative Movement* (London: Allen & Unwin, 1938, p. 212).
3. Cole, op. cit., p. 324; R. McKibbin, *The Evolution of the Labour Party 1910–1924* (Oxford: Clarendon Press, 1974, pp. 178–91).
4. 'Mrs Barton', *Minutes of Evidence taken before the Royal Commission on Divorce and Matrimonial Causes*, (1912), 3 (Cd. 6481) PP 1912–13, **XX**, p. 172.
5. 'Report of Women's Guild', CCR, 1919, p. 303.
6. *Co-operative News*, 4 March 1922, p. 13.
7. Letter from Mary Booth, *Co-operative News*, 9 December 1922, p. 12.
8. Letter from Florence R. Toon, *Co-operative News*, 16 December 1922, p. 12; the General Secretary, Honora Enfield, speaking at the annual All Councils meeting, *Co-operative News*, 3 February 1923, p. 12.
9. Mrs Butler (Yorkshire Section), All Councils, *Co-operative News*, 3 February 1923, p. 12.
10. *Co-operative News*, 31 January 1925, p. 12.
11. *Co-operative News*, 4 July 1925, p. 7.
12. *Co-operative News*, 28 February 1925, pp. 12–13.
13. *Co-operative News*, 30 January 1926, p. 12.
14. *Co-operative News*, 30 January 1926, p. 12; 3 July 1926, p. 16. The 1926 Congress also received the report of an Inquiry Committee set up two years earlier to consider ways of coping with increased membership. The new leadership took issue with many of its recommendations – such as the devolution of power to the Sections, and a reduction in the General Secretary's salary – and only adopted those which conformed to its own priorities. See G. Scott, ' "The working-class women's most active and democratic movement": the WCG from 1883 to 1950', Sussex University D.Phil., 1988, p. 241.
15. *Co-operative News*, 28 January 1928, p. 12.

16. *Co-operative News*, 23 June 1928, p. 13.
17. *Co-operative News*, 16 February 1929, p. 16.
18. Ibid.
19. *Co-operative News*, 23 June 1928, p. 13 (Mrs Wimhurst was the 1913/14 Guild President).
20. *Co-operative News*, 12 February 1927, p. 17.
21. *Co-operative News*, 11 February 1928, p. 17.
22. *Co-operative News*, 2 February 1929, p. 17. The subscription was now set at two shillings a year per member; fixed national subscriptions apart, branches had previously determined these charges.
23. WCG, *Annual Report*, 1929–30, p. 2.
24. *Co-operative News*, 29 June 1929, p. 12; her father was Samuel Bamford, *Co-operative News* editor, 1875–1898, and an early Guild supporter, J.M. Bellamy & J. Saville (eds), *Dictionary of Labour Biography* (DLB), I (London: Macmillan, 1972).
25. WCG, Central Committee Minutes, 7 November 1929.
26. *Co-operative News*, 31 August 1929, p. 13.
27. *Co-operative News*, 28 September 1929, p. 13.
28. *Co-operative News*, 21 September 1929, p. 16.
29. *Co-operative News*, 23 November 1929, p. 13.
30. *Co-operative News*, 30 November 1929, p. 13.
31. *Co-operative News*, 23 November 1929, p. 13.
32. *Co-operative News*, 14 December 1929, p. 13; a number of branches in the Plymouth area did disaffiliate, and the status of their relationship with the Guild continued to be an issue for the CC for several years.
33. CC Minutes, 24 January 1930.
34. Ibid.
35. CC Minutes, 10 and 11 April 1930.
36. *Co-operative News*, 23 June 1928, p. 12; WCG, *Annual Report*, 1928–9, p. 24. This hostility reflected general resentment in the labour movement at the growing affluence of officials, but also stemmed from the fact that Davies and Harris had given their services gratis.
37. CC Minutes, 27 and 28 September 1928. When Mrs Barton lost the election, however, one of the party executive's complaints against her was that she had interrupted her campaign to attend the Guild Congress, CC Minutes, 20 and 21 September 1929.
38. *Co-operative News*, 10 May 1930, p. 12.
39. CC Minutes, 10 and 11 April 1930.
40. *Co-operative News*, 29 March 1930, p. 12.
41. CC Minutes, 26 and 27 May 1930.
42. *Co-operative News*, 24 May 1930, p. 12.

43. *Co-operative News*, 5 July 1930, p. 16.
44. *Co-operative News*, 28 June 1930, p. 5.
45. *Co-operative News*, 5 July 1930, p. 16.
46. By women from NUSEC, successor of the NUWSS, to create a non-partisan, citizenship-centred, urban equivalent to the Women's Institute movement that had been founded in 1915. See M. Stott, *Organization Woman: The Story of the Townswomen's Guilds* (London: Heinemann, 1978); I. Jenkins, *The History of the Women's Institute Movement of England and Wales* (Oxford University Press, 1953). For the significance of the WI and the TG in relation to organized feminism, see M. Pugh, *Women and the Women's Movement in Britain, 1914–1959* (London: Macmillan, 1993).
47. CC Minutes, 10 and 11 April 1930.
48. *Co-operative News*, 14 May 1932, p. 17.
49. This perception may well have been connected with the fact that Guild branches began to compete on the same terrain as the TGs by introducing more domestic crafts in connection with Co-operative sales promotion, for which see Chapter 8.
50. R. Miliband, *Parliamentary Socialism: a Study in the Politics of Labour* (London: Merlin Press, 1973, p. 118; CC Minutes, 6 and 7 April 1927.
51. *Co-operative News*, 7 March 1937, p. 12; in 1926 and 1927, for example, Labour leaders disaffiliated 23 Constituency Labour Parties which refused to accept the ban on Communists, Miliband, op. cit., p. 153.
52. WCG, *Annual Report*, 1934–5, p. 5. So did other members of the rank and file; Ellen Wilkinson, for example, described the Leicester Society cobblers staying up all night to repair the marchers' ruined boots, E. Wilkinson, *The Town that was Murdered* (London: Gollancz, Left Book Club edition, 1939, p. 206). For the NUWM and the marches, see J. Stevenson and C. Cook, *The Slump: Society and Politics during the Depression* (London: Quartet, 1979, chs. IX and X).
53. CC Minutes, 2 and 3 May 1932; 2 and 3 October 1932.
54. CC Minutes, 22 and 23 May 1933.
55. *Co-operative News*, 3 December 1932, p. 16.
56. Communist Party member and wife of its leader, see K. Morgan, *Harry Pollitt: Lives of the Left* (Manchester University Press, 1993).
57. CC Minutes, 23 and 24 January 1935.
58. Wording which reflected continuing hostility to the Labour Party among many guildswomen.
59. Annie E. Corrie, letter, *Co-operative News*, 15 February 1936; p. 12.
60. *Co-operative News*, 11 April 1936, p. 8.
61. CC Minutes, 22 and 23 January 1936.

62. CC Minutes, 27 February 1936.
63. *Co-operative News*, 28 March 1936, p. 16.
64. *Co-operative News*, 8 February 1936, p. 13.
65. *Co-operative News*, 22 February 1936, p. 16.
66. *Co-operative News*, 15 February 1936, p. 12.
67. The Co-operative Party did not introduce a ban, Cole, op. cit., p. 333.
68. *Co-operative News*, 29 February 1936, p. 12.
69. Ibid., p. 16.
70. *Co-operative News*, 22 February 1936, p. 16.
71. Interview with Mabel Cumins, Brighton, February 1982.
72. *Co-operative News*, 21 March 1936, p. 16.
73. *Co-operative News*, 22 February 1936, p. 16.
74. *Co-operative News*, 29 February 1936, p. 16.
75. *Co-operative News*, 28 March 1936, p. 16.
76. In 1934, the TUC took steps to exclude from the trades councils those associated with the Minority Movement, and then members of Communist and Fascist organizations; these regulations were known by their opponents as 'black circulars'. See Alan Clinton, *The Trade Union Rank and File: Trades Councils in Britain, 1900–40* (Manchester University Press, 1977, p. 152).
77. *Co-operative News*, 28 March 1936, p. 16.
78. *Co-operative News*, 11 April 1936, p. 8.
79. *Co-operative News*, 16 May 1936, p. 12.
80. *Co-operative News*, 16 May 1936, p. 12.
81. *Co-operative News*, 16 May 1936, p. 12.
82. *Co-operative News*, 9 May 1936, p. 16.
83. *Co-operative News*, 6 June 1936, p. 20.
84. CC Minutes, 6 and 7 April 1936.
85. *Co-operative News*, 21 March 1936, p. 12.
86. CC Minutes, 6 and 7 April 1936.
87. *Co-operative News*, 2 July 1938, p. 12.
88. CC Minutes, 11 and 12 January 1939; 12 and 13 March 1939.
89. *Co-operative News*, 1 April 1939, p. 16.
90. *Co-operative News*, 15 April 1939, p. 20.
91. *Co-operative News*, 15 April 1939, p. 20.
92. *Co-operative News*, 17 June 1939, p. 17; CC Minutes, 15 and 16 May 1939.
93. *Co-operative News*, 17 June 1939, p. 7.
94. Contrary to the claim that the Guild 'kept open house for communist and ILP as well as Labour women', P. Graves, *Labour Women in British Working-Class Politics 1918–1939* (Cambridge University Press, 1994, p. 210).
95. Interview with Kitty Fitzgerald, *The Leveller*, December/January

1982/3, no. 90, p. 12.

96. Bessy Wilde made this comment during a session on the WCG organized by Sheffield Women's History Group, at History Workshop, Sheffield, 1982.

97. C. Salt, P. Schweitzer & M. Wilson (eds), *Of Whole Heart Cometh Hope Centenary Memories of the Co-operative Women's Guild* (London: Age Exchange Theatre Company, 1983, p. 31).

98. Interview with Mrs Cumins, Brighton, February 1982.

99. For women's involvement with peace movements, see J. Liddington, *The Long Road to Greenham Common, Feminism and Anti-Militarism in Britain since 1820* (London: Virago, 1989); S. Oldfield, *Women Against the Iron Fist: Alternatives to Militarism, 1900–1989* (Oxford: Blackwell, 1989); A. Wiltsher, *Most Dangerous Women: Feminist Campaigners of the Great War* (London: Pandora, 1985). For a laudatory account of Guild pacifism, N. Black, 'The Mother's International: the WCG and Feminist Pacifism', *Women's Studies International Forum*, 7, no. 6, 1984, pp. 467–76 (thanks to Jean Gaffin for this reference).

100. Barton's anti-war activity went back to the Boer War; she attended peace meetings in the 1914–18 War, and was involved in the National Peace Council and the No More War Movement in the 1920s; H.F. Bing (1898–1975), a First World War Conscientious Objector, was a good friend of hers; *Co-operative News*, 15 January 1927, p. 12; 29 May 1937, p. 13; WCG, *Annual Report*, 1924–25, p. 8, 1926–27, p. 6; *DLB*, I.

101. WCG, *Annual Report*, 1928–29, p. 22.

102. *Co-operative News*, 1 July 1933, p. 12.

103. *Co-operative News*, 4 February 1933, p. 14. All Councils was the annual meeting of Sectional Councils.

104. *Co-operative News*, 1 July 1933, p. 12.

105. WCG, *Annual Report*, 1935–6, p. 13.

106. *Co-operative News*, 10 October 1936, p. 13.

107. WCG, *Annual Report*, 1938–9, p. 17.

108. D.A. Martin, *Pacifism An Historical and Sociological Study* (London: Routledge, Kegan and Paul, 1965, p. 109).

109. For a detailed discussion of this divergence see M. Ceadel, *Pacifism in Britain 1914–45: The Defining of a Faith* (Oxford: Clarendon Press, 1980).

110. *Co-operative News*, 1 August 1936, p. 12.

111. *Co-operative News*, 11 July 1936, p. 13; 18 July 1936, p. 12; 25 July 1936, p. 17.

112. *Co-operative News*, 26 September 1936, p. 12; and see Liddington, op. cit., pp. 162–6 for details of this debate in Hampstead Garden Suburb Guild.

113. 'Where is Our Faith? Peace the Rallying Cry', report of Mrs McKay (ex-national president) at All Councils, *Co-operative News*, 6 February 1937, p. 12.
114. *Co-operative News*, 3 April 1937, pp. 3–4; Co-operative Congress a few weeks later endorsed the collective security position, *Co-operative Congress Report*, 1937, p. 124.
115. See Miliband, op. cit., ch. VIII for a detailed discussion of Labour Party debates on these issues.
116. WCG, *Annual Report*, 1936–7, p. 16.
117. Ibid., 1937–8, p. 10.
118. Rose Simpson's career as General Secretary came to an ignominious end when she was obliged to resign in November 1939 amidst charges of incompetence and financial improprieties in her management of the new monthly Guild journal, *The Guildswoman*, which appeared briefly that year. The auditors found a deficit on its accounts, and the CC was shocked to discover that she had employed two men on its staff – a friend, and her brother – without its knowledge. CC Minutes, 11 November 1939; J. Gaffin & D. Thoms, *Caring and Sharing The Centenary History of the Co-operative Women's Guild* (Manchester: Co-operative Union, 1983, pp. 119–20).
119. *Co-operative News*, 6 May 1939, p. 12; CC Minutes, 15 and 16 May 1939.
120. *Co-operative News*, 20 November 1937, p. 12.
121. Ibid., p. 12.
122. *Co-operative News*, 25 December 1937, p. 12.
123. See Miliband, op. cit., p. 257.
124. *Co-operative News*, 4 June 1938, p. 2.
125. WCG, *Annual Report*, 1938–39, p. 17.
126. *Co-operative News*, 25 June 1938, p. 8.
127. *Co-operative News*, 29 October 1938, p. 16.
128. *Woman's Outlook*, XIX/490, 30 July 1938, p. 407.
129. P. Kennedy, *The Realities behind Diplomacy: Background Influences on British External Policy, 1865–1980* (London: Fontana, 1985, pp. 290–301).
130. *Co-operative News*, 8 October 1938, p. 12.
131. *Co-operative News*, 22 October 1938, p. 16.
132. *Co-operative News*, 1 December 1938, p. 12.
133. *Co-operative News*, 10 December 1938, p. 1.
134. WCG, *Annual Report*, 1938–9, pp. 2–3.
135. Ibid.
136. *Co-operative News*, 18 February 1939, p. 16; Mrs Johnston Elliott was an influential Co-operator, and a runner-up in the 1937 General Secretary election.

137. *Co-operative News*, 1 July 1939, p. 12.
138. J.B.S. Haldane, *ARP* (London: Gollancz, 1938, p. 10).
139. *Co-operative News*, 17 June 1939, p. 8.
140. *Co-operative News*, 1 July 1939, p. 12.
141. *Co-operative News*, 15 July 1939, p. 12.
142. WCG, *Annual Report*, 1939–40, p. 20.
143. *Co-operative News*, 17 June 1939, p. 8.
144. CC Minutes, 28 and 29 November 1938; *Co-operative News*, 10 December 1939, p. 1.
145. WCG, *Annual Report*, 1938–39, p. 3.
146. *Co-operative News*, 31 January 1942, p. 13.
147. Discussion at All Councils, *Co-operative News*, 31 January 1942, p. 12.
148. *Co-operative News*, 28 March 1942, p. 13.
149. *Co-operative News*, 21 March 1942, p. 12.
150. *Co-operative News*, 14 February 1942, p. 18.
151. *Co-operative News*, 25 April 1942, p. 12.
152. *Co-operative News*, 19 June 1943, p. 12; CC Minutes, 11 August 1943.
153. *Co-operative News*, 15 May 1943, p. 13.
154. See Ceadel, op. cit., especially chs. 15 and 16, for the growth of pacifist sectarianism.

Chapter Eight

Compromises

As the preceding chapters have shown, during the 1920s the Guild's cutting edge was blunted as its radical policies were sacrificed to Labour Party orthodoxy. At the same time its democratic organizational form was recast to produce strong centralized control, which in the 1930s served to bolt the organization to an inflexible, and ultimately, for many members, untenable pacifist position. Yet despite the signs of gradual decay, between the wars the Guild remained a leading working-class women's organization. Its size – membership grew from 50,600 in 905 branches in 1921, to 87,246 in 1,819 branches by 1939 – and its position in the mighty Co-operative movement combined to give it an authoritative voice in a variety of local and national public forums. But what kind of voice? How did the Guild represent working women?

The Guild did not abandon the cause of feminism during the inter-war years, but its residual loyalty to the principle of women's rights was now conditioned by the political and organizational transformations which it had undergone. The growing concern with party politics, and then with pacifism, both served to reduce the proportion of the Guild's energies devoted to women's issues, while the working-class feminism pioneered by the Guild before the war did not survive its growing attachment to the Labour Party. As birth control and then family endowment were defeated by dominant interests within the latter, the Guild closed down its investigation of the problems associated with unwanted pregnancies and married women's economic dependence; and the key question of sexual inequality in the private sphere disappeared not simply from its policy, but from its conceptual apparatus. Thus, by the late 1920s its social policy was geared to the improvement of family life rather than the specific needs of working women, and offered an uncomplicated view of women in the home, fulfilling their natural role as wives and mothers.

What survived was the politically less contentious, rights-based feminism, focused on equal opportunity in the public sphere, which was in the main compatible with Labour Party policy. Here the Guild was still active. The problem, however, was that while the gender issues possessing strong rank-and-file appeal, and the potential to involve the whole organization, had been dropped in line with Labour policy, the demands with which the Guild did persist – for more women on public bodies and equal employment rights for married women – had only minimal resonance with the mass of the membership. Before 1920 organizational unity had been generated by campaigns for social reform which had general relevance to working women and were buttressed by feminist principles. The equal-rights issues pursued by the Guild between the wars did not touch the lives of working women to the same extent, and often had little but lofty principles to offer. Stripped of content that was capable of promoting sexual equality without privileging women with superior talents or resources, the Guild's continuing feminist efforts tended to divide rather than unify the membership, by highlighting their different social circumstances rather than their common sexual experience.

The ideological backdrop for these shifts was the growth of an anti-feminist discourse about ordinary housewives as the nurturing force in society: mothers of the race, chancellors of the domestic economy. As the living standards of those in work rose and new mass markets opened up, the spending power of the working-class wife gained in importance. Advertising targeted married women, developing methods of persuasion which described and elaborated their responsibilities as wives and mothers. In the absence of a relevant feminist analysis, or any oppositional view of working-class womanhood, the Guild became increasingly porous to the mainsteam representations of femininity that were transmitted through Co-operative channels, as well as through other cultural agencies, and by the 1930s its representation of working-class femininity was indistinguishable from the dominant forms.

Guild literature between the wars did continue to provide trenchant feminist critique. An editorial in the 'Women's Pages' at the beginning of 1929, for example, noted that despite the 1928 franchise reform, 'we are still far from complete emancipation'.[1] Another, in 1933, detected 'a revival of the old and outworn dictum, "Woman's place is at home." ' If guildswomen were not vigilant, their daughters would have to fight again 'for recognition as responsible citizens and workers worthy of a "living" wage.' The Guild, it continued, was the 'champion of the *Woman* in the Home, while at the same time striving to give her a wider outlook and openings for service OUTSIDE her home.'[2]

Taking stock of the previous 50 years, *The Guild Yesterday and Today* (1933) registered the fact that the 'growing position of women in social and political life, and her increasing self respect and dignity, have made possible great social changes in other directions. If the Guild is, to some extent, the product of this development, it is also in no small degree a pioneer, and the history of the Guild is the history of the movement for women's emancipation from the prejudices of the past.'[3] Yet there was a need for vigilance. A 'bitter attack' was 'being made against married women at the present time, reducing their sick benefits, cutting their unemployment pay, and depriving them of that fundamental human right, the right to support themselves and earn their own living'. Mainly as a result of 'their lack of organisation and collective resistance', this 'vulnerable group' was being treated as 'some peculiar species of sub-normal humanity' and 'forced into complete dependence upon their menfolk.'[4]

These pieces were all unsigned: the editorials probably came from the pen of Mrs Bamford Tomlinson, while *The Guild Yesterday and Today* reads like the work of Margaret Llewelyn Davies. But whatever their provenance, they are more reminiscent of what the Guild had been than what it had become, and there was a conspicuous absence of campaigning initiatives to build on these critical insights.

On the contrary, the active feminism of the Guild had become increasingly ensnared in the contradictory effects of women's achievement of citizenship rights. Enfranchisement had tended to underline differences within the women's movement, between those who wanted an end to formal discrimination and those who viewed sexual inequality as having structural causes. For the feminist élite, citizenship rights more or less completed a long struggle for equality of opportunity, enabling energetic and talented individuals to prove themselves on the same terms as men. As Ray Strachey wrote in 1928, 'the main fight is over, and the main victory is won. With education, enfranchisement, and legal equality all conceded, the future of women lies in their own hands.'[5] In the early 1920s, guildswomen were still prepared to argue that equality of opportunity existed in theory but not in practice, and for reasons that dictated social as well as legal reform. Increasingly, however, senior guildswomen inclined to the view that it was now up to the women themselves to demonstrate their worth, and began to use the language of an achieved emancipation, emphasizing women's responsibilities rather than their entitlements.

The requirement that women take their place alongside men as equals, rather than draw attention to the ways in which they were disadvantaged by their gender, was an unstated condition of their admission to the political parties and as strong, if not stronger, in the Co-operative Party as elsewhere. Despite the Guild's importance, it was not awarded direct representation on the Parliamentary Committee on the grounds that Co-operative women already enjoyed equality: 'sex is no barrier to any position in the co-operative movement ... women have equal opportunity with men, and therefore, there is no need for special privileges.'[6]

Initially, guildswomen challenged this view. 'We wish with all our hearts that it were not necessary to emphasise the fact that women – as women – still have to fight for equality of opportunity even in a movement which professes to give equal opportunities to all', complained an article in the 'Women's Pages' in 1920.[7] As Mrs Cottrell (CU Midland Sectional Board) pointed out: 'men and women do not start equally from scratch. Women as a whole are handicapped. The wives and mothers who form the bulk of our co-operative women are not disqualified, but with a few exceptions they are debarred from active participation in official management by the very fact of being responsible for the management of their homes.'[8] Gradually, however, senior guildswomen came to appreciate that to labour the disabilities of sex would, in effect, be to prejudice the chances of women winning nominations. As Eleanor Barton remarked in 1924, 'she had found that a woman has got to stand out far and away above men if she is to be chosen at all'.[9] Increasingly, the emphasis switched from the objective difficulties facing women to what they themselves must do. At a Southern sectional conference in 1924, for example, Mrs Close (CC) informed a delegate who asked how they might get more women MPs, that it was down to women voters: 'when women realise they need working women in Parliament they will put them in.' To a delegate who raised the problem of 'Labour candidates who believed that woman's place is at home', Mrs Close 'offered the consoling opinion that there were old-fashioned people in every movement, but they would all die out in the course of time, and the younger people would have a different education as voters, and hold more progressive views. When men made mates of their wives they would soon become proud of their services.'[10]

Notwithstanding such rhetoric, views expressed in the Co-operative Party demonstrated that sexual discrimination was alive and well. Pressed on the issue of the difficulty women faced in gaining safe seats at the 1926 Party Conference, the chairman, Alfred Barnes (MP), had to admit that the idea of women in Parliament was still not widely accepted. Female candidates could not 'be forced on the constituencies. There was still a certain amount of prejudice against women in political circles; it had to be broken down.'[11] Yet the Party spectacularly failed to break down this prejudice, and the continuing failure to return a woman MP was regularly aired at Conference until 1945, when three guildswomen won seats.[12]

An exchange at the 1931 Party Conference indicated that 'prejudice in the constituencies' was only part of the problem. Some activists saw safe seats as a form of discrimination. Thus, when Mr Derbyshire (Manchester) pointed out that unlike the other parties they had not a single woman MP, and that as the movement was 'largely based on womenfolk they should have special consideration', Mrs Shimmin (London Political Committee) was quick to rise to her feet. 'I do object', she retorted, 'at this time of day to arguing on any question on a sex basis. Women ask for equal citizenship with men, for equal opportunities and rights, and surely a natural corollary of that will be equal responsibilities.'[13]

Despite the impediments blocking them from the highest offices in the Co-operative Party, the main tendency among senior guildswomen was to follow Mrs Shimmin in abjuring any attempt to explain women's under-representation in terms of structural disabilities. The CC was sensitive to the Guild's 'unsatisfactory' position in the Co-operative Party, and the lack of local and national support for Mrs Barton in her campaigns.[14] At All Councils in 1930, senior officials received the news that Mrs Barton had not been nominated as a Parliamentary candidate for Nottingham Central as 'a terrible snub', and condemned the absence of a Co-operative woman MP as 'regrettable' and 'a disgrace'. But Mrs Moore (CC) was quick to turn the discussion away from the charge of sex discrimination. Whatever prejudice Co-operators faced in the labour movement,[15] she argued, 'the responsibility rested with themselves'.[16] As the Guild embraced the view that women now possessed sufficient formal equalities to help themselves, arguments about their disadvantages seemed like a liability. Thus, in 1937, an editorial in the 'Women's Pages' claimed that it was 'not feminism' that prompted the wish for another woman to replace Mrs Cottrell, then retiring from the CWS Board of Directors, but 'common sense'.[17]

If women of sufficient worth could rise to the top by virtue of their individual talents, then, surely, it followed that those who stayed at the bottom had only themselves to blame; and that the concept of an apathetic mass could further be deployed to explain why more women were not successful in getting elected. Thus prominent guildswomen began to suggest that ordinary women, inside and outside the Guild, were inept or ignorant, or both. As Barton pronounced in 1928:

> Women can still claim today that they are not responsible for the distress and injustice that is rife in the country, but after the coming General Election they will not be able to make such a claim. Then they will have to take the credit or the blame for the Government that is returned, and women Co-operators have a wonderful opportunity now that they all have the vote of seeing that their Co-operative principles are put into practice nationally.[18]

In 1931, at All Councils, Mrs Ganley argued that 'more women on public committees, and in public affairs would greatly improve the prospects of future mothers. But women', she claimed, 'did not care. In many cases they did not understand, and, mainly, they were apathetic.'[19] When she stood for election to Essex County Council in 1931, Mrs Ranson found 'tragic apathy' and 'deplorable ignorance' among working-class voters, and an appalling lack of commitment among her fellow members. 'When are guildswomen,' she wrote bitterly, 'going to cease making any and every kind of excuse to get out of what is their obvious and important duty?'[20] Mrs Marsden (Sectional Council), speaking at Oldham District Conference in 1932, 'deplored' the fact that 'Oldham had no women on co-operative bodies, but pointed out that this was their own fault'; they needed to use their 'united strength' to get women on to committees.[21] In a similar vein, in 1936 Mabel Langford claimed that political infiltration of the Guild was successful, because many members were 'either uninterested or unaware of what is happening.'[22]

This kind of mistrust or even contempt for the rank and file was a corollary of the stance taken in the mid-1920s, as the ascendant Labour-dominated leadership sought to impose electoral unity on the politically heterogeneous Guild. Unable to set political conditions for membership, which would have damaged recruitment, the income from subscriptions, and the standing of the organization, the new regime under Eleanor Barton chose to impose party discipline on the official caste. The resulting rule changes drove a wedge through the organization, implicitly categorizing members as loyal or disloyal. The latter were tolerated, but not appreciated; and those who took local initiatives unconnected with the official labour movement were viewed as subversive elements to be silenced or, better, rooted out, as an increasing proportion of the administrative energies of the Guild were devoted to this policing operation.

The election of guildswomen on to public bodies certainly assumed greater importance. We need 'a big push to put women forward both locally and nationally,' Barton told Sheffield guildswomen in 1933. 'They should put forward a woman for each Co-operative Union Section. ... They also wanted more co-operative women as magistrates; they wanted more women on management and educational boards, and also as CWS directors.'[23] For hundreds of women, the Guild provided a springboard for careers in the labour movement and municipal politics. Mrs Matt Lewis, CC member and Guild president 1944–5, was the first Labour woman to gain a seat on Aberdare district council; at various times she served on the Labour Party parliamentary panel and the Co-operative Party executive.[24] Mrs Ganley, longstanding Guild member and a director of the London Co-operative Society, served as a magistrate from 1920, and sat on Battersea Borough Council and the London County Council; in 1945 she became MP for Battersea South.[25] By 1939, in addition to its many seats on Co-operative bodies, the Guild could boast 2 mayors, 18 mayoresses, 24 aldermen, 24 county councillors, 255 city, town or urban district councillors, and 137 magistrates.[26]

Yet while energetic guildswomen worked their way up through the committee structure, obtaining Co-operative and municipal offices, the bulk of the membership now seemed to exist mainly as a vehicle for their ambitions. In 1938, three years after joining, one militant but anonymous guildswoman wrote perceptively about the Guild hierarchy. 'The machinery of organisation works,' she observed in the Guild journal, *Woman's Outlook*, 'but what are the results? Surely very little compared with what we could do. The only concrete results that I can see is that in working it from committee members upwards, social-minded, not always Socialist, women get knowledge and opportunity.' All well and good, she went on, 'but are 80,000 women to be used simply as stepping stones? It appears to me to have amounted to that with teas and dances thrown in, not always cheaply ...'[27]

Ranged alongside the Guild's sustained efforts to increase women's representation on public bodies was its most explicit feminist position of the inter-war years: the defence of married women's right to work. Yet this too not only failed to provide the basis for united action, but had a divisive effect, because it largely ignored the very different kinds of employment opportunities that were available to guildswomen according to their social class.

The question was first taken up by the WCG in 1922, following a NUSEC[28] initiative to highlight the problem as the post-war recession set in.[29] The subject was discussed at All Councils, and a paper produced for discussion at sectional conferences. All Councils unanimously passed a resolution which opposed 'the exclusion of married women from employment', on the ground that it would cause 'serious dangers and hardships'. The marriage bar would enforce economic dependence by denying wives the protection of their own earnings; it would curb women's entry into the professions and skilled trades, confining them to low-paid, unskilled work; it would cause hardship in individual cases, and encourage objectionable inquisitions by employers, concealment, and 'irregular relations' by employees. Furthermore, it would deprive the community of valuable workers, and married women of direct representation in Parliament and on other public bodies. Accordingly, there should be 'no barrier of sex or marriage in regard to the holding of paid positions, and no differentiation in the scale of payment.'[30]

These arguments were elaborated by Eleanor Barton in a Guild pamphlet, *Married Women and Paid Positions*, published late in 1922,[31] and recurrently taken as a special subject between the wars.[32] Barton set out to demolish the objections commonly advanced against married women working, using both feminist and class-based arguments. Firstly, there was the traditional view that the wife should be kept by her husband, in itself problematic as it perpetuated the false notions that married women's work at home had no value and that she was not an equal partner in the marriage. Aside from the many married women who were not maintained for various reasons – bad husbands, sick husbands, unemployed husbands, etc. – this wrongly assumed that all married women were fitted for full-time domesticity, and denied them the opportunity to develop other talents and skills. 'Once give way to the pressure,' stated Barton, 'and the thin end of the wedge will be used to force women back into their homes, with no outside interests at all.'[33]

Another objection was that in times of unemployment it was unfair for two wages to go into one home. Perhaps so; but as Barton pointed out: 'If we really mean that, why restrict it to man and wife?'[34] Why should a son or a daughter of an employed man bring in a wage, or each of three bachelors sharing a flat? Equally mistaken was the notion that 'the married woman should go in order to make room for the single one.'[35] Setting aside the difficulty of replacing particular skills and experience, was it to be assumed that all single women were more in need of paid employment than all married women? And who would adjudicate

239

between contending claims? Would there be an inquisition into everyone's circumstances prior to making appointments? In a society that took huge disparities between the incomes of households and of individuals for granted, the application of such criteria solely to married women smacked of sexual discrimination, not social justice. The only proper criterion for employment was 'of capability and efficiency to do the work.'[36]

In essence, this remained the Guild's official view of the question throughout the inter-war years. While firmly rooted in equal rights feminism, it was broadly consistent with the Labour Party and the SJC's formal support for married women's right to work, a position which reflected the fact that discrimination on the basis of marital status would ultimately damage the trade-union side in collective bargaining by allowing employers to use single male workers to undercut married ones.[37] In the late 1920s, this labour–feminist convergence was weakened, when the issue of protective legislation for industrial women exposed fundamental incompatibilities within the women's movement between a liberal feminist insistence on formal equality, and a more pragmatic welfare feminist acceptance of sexual distinctions. For the pure equal rights feminist groups, such as the Open Door Council (ODC), founded in 1926, any special treatment of women constituted oppressive sexual discrimination. But the labour women, including the WCG, along with 'new feminists' such as Eleanor Rathbone of NUSEC, argued that such discrimination was necessary, given the physiological differences between men and women.[38]

Eleanor Barton introduced the subject of protective legislation at All Councils in 1930. She warned that ODC members were agitating for the abolition of legislation which benefited women. 'They were pleading for women on the lines of equality', she said, 'and many guildswomen were going with them without giving the matter serious thought. In her opinion the ODC was not speaking for industrial, but professional women.'[39] Yet alongside its formal support for protective legislation, and a tendency during the 1930s to place more emphasis upon the trade-union arguments against the marriage bar, a strong body of opinion in the Guild continued to press the unalloyed feminist case. A 1930 Congress resolution, for example, technically in line with the ODC position, called for legislation to bring about the equality of the sexes in all trades and professions, for all avenues of work to be open to women on the same terms as men, with equal opportunities for advancement, equal pay for the same work, and an end to discrimination against married women.[40]

Support for this equal rights principle persisted in the Guild thoughout the 1930s, with frequent condemnations of the prejudice against married women's employment. An article in *Woman's Outlook* in July 1938 argued that those who 'declare bitterly that women keep men out of jobs', failed to appreciate that acceptance of the marriage bar and, implicitly, the notion of the family wage perpetuated the low rates paid to women workers, and in turn undercut the position of male workers. In non-unionized workplaces, women's wages were less than half those of men, and there was an urgent need to increase the proportion of women workers in trade unions (currently under a million of the four million women employed). Side by side with this defence of working-class interests, the article also put the feminist case, stressing that women should have the freedom to make a choice in the matter: 'We realise that every woman does not want to tie herself to a home, and that some are not only happier, but more useful to the community, doing outside work. The married woman has a right to please herself whether she works or not ...'.[41]

Overall, the WCG was able to maintain a feminist defence of married women's right to work that was consistent with its primary allegiance to the Labour Party and the SJC. It is ironic, therefore, that the Guild was internally divided on the subject: despite official support for the position, and earnest attempts at conversion, many members refused to accept that married women did have a right to work, often to the embarrassment and disapproval of their more enlightened colleagues.

When married women's employment was first taken as a Guild subject in 1922, delegates at the Lancashire sectional conference were of the opinion that married women working 'blocked their single sisters and was swelling the ranks of the unemployed', although Honora Enfield pointed out that this was 'too narrow a view'.[42] At a South Metropolitan conference in September 1922, the district secretary introduced the subject 'in a broad and unbiased manner while the discussion following centred mainly

241

round unemployment and the old question of the mother's place being in the home.'[43]

As trade improved, the issue faded. But it flared up again in the late 1920s as the recession began to bite and married women once again found themselves in the front line for redundancies. The division between 'advanced' and 'backward' opinion emerged once again in Guild discussions. In 1929 the Oldham Industrial Society's decision to introduce a marriage bar[44] provoked a major debate among guildswomen. The move was promptly condemned by feminists. 'It cuts at the root of the question', the 'Women's Pages' leader commented, 'whether women shall be dominated by economic restraints set by men or gain the liberty to regulate their own lives and fortunes.'[45] Yet there were others who welcomed the measure. A branch secretary who respected 'the Guild principle of equality,' argued that, widows excepted, 'married women should stand down so that school leavers could get jobs.'[46] Typical of those taking the opposing view was a member, whose own Society already operated a bar, who believed that married women with husbands in work should not be employed, 'especially when economic conditions make it difficult for the single girl to earn a livelihood.' She held that 'no man has a right to get married unless he can keep his wife at home', but made it clear that this was as much a matter of practical expediency as of principle: 'a woman who goes out to work generally loses in the end, with washing to send out and a woman to pay for cleaning.'[47]

Similar convictions surfaced at the 1930 Congress, where three different amendments sought to remove married women from the ambit of the equal employment rights motion. Their supporters variously insisted 'that married women were the cause of young girls being unemployed'; that the majority of married women did not seek work out of necessity but for pocket money; that 'wives whose husbands were physically fit should not be employed', and that the market was already 'overstocked with married women workers.' The most liberal of them conceded only that married women's employment would be acceptable, 'providing sufficient work was available'.[48]

These claims were efficiently countered by seasoned Guild officials – all the amendments were defeated and the main resolution carried – yet the views expressed at Congress undoubtedly represented a solid body of opinion among the membership. In 1933, when 'Married Women in Paid Positions' again appeared as a Guild subject, a tactful piece in the 'Women's Pages' acknowledged that this question was 'most difficult and controversial. It is obviously necessary that an organisation of married women, who see both the hardship of watching two incomes go into one home and hardly one into another, and the necessity of many married women working to keep the home together, as well as the right of the married woman to order her own life as she thinks best, should thrash out this difficult matter.'[49]

For those well-versed in the philosophy of equal rights, the issue was cut and dried; and it was hard to see why fellow guildswomen should think otherwise. In the words of one branch president, 'married women have a right to work out their own destiny, just as married men do, and I cannot see how any progressive person can decide otherwise.'[50] At the 1922 Congress Mrs Ferguson (CC) had been blunt, contending that 'the women's minds were unbalanced at the present time, owing to what we had gone through and the unemployment chaos, and they were incapable of seeing the question in a right light'.[51] Rather more diplomatically, in 1930 Catherine Webb reminded Congress delegates that their resolutions 'were matters of principle. As women co-operators who had striven for nearly fifty years for equality, they had to consider the question in this light and not in that of local difficulties.'[52]

The fact that many guildswomen saw the question in a 'wrong light' could be attributed to the uneven diffusion of feminist ideas through the organization. Yet on other, arguably more controversial women's rights issues – notably fertility control – there was an unequivocal display of unity. The Birth Control resolution in 1923, for example, was approved almost unanimously, and in 1934 Congress called for the legalization of abortion by a majority of 1,340 to 20.[53] What this discrepancy suggests is that for the majority of the rank and file in this working-class women's organization, feminism was relevant not as a set of abstract ideals, but in the form of demands which would deliver obvious and immediate benefits to women in their everyday lives.

In pressing for birth control and legal abortion, the women were, as Margaret Llewelyn Davies observed of their stand on divorce law reform, 'dealing with what they know – with questions which concern them'.[54] Whatever their understanding of women's rights in theory, delegates shared a knowledge of the reality of unwanted pregnancies which informed their support for radical change. For some members, the question of married women's employment rights was embedded as a matter of principle; but for many, it posed the class-differentiated experience of employment, rather than the common experience of childbearing.

This is not to suggest that the Guild divided rigidly along class lines on this subject. The marriage bar was most visible in the case of teachers and civil servants. But guildswomen made sure that the threat it posed for working-class women was also emphasized. The organization had deep roots in Lancashire, where it was the custom for women to continue working in the mills after marriage. At All Councils in 1922, Mrs Proudfoot (NW Section) protested the laying off of married women cotton operatives; she also warned that 'Charwomen and caretakers will not be overlooked when the public authorities begin to cut expenses.'[55] A seasonal worker in a plush factory pitched her experience against the marriage bar, insisting, in a letter to the 'Women's Pages', that a woman 'who has brought up her family has a right to go out and work if she desires. Take my own case. If I had not been able to earn a little money, my children would have suffered in consequence, for my husband is an engineer and you know what that means to-day.'[56]

Yet the majority of guildswomen were dependent married women, whose earning potential – even in times of full employment – was low. For many, paid work was a matter of survival in desperate times; in some cases, a shameful admission of poverty; and in general, an increase in the workload, since their wages would not stretch to cover additional help in the home. A great gulf separated such women from those for whom employment was a matter of personal fulfillment and financial reward. Faced with such a prospect, women with limited job opportunities would be more inclined towards secure and better waged employment for their husbands, than the right of married women to work.

Two examples serve to illustrate this division in the Guild. Firstly, a resolution signed by six voting delegates was submitted to the 1922 Congress asking that, 'owing to the abnormal state of the labour market', the £300 a year post of Assistant Secretary, to which Mrs Barton had just been appointed, go to a London-based woman whose circumstances forced her to maintain herself. This proposal was vigorously attacked – Mrs Campbell (East Metropolitan District) insisted that the 'women had to keep a clear head on the married women's question. Was it going to help the position of women if they were not going to allow married women to work?' – and defeated. But the voting figures (207 to 322, with 100 absentions) are indicative of hostility, as well as what was perhaps a strategic indifference, to both the particular appointment and the general principle.[57]

Similar kinds of tensions were apparent at the 1930 Congress. Seconding the equal employment rights resolution, Mrs Lane (Bideford) focused on the rights of professional married women, in whose ranks she counted herself. Until provision was made for all women to remain at home on an economic basis, she demanded 'the right to carry on her career as a married woman.' She won applause when she pointed out that 'the people who were against married women working never raised their voices against the charwoman.' Yet having deplored the double standards of a labour market which exempted the most exploited class of married women workers from the marriage bar, Mrs Lane seemed to those present to identify herself as a member of the exploiting class, when she declared that a husband and wife should both be free to take paid work and 'have someone in to run the home'. Evidently, she touched a raw nerve in an audience composed of many women for whom paid work probably would entail running someone else's home: at this point 'the delegates dissented so loudly that the President had to appeal for an opportunity to proceed.' Later in the debate, a delegate opposed to the employment of married women, presumably addressing herself to Mrs Lane, burst out: 'You don't mind a woman scrubbing the hotel steps while a man at the top stands by to open the door; that is your outlook on life.'[58]

In theory, these dissenting women should have been sympathetic to the argument that the defence of married women's jobs was also a defence of working-class interests; in practice, many seem to have been convinced that the question was one of competition for diminishing resources. The Guild discussions show how economic insecurity tended to reinforce traditional ideas about a woman's place and reduce the receptiveness of working-class women to feminist ideas. In times of full employment and rising class confidence, it was possible to imagine better futures and to buttress the principle of women's rights with a vision of socio-economic change that would create real opportunities for working-class women. The Depression had the opposite effect, closing down the possibility of progressive transformation, and creating a state of uncertainty in which even the maintenance of the status quo was not guaranteed. There were many guildswomen whose situations clearly made it difficult for them to conceive of women's rights in isolation from the family economy. In a climate of rising unemployment, their approach was deeply defensive. Imagining that jobs would not be lost but redistributed, they pressed the claims of single men and women, and married men, believing not only that wives should be provided for by the 'family wage' brought in by husbands, but that this arrangement best served the interests of the working-class family.

In this context, many guildswomen were unwilling to support a cause which seemed to offer the greatest benefits to more privileged women. However much Guild speakers pointed out that married women employees of all classes were equally vulnerable to this form of discrimination, they could not square the circle by making employed women of all classes social equals. Even if married women's right to work were secured, the disparity between the charwoman and the teacher would remain.

The problem for the Guild by 1930 was to find feminist issues that were both consistent with its self-imposed policy constraints and relevant to the lives of its members. In the early 1920s, the employment question had been presented alongside family endowment and birth control, as one of a programme of reforms capable of improving the quality of working women's lives. Labour Party hostility to birth control and family endowment excluded the two demands of greatest benefit to working-class wives, leaving the issue which in and of itself seemed to promise least. Demands for equality of opportunity for married women – to take paid employment, or, for that matter, to hold public office – ignored the fact that some women were better placed than others to take advantage of such openings: as William Thompson wrote a century earlier, 'their rights might be equal, but not their happiness, because unequal powers under free competition must produce unequal effects.'[59] The absence of a leader possessed of Margaret Llewelyn Davies' visceral sense of how to carry the movement, and a conspicuous failure to imagine ways of transcending such potential conflicts of interest once parliamentarism had been embraced, conjoined to undermine the resonance of feminist ideas for the Guild as a whole, and to deprive the organization of what had been the dynamic core of its work – campaigning issues rooted in the experience of working women.

For all its continuing claims to be 'the housewife's champion',[60] it was as regards women's rights in the home that the Guild's retreat from its earlier working-class feminist stance was most apparent. A critical outcome of the Guild's pre-war campaigning work had been to 'draw back the embroidered curtain' to reveal the vulnerable and often abused situation of married women. During the 1920s, as a reflex of its proximity to the Labour Party, the organization ceased to promote demands that would tackle some of the worst problems confronting such women – unwanted pregnancies and economic dependence – and it abandoned its gendered analysis of the working-class family.

This retreat from the domestic sphere as a site of feminist contestation exposed the Guild to anti-feminist ideas about working-class femininity and the home,[61] which emerged as part of the new and idealized model of working-class domesticity that accompanied rising living standards and the expansion of mass consumption during this period.[62] The radical and empowering thrust of its earlier work evaporated, while its policies and its language became saturated with conventional images of, and assumptions about, women as wives and mothers. No longer a site of sexual inequality, the home was now represented in Guild literature as the focus of improvements in working-class welfare and living standards, to be achieved through social reform – maternity care, housing, and so forth – but also through the good offices of the Co-operative movement.

The Guild's base in the Co-operative movement closely

associated it with the changing pattern of working-class consumption between the wars. For those in work, living standards rose;[63] while developments in manufacturing brought a new range of mass-produced commodities into the shops. As the spending power of the working-class family increased, the housewife became the target purchaser for a variety of goods, ranging from tinned foods to vacuum cleaners. The marketing techniques adopted to promote sales did not simply ask women to buy, but spoke to the anxieties, aspirations and daily concerns of the 'ordinary housewife', in ways that defined and elaborated her duties in the home, confirmed her primary allegiance to it, and set higher standards for her work there.

The Guild's institutional setting, and the social character of the majority of its membership, meant that it was doubly implicated in this general reworking of separate-spheres ideology, and working-class femininity, to fit the circumstances of the more affluent working-class family. As a Co-operative auxiliary, the Guild was recruited to the project of boosting sales in the face of growing competition from private business.[64] It was thus actively associated with initiatives which offered married women a range of goods and benefits, while simultaneously defining ever more precisely her role and responsibilities as a housewife. As working-class housewives, many guildswomen were benefiting from rising living standards and becoming the object of the intensive and increasingly gendered advertising campaigns adopted in marketing within and without the movement. By the 1930s, the content of the Guild's sales promotion in the movement was seamlessly connected with the message contained in the adverts adorning the pages of Co-operative News.

In the Co-operative movement, loyal trading took on a new importance between the wars. Although total membership doubled between 1914 and 1938, the Co-operative share of retail trade increased by only 2.5 per cent.[65] The bulk of this trade was in basic foodstuffs, which accounted for a diminishing proportion of overall spending; and it was not fully exploiting its potential in other areas of retailing such as furniture and electrical goods. Consequently, in the 1930s, despite its huge membership and even discounting items (such as motor cars, alcohol and newspapers) that it did not supply, the Co-ops were only handling about one-ninth of total retail trade.[66] In the attempt to increase the average purchases of existing members, and to recruit new ones, the Guild, with well over a thousand branches, was a great asset.

A Joint Trade Committee was set up after the First World War, as part of the Guild's *rapprochement* with the Co-operative Union, and the Guild devoted an expanding proportion of its time to activities designed to promote CWS goods and loyal buying. 'Chocolate clubs' to publicize CWS 'Lutona' chocolate were set up; a CWS corsets sales drive was reported to have increased employment at the Desborough factory; and in 1925, 259 branches reported increases in the sales of CWS goods.[67] This work intensified as the market contracted during the late 1920s. The reaction against trading rivals, evident in the Guild's 1926 rule disqualifying wives of private traders from office, was one response to the growing pressure on the movement. In 1927 'a great push forward' was launched, 'to enrol guildswomen as missionaries on behalf of CWS productions.' Due to developments in 'big business' and 'modern shopkeeping', loyal buying was more important than ever,' Mrs Barton informed delegates at the Lancashire sectional conference. They were expecting great results, explained Mrs Hewitson (Northern Section) at the South Eastern Conference. 'The women had carried out campaigns on the minimum wage, the breakfast cup, chocolate clubs, and maternity, and they must put the same amount of enthusiasm into the present campaign.'[68]

As well as fulfilling obligations to the movement, greater emphasis on trade answered the organization's need for a distinctive, but politically anodyne, focus for branch activity. Here was something central to the Guild's identity with which every guildswoman could busy herself. For many members, however, the larger purpose of loyal buying – via trade to the Co-operative Commonwealth – was only dimly apparent. The lack of serious social and political education, of meaningful attempts to make connections between women's lives and the social aims of the movement, or, indeed, of a feminist critique of the domestic ideal, meant that in substance 'Push the Sales' and associated initiatives did more to strengthen, than challenge, the traditional domestic roles of married working women.

Joint Guild–CWS propaganda, which sought to relate loyal

purchasing to Co-operative values, also served to emphasize the importance of good housekeeping. A 1928 paper, 'Ideals and Homes', taken at sectional conferences, featured 'Mrs Newlyclean' explaining to 'Mrs Faintheart' that by purchasing Co-operative goods, she would be 'building up a wonderful movement' and 'bringing beautiful and well-made things' into her home. The CWS, she explained, were model employers, with light and airy factories. But now 'bad times and lack of trade, and worst of all, through lack of loyalty on the part of co-operators, there is unemployment at these factories, which could be run full-time if only all co-operators were loyal and true to themselves.' Mrs Faintheart grows more and more enthusiastic about CWS brushes, dusters, blankets, tea-sets, and so on, before being introduced to CWS clothing for women. 'What a lot I have learnt,' she gasps, conceding that: 'True ideals do need polishing as well as our houses, and I see now that it is only by putting ideals into practise that we can reach the Co-operative Commonwealth.'[69]

This initiative was treated with scepticism by guildswomen who took loyal buying for granted. The 'Women's Pages' editorial referred to 'several pages of somewhat stilted conversation', and when 'Ideals and Homes' was introduced by Mrs Barton at the Lancashire sectional conference, Mrs Blair (Liverpool) expressed surprise that it should be necessary to discuss such a paper at a Guild conference, and suggested that general managers and committee members be asked to explain why their stores were not better stocked with CWS goods.[70] Nevertheless, work of this kind was on the increase, and with it a growing emphasis on domesticity. 'Women are essentially home-makers,' declared Mrs Hewitson speaking on 'Ideals and Homes' at the Yorkshire sectional conference, 'but during these trying times of unemployment it was difficult to get what they wanted for their homes.'[71]

In 1930 the Guild launched 'The Big Push' for sales and membership: pamphlets, literature, concerts, meetings – 'every conceivable form of attraction to secure converts for the movement.' *Woman's Outlook* included interviews with three Co-operative women: 'Three little homes, three happy women, and the co-operative movement standing forth as a fairy godmother to each.'[72] Such CWS promotional material frequently played on images of good and bad housewives. 'It is a fact', announced an article in the 'Women's Pages' in December 1930, 'told to us by a school-teacher in a slum area of Manchester, that mothers there feed themselves and their families on fish and chips, and fancy iced cakes. Of the nutritious value of food, and good wholesome bread and butter, they have no conception.' The school in question was providing lectures to mothers on 'how to cook plain, cheap dinners, and on the most nourishing food to give to children.' This suggested 'a great undeveloped field in this direction which guildswomen can follow. WE think it would be a good work, both for co-operation and for the people in such areas, if guildswomen held gatherings in some hall, to which they could invite the women, and then talk to them of the advantages of co-operative productions, which are guaranteed good and nutritious.'[73]

Literature from the Joint Propaganda and Trade Committee in 1931 gave prominence to the role of the WCG in the campaign, and suggested special afternoon meetings to attract more members.[74] 'Push the Sales' became a major element of branch activity, with the introduction of special events such as 'Lutona' nights, when members baked cakes using the Co-op brand of cocoa. CWS Recipe Books were promoted, emphasizing that cocoa was 'a tasty ingredient for cakes and confectionary', as well as a fine beverage.[75] Branches were reminded that 'in these hard times it is a relief, even to guild programmes, to get away from the hard problems of economics, education, politics and other matters which trouble thoughtful minds so seriously. A happy "Lutona Night" is as refreshing as an evening at the pictures, and far more helpful to the cause of co-operation.'[76] Guild leaders regularly drew attention to the organization's 'value as an advertising medium', and in 1936 its ambitious two-year plan for membership and trade targeted an array of CWS goods for promotion by branches: soaps, jams, Belmont overalls and lingerie, Keighley wringers, tobacco, cigarettes, biscuits, Desborough corsets, and Dudley electrical appliances.[77]

'Push the Sales' work was almost indistinguishable from the wider marketing offensive aimed at the female consumer, and evident in the pages of Co-operative News. Emanating from the ruthless struggle for commercial survival in the USA of the

Depression, the cutting edge of advertising in the 1930s went beyond 'simple proclamation and reiteration' to 'new methods of psychological warfare',[78] which aimed to create demand by stimulating irrational as well as rational drives in potential customers, especially women.

Bold claims about the nutritional value of a product and its capacity to enhance the health, and hence the happiness, of the family began to appear in the adverts for foodstuffs produced by American and Canadian companies. 'Families with *real work* to do – all over the world', proclaimed one for 'Grape Nuts', with an illustration of a family at breakfast, mother pouring the tea, 'choose this as their *main food*'.[79] 'Shredded Wheat' was 'the food that's best year in year out', the 'food for growing children'. Copywriters spelt out the alleged risks attendant upon not using a product. A picture of a sickly child, for example, was accompanied by the stern warning: 'How can he be well if he's vitamin starved? Make sure he gets his full share of this essential health element by giving him a hot, sustaining breakfast of Shredded Wheat every day.'[80] Key words such as vitamin and element implicitly mobilized science to strengthen the validity of such claims.

The suggestion of maternal negligence was one of the earliest and most persistent themes of such advertising. Guilt was invoked and a means of atonement offered. 'Quaker Oats' adverts in the late 1920s depicted children glowing with health, engaged in energetic activities: a girl playing hockey – 'A picture of health. She's had the energy breakfast'; another, showing a small boy on a scooter, was accompanied by the worrying question: 'Does your boy get the sunshine breakfast?'[81] The ideal of sturdy, resilient children, protected from the cold and from illness, was conjured up in an 'Ovaltine' advert: a mother offering steaming mugs to two warmly clad children and the promise, 'Children are healthy right through the winter if "Ovaltine" is their daily beverage'.[82]

A series of 'Nestle's Milk' adverts demonstrated the evolution of selling techniques ruthlessly manipulating maternal anxieties. In 1929 a more prosaic, informative approach was still the norm, the product being recommended as an ideal acompaniment to tinned fruit. But in the early 1930s, a series entitled 'A Mother's Thanks' featured line drawings of mother and baby, and letters purporting to be from women whose ailing offspring had been saved by the use of 'Nestle's Milk'. 'Mrs V.S___, Cornwall' described how 'at six weeks I nearly lost him. Then the doctor said "Have you tried Nestle's?"' Another 'grateful mother's story' told of a two-month-old daughter, about whom people warned that 'I shouldn't be able to rear her as she was so thin and her legs and arms were like sticks.' But now on 'Nestle's Milk', she was gaining steadily. 'Anxious mothers', proclaimed these adverts, should use 'Nestle's', for 'it never disagrees'.[83]

Advertising was not subject to any codes of practice (the first step towards regulation of the industry came when the 1939 Cancer Act banned so-called cancer cures). But extravagant claims about the nutritional content of breakfast cereals and tinned milks were also licensed by a new and relatively unsceptical audience. Adverts of this kind also shamelessly tapped into the contemporary drive to increase maternal efficiency that had arisen from voluntary and public-sector initiatives to promote infant and child welfare. The identification of feckless mothers, rather than social and environmental factors, as the cause of high infant mortality, combined with anxieties about population decline to create a situation in which: 'Successful womanhood was becoming virtually synonymous with successful motherhood.'[84]

The ideal of a successful marriage as companionate and affectionate, rather than a functional partnership, was also entering the frame of working-class life; a key performance indicator laid down by advertising was the full-time housewife's attainment of culinary excellence to please her bread-winning husband. A 1929 advert for 'Libby's Corned Beef' shows a woman (standing) serving a steaming dish to a man (seated), while the caption reads: 'Good fare for a hungry man'.[85] A more sophisticated version of the same theme appeared ten years later, in an advert for 'Zett' fruit pectin jam-making compound. Under the title 'Her Jam-making made him boil!', a dishevelled woman is slumped in an armchair while her pipe-smoking husband stands lecturing her: 'I won't stand for you tiring yourself out like this, Joan – the jam you've made's not worth it!' She replies: 'Don't rub it in Bill, I know it's poor stuff but I've slaved over it all day.' The unfortunate 'Joan' is a twofold failure: not only is she worn out and, by implication, unable to attend properly to 'Bill'; but her fatigue is unredeemed by a preserve worthy of the name. 'Zett', it is suggested, would enable her to produce excellent jam, and still be fresh and relaxed for her husband when he returns from work.[86]

Co-operative advertising also drew upon traditional images of women in the home, but tended not to adopt the manipulative hard-sell techniques imported from America. The harsh verdict of Carr Saunders' authoritative survey of the movement in the late 1930s was that Co-operative market research and advertising were in the stone age, its low-cost advertising a false economy.[87] CWS posters showing flowers and butterflies, and bearing the legend 'Summer is here. Buy CWS Products', would not 'pass scientific tests of the psychology of consumers' reactions.'[88] To expand its share of the market and keep up with their capitalist competitors, the movement needed to undertake research 'into the mind of the consumers to be catered for. Market research and consumer psychology must take their place in the armoury of the co-operative wholesaler.'[89]

If not at the forefront of blatant emotional manipulation, Co-operative advertising was making greater attempts to persuade, as well as inform, housewives. In common with the private companies who bought advertising space in *Co-operative News*, its adverts set high domestic standards for women and offered idealized versions of family life. The main difference was that while the private companies, especially those from North America, threatened the 'stick' of unhealthy children or unhappy families as part of their psychological hard sell, Co-operative advertising relied more heavily on the 'carrot' of increased efficiency, or greater convenience for the housewife.

CWS advertising spoke to women as custodians of the well-being of the family and guardians of the household budget, promising high levels of performance, a reduction in time-consuming chores, and improvements in the quality of their lives. 'The youngest housewife can be an expert caterer in the first weeks of home-keeping', promised CWS. 'The experienced housewife does not worry about analyzing the quality of everything she buys. She simply says CWS.'[90] CWS goods were consistently presented as high quality and good value, with the extra bonus of savings through purchases. CWS 'Grato' yielded 'a black glossy policy' (illustration of a dazzling kitchen range); CWS 'Pelaw' floor polish, a 'clean, bright and lasting shine'; while CWS soaps were 'best for all housework'.[91] The emphatic and often pseudo-scientific tone of these informative adverts implied a masculine narrative voice; occasionally, the expert actually appeared in the picture. In one full-page advert, 'A Lesson for Careful Housewives', a man in a white coat in front of a blackboard instructs a group of women on the properties of 'Invincible' aluminium cooking vessels.[92]

CWS tinned foods would significantly reduce preparation time. An advert for canned vegetables, dramatically titled: 'She envied her her freedom when she might have enjoyed it herself', depicted a woman with her arms in the kitchen sink, staring wistfully out of the window at her neighbour, sunning herself in a deckchair. 'Pity the "woman-in-the-kitchen"', advised the caption, '"stewing over stove and sink", everlastingly cleaning, peeling, and preparing vegetables, while the sun in vain calls her out of doors.'[93] In addition to the attraction of extra leisure-time, CWS copywriters also appealed to feminine vanity. As well as doing the job 'quickly and efficiently ... as almost every woman knows', CWS 'Wheatsheaf' soap, it was claimed, did it 'without coarsening the hands'; by 1939, it was so improved that 'you'll find it makes washing and scrubbing almost a beauty treatment. It certainly prevents rough and reddened hands.'[94]

Domestic labour was either mindless drudgery to be minimized, or a science to be perfected. However, underlying both labour-saving and performance-enhancement, the image of maternal self-sacrifice was never far away. 'Mother Daren't Be Ill', announced an advert for CWS Cod Liver Oil: 'Keeping fit has its own special problems for mother because she just has to carry on, all day long, all the year round. Out in all weather shopping, in and out of crowded shops, washing in a steamy kitchen, scrubbing floors, cleaning windows on raw cold days.'[95] No wonder she needed the extra protection supplied by the product! But of course, such solicitude for her health also served to strengthen the message that it was her duty to persevere, whatever the cost to herself.

An emergent theme of this advertising was the quality of family life. The decline in family size, the development of infant and maternity care, the expansion of suburban housing, and other changes in lifestyles – these contributed to an image of the nuclear family as the source of the best things in life: physical and emotional comfort, leisure and recreation. And in all of them there was scope for quantitative and qualitative improvements by using CWS commodities. Tea-time was marketed as a family institution, an intimate occasion in which small luxuries could be enjoyed by mother and children, and father, too, if he was home from work in time. CWS currant bread would be 'enjoyed by all the family'; CWS 'Jelly Joys' produced a 'chorus of delight'; CWS biscuits would 'quickly disappear to the obvious enjoyment of the family' and yet, being CWS, there was no need for the housewife to 'sigh at the expense' because of the 'extra bite ... the Dividend. This is mother's extra share.'[96]

On a grander scale, Co-operative marketing was alert to the exodus from the inner cities to the leafy suburbs. A Co-operative Permanent Building Society advert portraying children playing on a swing, and headed 'They Live in the Country Now', epitomized the ascendant child and home-centred values of the 1930s: 'Susan and Jeffrey are the pride of the family. Bless their hearts, it was mainly in their interest that Father and Mother moved out into the country where they could have the benefit of a bright modern home with plenty of fresh air and a large piece of garden to play around in.'[97] Adverts for CWS seeds – 'Have a brighter garden this year' – and the CWS 'Invincible' lawnmower likewise projected images of families enjoying private rural idylls, while the desirability of increased proximity to nature was signalled in full-page CWS features showing young couples out on picnics in the country and at the beach.[98]

The diminishing cost of foodstuffs and other essentials relative to wages, combined with the rapid spread of electricity – to almost two-thirds of all homes by 1938 – brought such luxury items as radios, vacuum cleaners, and irons within the reach of a growing proportion of skilled working-class families. Radio sets for domestic use strengthened the growth of home-based leisure activity. By the late 1930s, the CWS 'Defiant' Radio, first produced in 1933, was 'obtainable from all Co-operative Stores', price £7.10s, bringing 'the Voice of the World into your home'.[99] Other electrical goods were heavily marketed as labour-saving devices. An advert for CWS 'Dudley' electric fires featured a woman admiring one – with good reason. They promised more effective heat, and an enormous reduction of the grinding hard labour associated with coal fires.[100] For those not yet 'connected', CWS offered another alternative to the coal fires: 'Valor' oil heaters had the advantage of being portable. The message – 'heat goes everywhere with you' – was underlined by an illustration of a child being escorted to bed by both parents, father carrying the stove.

'WASHDAY WAS A NIGHTMARE' , confessed 'Mrs H.', until she got a CWS 'Climax' [sic] washing machine.[101] The CWS 'Dudley' vacuum cleaner, price ten guineas, enabled one to 'spring-clean cleanly', 'banishing the dustpan'; a picture of a woman carpet-beating was captioned 'She wants a Society carpet sweeper!'. When the commodity being marketed exceeded the terms of a normal weekly budget, the real power behind the household economy was introduced. Thus, one CWS window display of electrical goods featured a poster inviting the male customer to: 'Give your wife the Gift of more leisure in 1938. Give her a guaranteed "Dudley" Electric Vacuum Cleaner.'[102]

Advertising of this kind between the wars did not invent the sexual division of labour. Yet it projected an influential version of the working-class family and of working-class femininity: the full-time housewife, whose occupation was to improve the quality of the domestic services she provided for her husband and children; a male provider, enjoying home life and actively engaged with his wife; and two or three children signifying an investment in the future. The whole picture was informed by an assumption of continued, if modest, improvements in the familial standard of living. Here, then, were representations of the basic unit of a burgeoning domestic consumer economy, replicating the gendered values and roles associated with the 19th-century middle-class ideal of family life but in a 20th-century context of rising incomes, mass production, and labour-saving technology. This emergent model of the working-class nuclear family could not encompass the servants and solid bourgeois prosperity of its Victorian antecedent. But it did mobilize the same resonant images of the domestic sphere as a place of comfort and affective relationships, underwritten by the increasingly affluent male worker and serviced by the selfless wife and mother.

At the turn of the century, the WCG had commanded the requisite critical tools to resist and redefine constraining versions of working-class femininity. By the 1930s, however, it had lost the ideological and conceptual apparatus necessary even to grasp the value of such an initiative. Subservience to Labour Party policies, the growing distance between the leadership and the rank and file, and the expansion of its trading work in the movement, had irreparably damaged the Guild's ability to represent the interests of working-class wives in a progressive and empowering manner. The leadership's concern to develop the capacities and talents of ordinary members had been superseded by a suspicious and critical attitude towards the rank and file, which valued them more as passive shoppers and voters than as active participants. The demand for feminist rights in the public sphere, instead of being related to the situation of working-class women, had been detached from the issue of social inequality in ways that seemed to privilege the interests of middle-class women; consequently, the Guild's advocacy of formal employment rights for married women failed to win the support of many of its working-class members. Far from problematizing women's oppression within the home, the Guild's social policy and its Co-operative work now promoted an idealized image of the domestic sphere as the centre of women's existence, and the summit of their aspirations – an image that was not to be challenged until the rise of the women's liberation movement in the 1970s.

Notes

1. *Co-operative News*, 5 January 1929, p. 3.
2. *Co-operative News*, 14 January 1933, p. 12.
3. WCG, CC, *The Guild Yesterday and Today* (Manchester: CWS, 1933, p. 5).
4. Ibid., p. 9.
5. R. Strachey, *The Cause* (1928) (London: Virago, 1978, p. 384).
6. *Co-operative News*, 6 March 1920, p. 13.
7. *Co-operative News*, 28 February 1920, p. 12.
8. *Co-operative News*, 6 March 1920, p. 13.
9. *Co-operative News*, 16 February 1924, p. 12.
10. *Co-operative News*, 17 May 1924, p. 12.
11. *Co-operative News*, 5 February 1926, p. 4.
12. Co-operative candidates returned in General Elections (all male):

1922: 4; 1923: 6; 1924: 5; 1929: 9; 1931: 1; 1935: 9; successful in 1945: Mrs Mabel Ridealgh (Ilford North); Mrs Caroline Ganley (Battersea South); Mrs Edith Wills (Duddeston).

13. *Co-operative News*, 11 April 1931, p. 7.
14. CC Minutes, 27 and 28 September 1928; 20 and 21 September 1929.
15. For hostility towards Co-operative candidates in the constituencies, see R. McKibbin, *The Evolution of the Labour Party 1910–1924* (Oxford: Clarendon Press, 1974, p. 288).
16. *Co-operative News*, 1 February 1930, p. 12.
17. *Co-operative News*, 16 January 1937, p. 12.
18. Eleanor Barton JP, *Woman – in the Home, the Store and the State*, Manchester, n.d. (?1928), p. 6.
19. *Co-operative News*, 31 January 1931, p. 12. For a critical analysis of this kind of deprecation of non-participation, see S. Yeo, 'On the Uses of "Apathy"', *European Journal of Sociology*, **XV** (1974) pp. 279–311.
20. *Co-operative News*, 21 March 1931, p. 12.
21. *Co-operative News*, 15 October 1932, p. 17.
22. *Co-operative News*, 22 February 1936, p. 16.
23. *Co-operative News*, 11 February 1933, p. 12.
24. *Co-operative News*, 22 April 1933, p. 16.
25. See entry in the revised edition of the *Dictionary of National Biography* (Oxford: Clarendon, forthcoming).
26. J. Gaffin & D. Thoms, *Caring and Sharing The Centenary History of the Co-operative Women's Guild* (Manchester: Co-operative Union, 1983, p. 88).
27. *Woman's Outlook*, **XIV**, no. 491, 6 August 1938, p. 447.
28. National Union of Societies for Equal Citizenship, formerly the NUWSS.
29. NUSEC wanted Guild representation on a joint committee to deal with the question; without an official policy the CC declined but asked to be kept informed; at its next meeting it was agreed that the General Secretary, Mrs Layton and a Sectional Council member would attend a conference convened by NUSEC in February 1922, WCG Central Committee Minutes, 2 and 3 November 1921; 26 January 1922.
30. *Co-operative News*, 11 February 1922, p. 9; Report of Women's Guild, CCR, 1922, p. 184.
31. Eleanor Barton (JP), WCG, *Married Women and Paid Positions: A Plea for Solidarity Amongst the Workers* (Manchester: CWS Printing Works, 1922).
32. Special Subject: WCG, *Annual Report*, 1922–3, p. 2; 1933–4, p. 4; 1934–3, p. 4; 1935–6, p. 3.
33. Barton, *Married Women and Paid Positions*, p. 3.

34. Ibid., pp. 4–5.
35. Ibid., p. 6.
36. Ibid., p. 12.
37. Labour Party, *International Regulation of Women's Work, History of the Work for Women Accomplished by the International Labour Organisation*, London, 1930. See P. Graves, *Labour Women in British Working-Class Politics 1918–1939* (Cambridge University Press, 1994, pp. 138–51) for the debate over protective or restrictive legislation.
38. See, for example, the debate on equality between Eleanor Rathbone and Elizabeth Abbott of the Women's Freedom League, *The Woman's Leader and the Common Cause*, 11 February 1927, **XIX**, no. 1, pp. 3 and 4. For the relationship between 'new feminism' and the decline of the women's movement, see M. Pugh, *Women and the Women's Movement in Britain 1914–1959* (London: Macmillan, 1993, ch. 8).
39. *Co-operative News*, 1 February 1930, p. 12.
40. *Co-operative News*, 5 July 1930, p. 17.
41. *Woman's Outlook*, **19**, no. 289, 23 July 1938, p. 376.
42. *Co-operative News*, 6 May 1922, p. 12.
43. *Co-operative News*, 30 September 1922, p. 12.
44. Oldham Society gave six months' notice to married women employees, and those due to marry in the next half year, with the right of appeal in cases of hardship; in future any female employee was to resign on marriage, *Co-operative News*, 3 August 1929, p. 12.
45. Ibid.
46. *Co-operative News*, 10 August 1929, p. 12.
47. Ibid.
48. *Co-operative News*, 5 July 1930, p. 17.
49. *Co-operative News*, 29 July 1933, p. 17.
50. *Co-operative News*, 10 August 1929, p. 12.
51. *Co-operative News*, 24 June 1922, p. 12.
52. *Co-operative News*, 5 July 1930, p. 17 (voting figures not given).
53. WCG, *Annual Report*, 1934–5, p. 23. In 1935 Labour Party discussion of abortion reform was blocked by suspicions of Communist Party involvement, see Graves, op. cit., p. 199.
54. MLD to L. Woolf, n.d. (?summer 1915), Monks House Papers (MHP), University of Sussex.
55. *Co-operative News*, 2 September 1922, p. 13.
56. *Co-operative News*, 24 August 1929, p. 13.
57. *Co-operative News*, 24 June 1922, p. 12.
58. *Co-operative News*, 5 July 1930, p. 17.
59. William Thompson, *Appeal of One-Half the Human Race, Women,*

against the Pretensions of the Other Half, Men, to Retain them in Political, and thence in Civil and Domestic Slavery (1825), (London: Virago, 1983). Thompson was discussing structural inequalities between men and women but his point is also salient in relation to women of different classes.

60. *Co-operative News*, 14 January 1933, p. 12.
61. Using the 'same analytical framework as anti-feminists', J. Lewis, *Women in England 1870–1950 Sexual Divisions and Social Change* (Brighton: Wheatsheaf, 1984, pp. 104–5).
62. See Jeffrey Weeks, *Sex, Politics and Society: The Regulation of Society since 1800* (Harlow: Longman, 1989, p. 205).
63. H. Perkin, *The Rise of Professional Society: England since 1880* (London: Routledge, 1989, pp. 277–82).
64. See N. Killingback, 'Limits to Mutuality: Economic and Political Attacks on Co-operation during the 1920s and 1930s', in S. Yeo (ed.), *New Views of Co-operation* (London: Routledge, 1988).
65. Ibid., p. 216. In 1940 the total membership of retail societies was 8,717,000; by the end of the war more than a quarter of the civilian population, G.D.H. Cole, *A Century of Co-operation* (London: Allen & Unwin for the Co-operative Union, 1944, p. 377).
66. A.M. Carr, P. Sargant Florence and R. Peers, *Consumers' Co-operation in Great Britain: An Examination of the British Co-operative Movement* (London: Allen & Unwin, 1938, p. 480). By the late 1930s the Co-ops were handling nearly a quarter of Britain's liquid milk supplies, 27 per cent of the trade in sugar and preserves, and 18 per cent of other groceries, 14 per cent coal trade, 9 per cent boots and shoes, 6.5 per cent adult clothes, 3.5 per cent furniture and hardware, Cole, op. cit., p. 377.
67. WCG, *Annual Report*, 1924–5, p. 3.
68. *Co-operative News*, 30 April 1927, p. 13.
69. *Co-operative News*, 3 November 1928, p. 17.
70. *Co-operative News*, 10 November 1928, pp. 12–13.
71. *Co-operative News*, 15 December 1928, p. 13.
72. *Co-operative News*, 8 February 1930, p. 17.
73. *Co-operative News*, 6 December 1930, p. 13.
74. *Co-operative News*, 24 January 1930, p. 17.
75. *Co-operative News*, 29 October 1932, p. 16.
76. *Co-operative News*, 15 October 1932, p. 16.
77. WCG, *Annual Reports*, 1934–5; 1935–6.
78. See R. Williams, 'Advertising: the Magic System', *Problems in Materialism and Culture* (London: Verso, 1980, p. 180).
79. *Co-operative News*, 16 February 1929, p. 3.
80. *Co-operative News*, 3 February 1934, p. 9.
81. *Co-operative News*, 2 March 1929, p. 7; 16 February 1929, p. 9.

82. *Co-operative News*, 19 January 1929, p. 4.
83. *Co-operative News*, 12 January 1929, p. 10; 10 February 1934, p. 7; 10 March 1934, p. 9; 7 April 1934, p. 9.
84. D. Gittins, *Fair Sex, Family Size and Structure 1900–1939* (London: Hutchinson, 1982, p. 52); see also J. Lewis, *The Politics of Motherhood: Child and Maternal Welfare in England 1900–1939* (London: Croom Helm, 1980).
85. *Co-operative News*, 25 March 1929, p. 3.
86. *Co-operative News*, 8 July 1939, p. 3.
87. It was estimated that Co-op stores spent 0.2 per cent of their sales on advertising, less than a tenth of British department stores (2.64 per cent in 1932); in the USA the figure was between 2.4 per cent and 4 per cent Much CWS packaging was deemed 'unattractive or positively repulsive', its brand names (e.g. "Lustre" and "Cogent" cigarettes; Territorial sauce; I and U shoes; Federal bicycles, Lokreel tinned foods) displaying a woeful lack of attention to consumer preference. Carr Saunders, op. cit., pp. 372–3, p. 404.
88. Ibid., p. 405.
89. Ibid., p. 403.
90. *Co-operative News*, 10 February 1934, p. 4.
91. *Co-operative News*, 5 January 1929, p. 13; 14 September 1929, p. 13; 6 July 1929, p. 19.
92. *Co-operative News*, 27 October 1934, p. 20.
93. *Co-operative News*, 20 May 1939, p. 3 (Waveney canned veg.).
94. *Co-operative News*, 20 January 1934, p. 3; 7 January 1939, p. 12 (CWS 'Wheatsheaf' soap).
95. *Co-operative News*, 18 February 1929, p. 8 (CWS Cod Liver Oil).
96. *Co-operative News*, 5 January 1929, p. 3; 27 January 1934, p. 12; 8 September 1934, p. 3.
97. *Co-operative News*, 12 May 1934, Congress Supplement, p. viii.
98. *Co-operative News*, 3 March 1934, p. 8; 29 April 1939, p. 9; 22 July 1939, pp. 12 and 16.
99. *Co-operative News*, 28 July 1934, p. 3; Photograph, 'Modern London Collection', held at the London History Workshop Centre, 1985.
100. *Co-operative News*, 20 October 1934, p. 12; 21 January 1939, p. 4.
101. *Co-operative News*, 18 February 1939, p. 4; 9 September 1939, p. 3; 13 May 1939, p. 9; 25 November 1939, p. 3.
102. Photograph, 'Modern London Collection', held at the London History Workshop Centre, 1938.

Chapter Nine

Endings

In one of her earliest WCG *Annual Reports*, in 1894, Margaret Llewelyn Davies tentatively outlined her vision of its future development. They were often asked, she wrote, 'what does a branch do?' Her response came in two parts. Firstly, she made plain that while loyal to Co-operation, the Guild had a higher purpose than to serve its trading interests: 'we deprecate being judged merely by the material side of the help we give. We believe that such results naturally follow from the wider view of the movement that it is our desire to inculcate.' She then came to her main point: 'But we aspire to accomplish work which will not show itself in tangible form at the present moment. If we have helped to train women's minds (the need and desire for which is touchingly expressed to us by our members), developing in them a belief in the new social faith; and if we have helped to give women a field of action in which to carry out this faith, then the harvest of the seeds we are sowing will be reaped by future generations.'[1]

For someone with the perspicacity of Margaret Llewelyn Davies, the Co-operative movement presented a rich and unique resource for the organization of working women. Under her leadership, the WCG grew into a rank-and-file organization capable of articulating working women's most radical impulses. It was soon established as the most left-wing element of the Co-operative movement, associated through its Citizenship and Co-operative work with both the women's movement and with working-class politics. As a distinctively feminist wing of the working-class movement, the Guild's work during this period converged with, and importantly enhanced, the growing momentum of the women's movement. This high-point of 'first-wave feminism' consisted in a rich culture of organizations, networks and individuals which sustained the suffrage campaign, and a range of other initiatives for social, industrial and legal reforms to improve the position of women. All this served as an ideological and organizational resource for the WCG.[2] Its own contribution was not only to carry feminist ideas to married working-class women but also to feed back the latter's experience of married life and maternity in ways that significantly extended the scope of feminism, demanding not only women's entry into the public sphere but social intervention to secure justice in the private sphere.

Underpinning this substantive commitment, the Guild's federal constitution and its educational methods were carefully geared to the project of politicizing an ideologically heterogeneous membership, drawn from the wider trading movement, by focusing on the needs of working-class housewives. The guarantee of branch autonomy, whereby local guilds could affiliate without being bound by national policy, recognized that this process would be gradual and uneven; unity of action was achieved through a focus on issues of relevance to the membership – as one long-standing guildswoman put it, 'laying down policy and educating branches up to it'.[3]

Twenty years on, the question, 'what do branches do?', could have been answered with a long list of campaigning and educational subjects which embraced trade unionism, Co-operation and women's rights. Yet beneath the attempt to characterize the Guild by reference to its branches' activities lurks a more intractable issue: what *kind* of organization was the WCG? The official designation – an auxiliary body of the consumers' Co-operative movement – does not answer the question precisely because Co-operation was so broad that its component parts could, and did, assume a variety of different forms. Under Davies, the Guild's preferred label was 'a trade union for married women', a phrase which had the great advantage of explicitly aligning the Guild with organized labour. Certainly, the WCG found its most distinctive identity in representing the interests of working-class housewives to government on specific issues. Yet while the resonance of the term derives from the implied equivalence of the relationships between a trade and an employer, on the one hand, and domestic labour and the state, on the other, the absence of a contractual relationship obviously refutes the claim that the Guild was a trade union. Was it then a pressure group for working-class housewives? The head office, especially in the years of the Citizenship Sub-Committee, unquestionably became very skilled at Parliamentary lobbying. But pressure groups or, for that matter, large campaigning organizations, do not generally have such a broad range of concerns as the Guild. Still less, however, was the Guild a party: it had no programme, no ambition to achieve power itself; indeed, prior to the formation of the Co-operative Party, its politics were never more than implicit.

So, neither a trade union, nor a pressure group, neither a campaigning body nor a party, the Guild under Davies' leadership does not fit any of these general categories of left-wing organization. It was, for a brief period, a unique phenomenon in the history of progressive movements, both in Britain and internationally. As Davies' reference to the 'new social faith' suggests, it was a vehicle to involve working women in the making of socialism. It endeavoured to express the common interests of working-class women, while concentrating on the concerns of the majority of them who were housewives. Here was an organization, then, capable of effective education, agitation and advocacy on single issues, while constantly preparing and building for social transformation on a far larger scale.

Importantly, what the WCG became through Davies' contribution cut with the grain of British working-class and feminist experience prior to the First World War. In the years prior to 1914, to someone of Davies' deeply held democratic convictions, syndicalist-inspired industrial militancy, the growing convergence of the suffrage movement and organized labour, and the Guild's growing radicalism, all alike suggested that the sheer weight of a progressive working-class mobilization would be sufficient to overwhelm capitalism. Had there been a decisive break with the prevailing political order, then it is possible to imagine the Guild developing as a kind of council or soviet of housewives. 'I cant [sic] help feeling', Davies wrote to Leonard Woolf in 1922, reflecting on the nature of the ideal democratic form, 'that democracy is more "democratic" if it is as inclusive &

representative of "interests" as possible – & not merely an expression of a majority of individuals.' Displaying her personal and political sensitivity to the normally masculine character of such majorities, she added in the margin: 'I suppose I feel this being a woman.'[4] For Davies, the Guild was the instrument by which the interests of the social group most peripheral to working-class organization could be active and represented in the working-class movement. Yet the Guild could never be more than a part of the whole, and ultimately the limits of its role were conditioned by the ebb and flow of those wider social forces.

In this respect, while Davies' explicit commitment to a socialist transformation, both as desirable in itself and as a necessary precondition for overcoming the oppressions of working-class women, is unambiguous, her legacy was not so unitary. A striking feature of the Guild project as it took shape under Margaret Llewelyn Davies was its avoidance of explicit political debate and discussion. The content of Guild policy during Davies' leadership implicitly reflected the essence of her commitment to socialist values. Davies believed that the interests of working-class women were incompatible with those served by the capitalist system. She also believed that while the isolation and oppression that characterized their lives obscured this fact, given access to association and knowledge they would inevitably begin to contribute their collective strength to the project of social transformation. Accordingly, she attempted to enshrine the Guild's progressive qualities in a constitution that safeguarded rank-and-file initiative, and in a set of aims that committed it to the promotion of its members' interests. Perhaps the progressive external political circumstances made it easier for her not to confront the key problem about Guild organization acutely posed after her retirement: that neither its form nor its content could ultimately be protected from a leadership with a different conception of its primary purpose. Yet the absence of explicit political discussion – about strategies for fundamental change, and the Guild's role as part of the social agency through which such change might be achieved – rendered the organization ill-equipped to defend its unique achievement as the wider political climate changed, and a different Guild leadership took power, following Davies' retirement.

Thus, during the 1920s, the Guild's commitment to an auton-omous politics of working women dissolved as a consequence of rapid change in both its external and internal circumstances, which brought a new generation of leaders to the fore. The vote, and the birth of Co-operative politics, drew the Guild into an alliance with the working-class parties that rapidly *weakened* the feminist and socialist allegiances underpinning its former radicalism. Senior guildswomen, inspired now by personal as well as political ambition,[5] accepted that admission into this formerly masculine domain precluded the Guild maintaining its indepen-dence. As the WCG was incorporated into Labour–Co-operative electoral politics, its militant advocacy of the rights of working women was superseded by the adoption of moderate demands for social reform, evincing henceforth little of its former sensitivity to gender relations.

Labour's determination to avoid issues that were perceived to be contrary to trade-union interests, or divisive, or scandalous vote-losers, steadily undermined the Guild's residual engagement with the representation of working-class wives. The space in which to develop a critical analysis of women's position within marriage – one that acknowledged the problem of economic dependence and the possibility of tyrannical and selfish husbands – was foreclosed by the primacy of parliamentary politics. As the Guild evacuated the site of its commitment to working-class feminism, it abandoned the concept of a political agenda that reflected the circumstances of the lives of working women, and implicitly endorsed Mrs Harrison Bell's deprecation of 'any Party interfering in the intimate relationships between husbands and wives, fathers and mothers and children.'[6]

The supposed equality or freedom of action for women in the public sphere now informing the Guild's discourse about working women was buttressed by a gender-blindness as regards the private sphere. Lacking the imagination or the political will to think outside the Labourist frame, those advocating the moderate social reforms now promoted by the Guild tended to confirm, rather than to contest, women's primary identity as wives and mothers. The needs of working women were collapsed into a broader and more anodyne concern for the welfare of the working-class family: marriage was once again conceived as a private arena; the home as the site of all that was most positive and unproblematic about social existence.

There was a loss, too, of the democratic socialist values that had previously guided the Guild. According to the earlier model of participatory democracy, the national legislature was only one among a number of methods available for securing social justice. Davies' successors, however, adopted an exclusively parliamentary view of politics, informed by a Fabian conception of social change as something that would be secured *for* the people rather than *by* them. The democratic checks and balances nurtured in the Guild – rank-and-file autonomy, consultation and accountability – not only ceased to be valued in themselves but were increasingly regarded as impediments to the realization of a Labour Government. Similarly, the forms of rank-and-file mobilization that had once been used to great effect now appeared to the leadership as a political threat to be contained. The Guild was steadily transformed into a more hierarchical and autocratic organization whose constitution enabled the leadership to maintain firm control of policy, and suppress dissenting voices. The idea of campaigns representing the interests of the membership, or political education geared to their everyday concerns, were by now considered at best redundant, and at worst inimical to the Guild's revised project.

These strategic shifts cannot simply be understood as expressions of the political will and the personalities of the women who dominated the WCG. In the new political environment of the 1920s, even a leader of Davies' calibre would have had to carry out a radical overhaul of the Guild's approach to campaigning work to sustain a role commensurate with its own traditions. In the absence of such talent and inspiration, the Guild was swept along on the tide of Labourism. That the new leadership was able so effectively to alter the Guild's orientation in the 1920s was itself a consequence of, or at least facilitated by, wider transformations in the balance of forces affecting the working-class movement. The inter-war period in Britain saw major set-backs for trade unionism, a steady downturn in rank-and-file militancy, and an increase in the power of labour's industrial and political leadership; all this was underpinned internationally by rising unemployment, the onset of the Great Depression, socialist defeats and the rise of Fascism.

Of course the character of the Guild leadership mattered but both the nature and success of its project cannot be explained in isolation from these contextual factors.

These developments demonstrate that Davies was mistaken in her belief that the Guild's politics could somehow be inscribed in its social composition and constitution. Ultimately, her conception of the WCG as an ongoing project proved to be an unrealizable ideal. Its radicalism prior to the First World War was not the reflex of its social base, but the product of contingent circumstances (including Davies' leadership), and was consequently destined not to survive the altered conditions of the 1920s. Yet although shortlived, that radicalism was still expressive of an inventive and exciting approach to the organization of working-class women. Without national or international models to emulate, the Guild leadership evolved a method of working in which involvement with specific issues directly affecting the rank and file facilitated a rolling process of wider politicization around both class and gender inequality.

The changes supervening between the wars, the loss of a clear focus on the members' interests, and the constitutional amendments associated with the political rule, effectively transformed the WCG into a two-tier structure consisting of a bureaucratic, élite leadership, and a subscribing but largely impotent mass membership. Senior members of the Guild were able to 'represent their members' interests' on an array of national bodies, speaking for, yet unaccountable to, tens of thousands of women. The priority for the leadership was no longer to 'bring into active life' ordinary Co-operative women but to put the Guild at the service of the causes which they supported. Chief among these, from the late 1920s, were right-wing Labour–Co-operative politics, a malignant anti-Communism, and an unyielding commitment to absolute pacifism.

These changes had a number of different effects, which gradually perished the fabric of the organization. In the short term, at least, recruitment continued to track the growth of the wider movement. And yet there were signs of an identity crisis. Although still promoting itself as a democracy of working women, the Guild was not doing very much to justify the title. The leadership's suspicion of rank-and-file initiative, and its concern to safeguard the Guild against the incursion of Communists and other undesirable elements, limited the opportunities for joint action. Peace work, and Co-operative–Labour politics, gave some focus to branch life. But neither really filled the vacuum left by the loss of the single-issue campaigns, and both were the focus of considerable internal conflict throughout the 1930s. Increasingly, it was schemes to promote Co-operative sales, often amounting to cake-baking competitions, that became the most common item on Guild programmes. This resurgence of the domestic arts tended to eliminate what had been a sharp distinction between the WCG and its apolitical main competitors for new members, the Townswomen's Guild and the Women's Institutes, which were already making better provision in this area. If it was the case that prospective WCG members were being won to these organizations, then it was in part symptomatic of the Guild's own transformation, and a problem of its leadership's making.

The outbreak of the Second World War interrupted a period in which the Guild had been 'running on empty', its leaders increasingly oblivious to the situation of the women whose interests were supposed to be the organization's first concern. War explicitly posed the contradiction between the Guild's first priority, absolute pacifism, and its other main commitments, not only to Labour–Co-operative politics, but to the promotion of women's public role. Large numbers of guildswomen found that the pacifist faith excluded them from involvement in the burgeoning field of voluntary social work to which they were drawn; unable to change Guild policy, many left the organization, while others ignored official policy and undertook war work despite it.

As well as exposing the inadequacy of absolute pacifism as the basis for a broad-based women's organization, the war brought changes that further underlined the distance between the Guild leadership and ordinary Co-operative women. In first place among its effects, the 1945 landslide Labour victory, which brought three guildswomen into the House of Commons,[7] terminated any possibility of the WCG playing an oppositional role. Guildswomen were frequently reminded that it is 'no longer a Government of "THEY", with "WE" as the electorate on the opposite side of the fence: it is our Government, and we with them, must play our part in the fight.'[8] The Guild CC now became a buffer zone between a potentially awkward rank and file, and the Parliamentary Labour Party, refusing to countenance even quite minor complaints from branches. In May 1946, for instance, the CC decided that a criticism of the price of utility clothing was unjustified, while one concerning MPs' salaries was 'in the hands of the electors'. A protest about smaller loaves was rejected because the CC did not believe the Government would take such action without consulting the bakers, and in answer to a suggestion that a delegation of working people should be organized to visit the USA, the CC replied that they had faith in the Labour Government's ability 'to represent the views of ordinary people in America and elsewhere'.[9] With the exception of a continued and vigorous persecution of actual or suspected Communists, Guild politics were suspended until the return of a Conservative government. 'Now that their own people were in power and the basis of the new order was laid,' the General Secretary, Cecily Cook, told a Guild conference in 1949, 'they must learn to become capable administrators.'[10]

A Labour government in office, and the welfare state taking shape, had effectively bankrupted the Guild's strategies for improving the position of working women. Certainly, full employment, social security, better housing and health care, alongside the greater availability of labour-saving devices, and smaller families, were all helping to make married women's lives easier. But residual fears about population decline, the drive to normalize society with its emphasis on home life, the closure of nurseries, growing attention to the psychological aspects of mothering, the continuing reliance on female stereotypes in advertising, and layers of other cultural influences, all projected powerful, anti-feminist images of women as feminine and desirable wives, caring and competent mothers, dedicated and efficient home-makers.

On the other hand, the massive mobilization of women for paid war-work had significantly accelerated the reversal, under way since the First World War, of a trend that was almost a century old. Since the early 19th century, working-class women's status in political and civil society had been determined almost exclusively by their responsibilities for male producers and children. The construction of an ideology of working-class domesticity during this period corresponded to the decline in married women's employment, which continued from the mid-19th century to the inter-war period. The image of the full-time housewife at the centre of working-class family life, projected by advertisers and assumed by policy-makers, thus conformed in kind (if not quality) to the real-life arrangements of the majority of the population. To an even greater extent than from 1914–18, the Second World War broke this pattern by setting a large-scale precedent for married women's paid employment; in the post-war years, despite a new ideological offensive concerning women's domestic role, part-time work for women after marriage became increasingly widespread and acceptable.[11]

As the WCG attempted to regain its lost membership, its confusion in the face of these shifts became fully apparent. Initially, its leadership resisted what it saw as the growing tendency of women's organizations to encourage feminine accomplishments. The 1947 Annual Report referred to the wide appeal of women's associations 'directed to fostering and stimulating improvement of the domestic arts, or a knowledge of handicrafts', but insisted that the Guild 'cannot and should not compete' since its main purpose was 'to provide education in Co-operation and Citizenship in order that we may establish the Co-operative order of society in which we believe.'[12] In the following year, however, noting reports from CC members that some branches were already taking initiatives of this kind, it too began to make more of 'cultural activities'.[13]

In October 1948, the launch of the Guild's 'New Look' campaign highlighted the absence of any critical framework for analysing the rapid changes affecting women's lives. 'Modern progress', it declaimed, 'had given the young woman, whom the Guild sought to interest, a standard of living both in her home and in industry, which was unknown in guild pioneer days and she had not the same incentive towards campaigning which older women had when conditions were bad. The appeal should now be towards cultural subjects.' They should develop 'the fields of leisure, art, music, craftmanship, and appreciation of beauty.' The job of the WCG today, explained Cook, 'is to teach the working housewife how best to use her leisure. If we do not do it, other organizations will.'[14]

What had disappeared from the WCG was any feminist analysis of women's role in the family. When Cecily Cook gave evidence before the Royal Commission on Population with other members of the SJC, she stressed that she would be opposed to any continuation of married women's wartime employment. A 'large proportion of women', she admitted, had been obliged by economic necessity to take on paid employment; but she insisted that 'they would much prefer to be in their homes and looking after their families. Women do look on home-making as a full time job,' she claimed, 'but they do require the resources to be adequate to carry out that job properly.'[15] Here were echoes of Beveridge's conviction that social security provision should put 'a premium on marriage' in recognition of the fact that in 'the next thirty years housewives as mothers have vital work to do in ensuring the adequate continuance of the British race and of British ideals in the world.'[16]

In 1950, an article in *Woman's Outlook* proclaimed that 'the glamour of a life career for women has quite definitely had its day.' Marriage, it went on, was 'the greatest career of all. But it needs more time and excellence than any other. So when marriage comes train for it and put all your qualities into it. Then you will be happiest of all.'[17] In an uncanny echo of the words of Mrs Ben Jones in the 1880s – warning that Guild work should not lead to 'the neglect of their household duties'[18] – at a district conference in Blackpool in 1951, Mrs Chorlton observed that 'we in the guild appreciate that the duty of the young mother is in her home. Her family takes up most of her time and she cannot neglect her domestic responsibilities to attend Guild meetings.'[19]

The Guild was by now actively transmitting the values it had contested half a century before. With an ageing membership and an autocratic leadership, it was in no condition to respond imaginatively to the changed circumstances of younger women. Meanwhile, in the postwar boom, the feminine ideal sketched out in the 1930s came to maturity: a glamorous young woman, with two children, a sparkling kitchen, and earning pin money to pay for such extras as an electric vacuum cleaner. The model pioneered by the WCG in the early decades of the century – the citizen wife supported by statutory provision, with democratic rights and entitlements in the domestic as well as the public sphere

– had been reduced to a welfarist strategy to buttress the traditional role of married women. With feminism at its lowest ebb for a century,[20] widely perceived to be outdated and irrelevant, it was in recognition of the apparent declining importance of 'one-sex organisations' that in 1963 the Guild changed its name to the Co-operative Women's Guild.[21]

By the time 'second-wave feminism' emerged in the late 1960s,[22] the CWG was culturally, politically, generationally, and organizationally insulated from the main centres of growth in women's issues. Yet while the advent of the Women's Liberation Movement (WLM) was not to halt the Guild's steady decline, it did bring a revival of the kind of vision that had inspired the latter's early and radical period of development. It was not exactly the case that history had turned full circle: 50 years on, feminism had to a great extent to be reinvented to take account not only of new forms of oppression but also of new resources for emancipation. Thus, demands were framed that could hardly have been conceptualized at the beginning of the century.[23] But intertwined with the new, there were also continuities. Certainly, many of the concerns of the early Guild reappeared as central themes of the agenda for women's liberation: the critique of the dominant feminine ideal; the identification of the family as a site of women's sexual and physical abuse; the right of women to freedom from unwanted pregnancies; the need to create democratic and inclusive forms of association; and the indispensability of women's autonomy. And echoing their first-wave predecessors, feminists in the WLM insisted that a women's movement worth the name needed to involve working-class women, that any adequate analysis of their situation needed to take account of both their socio-economic circumstances and the cultural, ideological and sexual aspects of women's oppression, and that their advancement required interventions capable of building bridges between the women's movement and working-class organizations.

These concerns were signalled, for example, in the scope of the demands of the WLM in the 1970s – for universal and substantial entitlements such as 24-hour nurseries, free contraception and abortion; and in such alliances between feminism and the labour movement as the TUC march for abortion rights in 1978.[24] Even so, there was an absence in the 1970s of an institutional setting that would support the self-organization of working-class women on the scale achieved by the early WCG. The peculiar circumstances of its genesis and development had passed: the Co-operative movement was no longer a mighty force attracting figures like Margaret Llewelyn Davies, and increasing numbers of working-class wives were now in some form of employment.

Yet if there was to be no national movement of working-class women, the social base of feminism was broadened by numerous community campaigns, and industrial struggles. Sheila Rowbotham cites one example from the early 1970s, when women workers at a shoe-making factory in Fakenham, Norfolk, constituted themselves as a workers' co-operative, the subject of a study by Judy Wajcman. One of their leaders, Nancy, stressed the importance of 'shared decision-making' in their new work situation. 'People', she said, 'aren't afraid to talk here … when we make a decision it's an overall decision by everybody.' She also felt that the co-operative had helped them 'to grow in self-confidence'. Although there had been challenges, the women had enjoyed their new work relations. One of them told Judy Wajcman: 'It's a home from home.'[25]

There are echoes here of the ways in which early guildswomen talked about their organization. For one Lancashire mother and former mill worker at the turn of the century, the 'great point' of the WCG 'is that we are so democratic; no patronage, but all to take their share in government.'[26] When Mrs Dickenson, a guildswoman and a miners' wife, arrived at St James' Hall in London, to speak at a public meeting during the miners' strike in 1893, she was encouraged to find other Guild members there. Their 'kindly welcome' took away her fear and nerves. 'It was then', she later wrote, 'I fully understood the power of our Guild, how we could make each other feel at home away from home.'[27] Eighty years apart, and in a producers' instead of a consumers' co-operative, it is striking that the Fakenham woman used the same image as the guildswoman: a 'home from home'. Both were seeking to communicate the sense of solidarity and empowerment generated by a form of organization that centred on the experience and needs of working-class women, still more accustomed to a domestic environment than a public one. It is also striking that both remarks were uttered, and indeed recorded, at a time when socialist *and* feminist politics were in the ascendant.

Projects which facilitate the self-organization of working-class women are rare. When they do emerge they express not only the grievances of those women but also the political conjunctures that enable their voices to be heard, while their demise will also be intimately bound up with wider political circumstances. Thus, the emergence of the modern WLM cannot be understood in isolation from the radical protest movements of the 1960s,[28] and the questions it posed about the intersection of the social and sexual division of labour were informed by Marxism as much as feminism. Its fragmentation during the 1980s was reflective of the general retreat of all radical agendas in the face of global economic recession and the associated policy reactions of conservative and social democratic governments, but also of internal fractures around issues of race, sexuality and class.[29]

In a similar vein, the contrasting phases of the Guild's history – the shift, from an outstanding women's organization characterized by a spirited defence of autonomy and a focus on the particular issues affecting working women in the movement for socialism, to one that became a mere appendage of Labour's electoral machine – show the work of leaders possessed of a political instinct for the different impulses of their times. The achievement of Margaret Llewelyn Davies and the early Guild leaders was to exploit to the full the circumstances available to them, moving boldly with the most progressive initiatives of their age, and in so doing harnessing the energies of the women who came into the Guild; their successors, on the other hand, were swept along by a current flowing within tightly imposed parameters, too mindful of external limitations to take risks or initiatives, and finally too myopic to nourish the vigorous rank and file that they had inherited. Thus, the authoritarian careerism of Eleanor Barton mirrored the stifling impact of Labourism upon working women's organization, against a background of working-class retreat, when gender politics became one of the main victims of those years in which the 'upward-drawing process of parliamentary "representation"' of the Labour Party, 'sucked dry so much of the activity and self-organization of women and men at the base.'[30]

Notes

1. 'Report of Women's Guild', *Co-operative Congress Report* (CCR), 1894, p. 62.
2. For example, Sarah Reddish, the first Guild organizer, was a key figure in the Lancashire suffragist movement, whose membership significantly overlapped with that of the Guild; left-wing feminists such as Isabella Ford (ILP), and Helena Swanwick (NUWSS), wrote papers for the Guild and spoke at Guild conferences.
3. *Co-operative News*, 16 February 1929, p. 16.
4. MLD to L. Woolf, Monday, n.d. (?February/March 1922). 'As regards democracy,' Woolf replied, 'you raise the most tremendous questions which have never, I think, been answered satisfactorily, L. Woolf to MLD, 9 February 1922, Monks House Papers (MHP), University of Sussex.
5. See Chapters 6 and 7.
6. Labour Party, *Annual Report*, 1927, p. 192.
7. A total of 23 Co-operative MPs were elected, including 3 women (see Chapter 8, note 12).
8. WCG, *Head Office Monthly Bulletin*, 8/4 May 1947.
9. WCG, Central Committee Minutes, 16 and 17 May 1946.
10. *Co-operative News*, 12 February 1949, p. 13.
11. The proportion of married women in paid work rose from 10 per cent in 1931, to 21.5 per cent in 1951 (no census in 1941), G. Joseph, *Women at Work the British Experience* (Oxford: Philip Allan, 1983, pp. 102–3); Lewis notes that by 1950 'the idea of part-time work for married women had become a solution to the problem of married women's status for feminists such as Eva Hubback, for policy-makers anxious to preserve male work incentives, and for trade unionists concerned to bargain for a family wage.' J. Lewis, *Women in England 1970–1950* (Brighton: Wheatsheaf, 1984, pp. 52 and 149–53).
12. WCG, *Annual Report*, 1946–7, p. 3.
13. CC Minutes, 13 and 14 April 1948.
14. *Co-operative News*, 30 October 1948, p. 8.
15. Oral Evidence and Written Evidence, *Royal Commission on Population* (1944–8), 3 vols., 105 pts, 1, Oral Evidence 16, 16 March 1948, Cecily Cook. Also giving evidence were Mary Sutherland (Labour Party chief woman officer), and Esther Martin (NUDAW). The Commission reported in 1949 (by which time concerns about the declining birthrate had been alleviated by the post-war 'baby boom'), *Report of the Royal Commission on Population*, 1949 (Cmd. 7695), PP 1948–9, XIX, 635.
16. W. Beveridge, *Social Insurance and Allied Services* (London: HMSO, November 1942, Cnd. 6404, p. 52).

17. *Woman's Outlook*, **XXX**, no. 873, 21 January 1950.
18. 'Presidential Address, 4th Annual Guild Meeting,' CCR, 1886, p. 89.
19. *Co-operative News*, 3 February 1951, p. 12.
20. E. Wilson, *Only Halfway to Paradise: Women in Postwar Britain: 1945–68* (London: Tavistock, 1980).
21. B. Groombridge, *Report on the Co-operative Auxiliaries*, Co-operative College Paper no. 7, Loughborough, 1960, p. 67; J. Gaffin & D. Thoms, *Caring and Sharing The Centenary History of the Co-operative Women's Guild* (Manchester: Co-operative Union, 1983, pp. 194–207).
22. For its beginnings see M. Wandor (ed.), *The Body Politic: Writings from the Women's Liberation Movement, 1969–72* (London: stage 1, 1972); for a succinct analysis of its origins, see V. Randall, *Women and Politics: an International Perspective* (London: Macmillan, 1987, pp. 218–24).
23. For example, the revolt against the explicit sexual objectification of women; the assertion of female sexuality; the assumption that women could have children and careers; the challenge to the traditional nuclear family.
24. S. Rowbotham, *The Past is Before Us: Feminism in Action since the 1960s* (London: Penguin, 1990, p. 66).
25. S. Rowbotham, 'Feminism and Democracy', in D. Held & C. Pollitt, *New Forms of Democracy* (London, Sage, 1986, pp. 92–3), quoting J. Wajcman, *Women in Control: Dilemmas of a Workers' Co-operative* (Milton Keynes: Open University Press, 1983).
26. M. Llewelyn Davies, *The Women's Co-operative Guild* (Kirkby Lonsdale: WCG, 1904, p. 35).
27. 'Report of Women's Guild', CCR, 1894, p. 60.
28. Notably the black civil rights movement in the USA, the opposition to the war in Vietnam, the international student movement. For an early discussion of political context, see J. Mitchell, *Woman's Estate* (London: Penguin, 1971).
29. L. Segal, *Is the Future Female?* (London: Virago, 1985, ch. 2).
30. H. Wainwright, *A Tale of Two Parties* (London: Hogarth Press, 1987, p. 165).

Bibliography

Unpublished Sources

Manuscript and Archival Material

Bishopsgate Reference Library, Co-operative Archive.
Central Committee Minute Books, Speakers' Notes and other records of the Co-operative Women's Guild, Brynmor Jones Library, University of Hull.
Co-operative Union Archive.
Fawcett Library, Newspaper Cuttings.
George Lansbury Papers, British Library of Political and Economic Science.
Gertrude Tuckwell Collection, TUC Library.
Gladstone Papers, British Library Manuscripts Department.
Leonard Woolf Papers, University of Sussex
Monks House Papers, University of Sussex.
Mass Observation Archive, University of Sussex.
'Material illustrating the work of the guild and kindred interests, manuscript, typed and printed papers, photographs, erstwhile property of Margaret Llewelyn Davies presented to the LSE after her death by L. Harris (1890–?1944)', 11 vols., British Library of Political and Economic Science.
Sheffield Co-operative Party Records, Sheffield Central Library Local Studies Department.

Papers

G. Holloway, 'A Common Cause? Class Dynamics in the Industrial Women's Movement, 1888–1918', Sussex University D.Phil. thesis, 1995.
G. Scott, 'The Politics of the Women's Co-operative Guild: Working Women and Feminism during the First World War', Sussex University MA Dissertation, 1981.

G. Scott, '"The working-class women's most active and democratic movement": the Women's Co-operative Guild, 1883–1950', Sussex University D.Phil. thesis, 1988.

Angela Tuckett, 'The Life and Work of Enid Stacey, 1868–1903', unpublished biography (thanks to Stephen Yeo for access).

'The Morgue', MS chronicle of the Llewelyn Davies family, 1750–1915, 7 vols., private collection (thanks to Chrys Salt for access).

Interviews

Mabel Cumins, Brighton, February 1982.
Mrs Palser, Sheffield, 24 July 1981.
Mrs Wilde, History Workshop, Sheffield, 1982.

Government Papers

Parliamentary Debates, House of Commons, Official Report Fifth Series, 1913, **LVI**, July 28–August 15, seventh volume of Session (London: HMSO, 1913).

Report of the Royal Commission on Divorce and Matrimonial Causes, 1912, (Cd. 6478), PP. 1912–13 **XVIII**

Minutes of Evidence taken before the Royal Commission on Divorce and Matrimonial Causes, 1912, **I** (Cd. 6479), PP 1912–13 XVIII; **II** (Cd. 6480), PP 19112–13 XIX; **III** (Cd. 6481), PP 1912–13 XX.

Appendices to the Minutes of Evidence and Report of the Royal Commission on Divorce and Matrimonial Causes, 1912, (Cd. 6482), PP 1912–13 XX.

Report of the Royal Commission on Population (1949), (Cmd. 7695), PP 1948–8 XIX 635.

'Royal Commission on Population, 1944–48. Oral Evidence and Written Evidence', Oral Evidence, 1–21 (and Written Evidence, 1–87), 1944–8, 3 Vols. 105 pts.

Newspapers and Periodicals

(i) Co-operative publications

Co-operative News
Review of International Co-operative Alliance
Reynolds News
Woman's Outlook

The Guildswoman
Co-operative Congress Annual Reports
WCG Annual Reports
WCG, Head Office Monthly Bulletins

(ii) Other publications

Birth Control News
The Englishwoman
The Common Cause
The Labour Woman
The Woman Worker
The Times
Labour Party Annual Reports

TUC Annual Reports

Labour Party, *International Regulation of Women's Work, History of the Work for Women Accomplished by the International Labour Organisation*, London 1930.

WCG Publications (in chronological order)

(For a full listing of Guild publications, see T. Mizuta, 'A Bibliography of the Co-operative Women's Guild', *The Journal of Social Sciences*, Nagoya Economics University & Ichimuragakuen Junior College, no. 46, November 1988; no. 47, March 1989).

M. Llewelyn Davies, *The Relations between Co-operation and Socialistic Aspirations*, a paper read at the Congress held at Glasgow (Manchester: Co-operative Union Ltd., 1890).

S. Reddish, *Women's Guilds With Special Reference to their Claims on the Attention and Support of Educational Committees* (Bolton: Co-operative Educational Committees' Association, 1890).

WCG, *Outline of Work with Model Branch Rules* (Manchester: Co-operative Printing Society, 1891).

C. Black, WCG Manchester Festival, *A Natural Alliance* (London: Co-operative Printing Society, 1892).

C. Webb, *Co-operation as applied to Domestic Work*, Annual Meeting, Leicester, June 1893, WCG, 1893.

Mrs Woodward (Birmingham), *Women as Shareholders and Officials in the Co-operative Movement*, Annual Meeting, Leicester, June 1893, WCG, 1893.

R. Nash, *Investigation Papers – I: Reduction of Hours of Work for Women, somepoints in the Time Regulations of the Factory Act* (Kirkby Lonsdale: WCG, ?1895).

L. Harris, *Investigation Papers – II: Abolition of Overtime for Women* (Kirkby Lonsdale: WCG, ?1895).

L. Marsh Phillipps, *Investigation Papers – III: Evils of Home Work for Women* (Kirkby Lonsdale: WCG, ?1895).

I.O. Ford, *Investigation Papers – IV: Women as Factory Inspectors and Certifying Surgeons* (Kirkby Lonsdale: WCG, ?1895).

WCG, *How to Start and Work a Branch* (Kirkby Lonsdale: WCG, 1896).

E. Carr, M. Llewelyn Davies, A. L. Martin & A. Sharp, *Why Working Women Need the Vote*, Sectional Conference papers, March 1897 (Kirkby Lonsdale: WCG, 1897).

WCG, *Co-operation in Poor Neighbourhoods* (Kirkby Lonsdale: WCG, 1899).

M. Llewelyn Davies, *A Co-operative Colony*, papers reprinted from Co-operative News, dealing with a scheme of Co-operation for Poor Neighbourhoods (Kirkby Lonsdale: WCG, ?1900).

M. Llewelyn Davies, *A Co-operative Relief Column or How to Adapt Co-operation to the Needs of Poor Districts*, WCG Woolwich Congress, June 1900 (Kirkby Lonsdale: WCG, 1900).

WCG, *The Extension of Co-operation to the Poor: Report of an Inquiry made by the Guild, December 1901, January & February, 1902*, (Manchester, Co-operative Newspaper Society, 1902).

WCG, *Petition to the Co-operative Wholesale Society, Minimum Wage for Women Employees*, n.p., n.d.

R. Nash, 'Co-operator and Citizen', in B. Villiers (ed.), *The Case for Women's Suffrage* (London: Fisher & Unwin, 1907, pp.66–77).

R. Nash, *The Position of Married Women*, WCG Annual Congress 1907 (Manchester: CWS Printing Works, 1907).

WCG, *A Co-operative Standard for Women Workers*, Annual Congress, 1908 (Kirkby Londsale: WCG, 1908).

WCG, *A Minimum Wage Scale for Co-operative Women and Girl Employees* (London: WCG, 1910).

WCG, *Working Women and Divorce: an account of the evidence given on behalf of the WCG before the Royal Commission on Divorce* (London: David Nutt, 1911).

WCG, *Lincoln Central Branch Coming of Age*, Lincoln, 1913.

M. Llewelyn Davies, *The Education of Guildswomen*, Annual Congress, 1913 (London: WCG, 1913).

WCG, *Divorce Law Reform: the Majority Report of the Divorce Commission*, Spring Sectional Conferences, 1913 (London: WCG, 1913).

L. Woolf, *The Control of Industry by Co-operators and Trade Unionists* (London: WCG, ?1913).

H.M. Swanwick, *Some Points of English Law affecting Working Women as*

Wives and Mothers, notes of two lectures of a guides' course given to members of the WCG (London: WCG, 1914).

L. Woolf, *The Control of Industry by the People* (London: WCG, 1915).

WCG, *The Self-Government of the Guild*, Annual Congress, 1915 (London: Co-operative Printing Society, 1915).

WCG, 'The Women's Co-operative Guild, 1895–1916: A Review of Twenty-One Years' Work', *Annual Congress Handbook* (London: WCG, 1916).

WCG Central Committee, *Divorce Law Reform*, London, 1918.

M. Llewelyn Davies, *The Vote at Last! More Power to Co-operation*, Co-operative Union Ltd., Political Pamphlet No. 2, Manchester, 1918.

WCG Central Committee, WCG: *Notes on its History, Organisation and Work*, London, 1920.

E. Barton, *Married Women and Paid Positions: A Plea for Solidarity Amongst the Workers* (London: WCG, ?1922).

WCG, *Notes for the Study of Family Allowance* (London: WCG, ?1925).

E. Barton, *The National Care of Motherhood* (London: WCG, 1928).

E. Barton, *Woman – in the Home, the Store and the State* (Manchester: Co-operative Union Ltd. for the Co-operative Party, ?1929).

WCG, *New Times and New Measures*, WCG Central Committee (London: WCG, 1929).

E. Barton, *Through Trade to the Co-operative Commonwealth* (London: WCG, ?1930).

WCG, *The Guild Yesterday and Today*, Central Committee of the WCG (Manchester: CWS, 1933).

E. Sharp, *Buyers and Builders: A Jubilee Sketch of the WCG 1883–1933* (London: WCG, 1933).

Official Publications about the WCG and its members

M. Llewelyn Davies, *The Women's Co-operative Guild* (Kirkby Lonsdale: WCG, 1904).

M. Llewelyn Davies (ed.), *Maternity Letters from Working Women* (1915) (London: Virago, 1978).

M. Llewelyn Davies (ed.), *Life As We Have Known It by Co-operative Working Women with an Introductory Letter by Virginia Woolf* (1931) (London: Virago, 1977).

C. Webb, *The Woman with the Basket: the History of the WCG, 1883–1927* (Manchester: The Guild, 1927).

J. Gaffin & D. Thoms, *Caring and Sharing The Centenary History of the Co-operative Women's Guild* (Manchester: Co-operative Union, 1983).

C. Salt, P. Schweitzer, M. Wilson, *Of Whole Heart Cometh Hope: Centenary Memories of the Co-operative Women's Guild* (London: Age Exchange Theatre Company, 1983).

Other Studies of the WCG

N. Black, 'The Mother's International: the WCG and Feminist Pacifism', *Women's Studies International Forum*, 7, no. 6, 1984, pp. 467–76.

J. Gaffin, 'Women and Co-operation', in L. Middleton (ed.), *Women in the Labour Movement* (London: Croom Helm, 1977).

G. Scott, 'Women's Autonomy and Divorce Law Reform in the Co-operative Movement, 1910–1920', in S. Yeo (ed.), *New Views of Co-operation* (London: Routledge & Kegan Paul, 1988).

G. Scott, ' "A Trade Union for Working Women": the WCG 1914–45', in S. Oldfield (ed.), *This Working Day World: Women's Lives and Culture(s) in Britain, 1914–45* (London: Taylor & Francis, 1994).

G. Scott, 'Basket Power and Market Forces: the WCG 1883–1920', B. Einhorn & E. Yeo, *Women and Market Societies* (Cheltenham: Edward Elgar, 1995).

Books and Articles

Dictionary of National Biography (Oxford University Press, various editions).

T. Adams, 'The Formation of the Co-operative Party Re-considered', *International Review of Social History*, **XXXII**, 1987–1, pp. 48–68.

Q. Bell, *Virginia Woolf: a Biography*, 2 vols. (1972) (London: Paladin, 1976).

J.M. Bellamy & J. Saville, *Dictionary of Labour Biography*, 9 vols. (London: Macmillan, 1972–92).

C. Benn, *Keir Hardie* (London: Hutchinson, 1992).

W. Beveridge, *Social Insurance and Allied Services*, November 1942 (London: HMSO, Cnd. 6404).

A. Birkin, *J.M. Barrie and the Lost Boys* (London: Constable, 1979).

H. Blackburn, *Women's Suffrage: A Record of the Women's Suffrage Movement in the British Isles* (1902) (New York: Kraus Reprint Co., 1971).

S. Boston, *Women Workers and the Trade Unions* (London: Lawrence and Wishurst, 1987).

S. Burman, *Fit Work for Women* (London: Croom Helm, 1979).

J. Butler, *Personal Reminiscences of a Great Crusade*, 1896.

A.M. Carr, P. Sargant Florence, R. Peers, *Consumers' Co-operation in Great Britain An Examination of the British Co-operative Movement* (London: Allen & Unwin Ltd., 1938).

M. Ceadel, *Pacifism in Britain 1914–45 The Defining of a Faith* (Oxford: Clarendon Press, 1980).

H.A. Clegg, *A History of British Trade Unions since 1889*, II, 1911–33 (Oxford: Clarendon Press, 1985).

A. Clinton, *The trade union rank and file: Trades Councils in Britain, 1900–1940* (Manchester University Press, 1977).

D. Nield Chew (ed.), *The Life and Writings of Ada Nield Chew* (London: Virago, 1982).

G.D.H. Cole, *A Century of Co-operation* (London: Allen & Unwin for the Co-operative Union, 1944).

G.D.H. Cole & R. Postgate, *The Common People 1746–1946* (London, Methuen, 1966 edn).

C. Collette, *For Labour and For Women: The Women's Labour League, 1906–1918* (Manchester University Press, 1989).

L. Davidoff & C. Hall, *Family Fortunes: Men and Women of the English middle class 1780–1850* (London: Hutchinson, 1987).

A. Davis, *American heroine: the Life and Legend of Jane Addams* (Oxford University Press, 1973).

H. Dewar, *Communist Politics in Britain: the CPGB from its Origins to the Second World War* (London: Pluto, 1976).

E. DuBois, 'Woman Suffrage and the Left: An International Socialist–Feminist Perspective', *New Left Review*, 186, March/April, 1991.

G. Elliott, *Labourism and the English Genius – The Strange Death of Labour England?* (London: Verso, 1983).

B. Einhorn & E. Janes Yeo, *Women and Market Societies* (Cheltenham: Edward Elgar, 1995).

M. G. Fawcett, *Women's Suffrage: A Short History of a Great Movement* (London: T.L. & E.C. Jack, 1912).

R. Fulford, *Votes for Women* (London: Faber, 1957).

L. Garner, *Stepping Stones to Women's Liberty Feminist Ideas in the Women's Suffrage Movement 1900–1918* (London: Heinemann Educational Books, 1984).

D. Gittins, *Fair Sex: Family Size and Structure 1900–1939* (London: Hutchinson, 1982).

P. Graves, *Labour Women in British Working-Class Politics 1918–1939* (Cambridge University Press, 1994).

P. Gurney, *Co-operative Culture and the Politics of Consumption in England 1870–1930* (Manchester University Press, 1996).

J.B.S. Haldane, *ARP* (London: Victor Gollancz, Left Book Club Edition, 1938).

C. Hall, 'The Early Formation of Victorian Domestic Ideology', in S. Burman, *Fit Work for Women* (London: Croom Helm, 1979).

R. Hall, *Marie Stopes A Biography* (London: Deutsch, 1977).

M.A. Hamilton, *Mary Macarthur* (London: Leonard Parsons, 1925).

D. Held & C. Pollitt, *New Forms of Democracy* (London: Sage, 1986).

J. Hinton, *Labour and Socialism A History of the British Labour Movement 1867–1974* (Brighton: Wheatsheaf, 1983).

S. Holton, *Feminism and Democracy: Women's Suffrage and Reform Politics in Britain 1900–1918* (Cambridge University Press, 1987).

A. James & N. Hills, *Mrs John Brown 1847–1935* (London: Albemarle St.W., 1937).

J. Joll, *The Second International, 1889–1914* (London, Routledge & Kegan Paul, revised edition 1974).

G. Joseph, *Women at Work: the British Experience* (Oxford, Philip Allan, 1983).

P. Kennedy, *The Realities behind Diplomacy: Background Influences on British External Policy, 1865–1980* (London: Fontana, 1985).

S. Kingsley Kent, *Sex and Suffrage in Britain 1860–1914* (London: Routledge, 1990).

S. Kingsley Kent, *Making Peace: the Reconstruction of Gender in Interwar Britain* (Princeton University Press, 1994).

H. Lee, *Virginia Woolf* (London: Chatto & Windus, 1996).

S. Lewenhak, *Women and Trade Unions: an outline history of women in the British trade union movement* (London: Benn, 1977).

J. Lewis, *Women in England 1870–1950 Sexual Divisions and Social Change* (Brighton: Wheatsheaf, 1984).

J. Lewis, *The Politics of Motherhood: Child and Maternal Welfare in England 1900–1939* (London: Croom Helm, 1980).

J. Liddington, *The Life and Times of a Respectable Rebel Selina Cooper 1864–1946* (London: Virago, 1984).

J. Liddington, *The Long Road to Greenham: Feminism and Anti-Militarism in Britain since 1820* (London: Virago, 1989).

J. Liddington and J. Norris, *One Hand Tied Behind Us* (London: Virago, 1978).

L.J. Macfarlane, *The British Communist Party: Its Origin and Development until 1929* (London: MacGibbon & Kee, 1966).

J. Macnicol, *The Movement for Family Allowances, 1918–45* (London: Heinemann, 1980).

D.A. Martin, *Pacifism An Historical and Sociological Study* (London: Routledge & Kegan Paul, 1965).

R. McKibbin, *The Evolution of the Labour Party 1910–1924* (Oxford: Clarendon Press, 1974).

R. Miliband, *Parliamentary Socialism: a Study in the Politics of Labour*, second edition (London: Merlin Press, 1973).

K. Millett, *Sexual Politics* (1970) (London: Virago, 1985).

J. Mitchell, *Woman's Estate* (London: Penguin, 1971).

K. Morgan, *Harry Pollitt: Lives of the Left* (Manchester University Press, 1993).

C.L. Mowatt, *Britain between the Wars* (1955) (Cambridge: Methuen University Paperback, 1983 edn).

S. Oldfield, *Women Against the Iron Fist: Alternatives to Militarism, 1900–1989* (Oxford: Blackwell, 1989).

S. Oldfield (ed.), *This Working Day World: Women's Lives and Culture(s) in Britain 1914–45* (London: Taylor & Francis, 1994).

E.S. Pankhurst, *The Suffragette Movement: an intimate account of persons and ideas* (1932) (London: Virago, 1977).

C. Pateman, *The Sexual Contract* (Cambridge: Polity, 1988).

M. Pember Reeves, *Round About a Pound a Week* (1913) (London: Virago, 1979).

H. Perkin, *The Rise of Professional Society: England since 1880* (London: Routledge, 1989).

S. Pierson, *Marxism and the Origins of British Socialism* (Cornell University Press, 1973).

A. Phillips, *Divided Loyalties: dilemmas of sex and class* (London: Virago, 1987).

A. Phillips, *Engendering Democracy* (Cambridge: Polity Press, 1991).

M. Phillips (ed.), *Women and the Labour Party* (London: Headley Bros., 1918).

S. Pollard, 'The Foundation of the Co-operative Party' in A. Briggs & J. Saville (eds.), *Essays in Labour History*, 2, 1886–1923 (London: Macmillan, 1971).

C. Porter, *Alexandra Kollontai: a biography* (London: Virago, 1980).

M. Pugh, *Women and the Women's Movement in Britain 1914–1959* (London: Macmillan, 1993).

V. Randall, *Women and Politics: an International Perspective*, second edition (London: Macmillan, 1987).

E. Rathbone, *The Disinherited Family* (first published 1924), introduction by Suzy Fleming, 'Eleanor Rathbone Spokeswoman for a Movement' (Bristol: Falling Wall Press, 1986).

P. Redfern, *The Story of the CWS: the jubilee history of the Co-operative Wholesale Society Ltd. 1963–1913* (Manchester: CWS, 1913).

J. Rendall, *Women in an Industrializing Society: England 1750–1880* (Oxford: Blackwell, 1990).

D. Riley, *'Am I That Name?' Feminism and the Category of 'Women' in History* (London: Macmillan, 1988).

S. Rowbotham, *A New World for Women: Stella Browne Socialist Feminist* (London: Pluto, 1977).

S. Rowbotham, *The Past is Before Us: Feminism in Action since the 1960s* (London: Penguin, 1990).

C. Rover, *Women's Suffrage and Party Politics in Britain, 1866–1914* (London: Routledge and Kegan Paul, 1967.

D. Rubinstein, *A Different World for Women: the Life of Millicent Garrett Fawcett* (New York: Harvester Wheatsheaf, 1991).

D. Russell, *The Tamarisk Tree* (London: Virago, 1977).

J. Ruskin, *Sesame and Lilies* (1865) (Oxford University Press, 1936).

L. Segal, *Is the Future Female?* (London: Virago, 1985).

G.B Shaw (ed.), *Fabian Essays* (London: Fabian Society, 1889).

N.C. Soldon, *Women in British Trade Unions 1874–1976* (Dublin: Gill and Macmillan, 1978).

R.A. Soloway, *Birth Control and the Population Question in England 1877–1930* (London: University of North Carolina Press, 1982).

G. Stedman Jones, 'Working-class culture and working-class politics in London, 1870–1900: Notes on the remaking of a working class', in *Languages of Class, Studies in English Working Class History 1832–1982* (Cambridge University Press, 1983).

C. Steedman, *Childhood, Culture and Class in Britain: Margaret McMillan 1860–1931* (London: Virago, 1990).

B. Stephens, *Emily Davies and Girton College* (London: Constable, 1927).

J. Stevenson & C. Cook, *The Slump: Society and Politics during the Depression* (London: Quartet, 1977).

L. Stone, *Road to Divorce: England 1530–1987* (Oxford University Press, 1990).

M. Stott, *Organization Woman: The Story of the Townswomen's Guilds* (London: Heinemann, 1978).

R. Strachey, *The Cause* (1928) (London: Virago, 1978).

B. Taylor, *Eve and the New Jerusalem* (London: Virago, 1983).

P. Thane, 'Visions of gender in the making of the British welfare state: the case of women in the British Labour Party and social policy, 1906–1945', in G. Bock & P. Thane (eds), *Maternity and Gender Policies: Women and the Rise of the European Welfare States, 1880–1950s* (London: Routledge, 1991).

P. Thane, 'Women in the British Labour Party and the Construction of State Welfare', in S. Koven & S.Michel (eds), *Mothers of a New World: Maternalist Politics and the Origins of Welfare States* (London: Routledge, 1993).

W. Thompson, *Appeal of One-Half the Human Race, Women, against the Pretensions of the Other Half, Men, to Retain them in Political, and thence in Civil and Domestic Slavery* (1825) (London: Virago, 1983).

W. Thornton, *On Labour; its wrongful claims and rightful dues; its actual present and possible future*, (1869); facsimile of second edition (1870), with a supplementary chapter on the Co-operative movement (Dublin: Irish University Press, 1971).

W. Thonnessen, *The Emancipation of Women: the Rise and Decline of the Women's Movement in German Social Democracy 1863–1933*, trans. Joris de Bres (London: Pluto Press, 1973).

H.A. Turner, *Trade Union Growth, Structure and Policy* (London: Allen & Unwin, 1962).

M. Vicinus, *Independent Women* (London: Virago, 1985).

M. Vicinus, *Suffer and Be Still: Women in the Victorian Age* (Bloomington: Indiana University Press, 1972).

H. Wainwright, *A Tale of Two Parties* (London: Hogarth Press, 1987).

J. Wajcman, *Women in Control: Dilemmas of a Workers' Co-operative* (Milton Keynes: Open University Press, 1983).

L. Wallis, *Life and Letters of Caroline Martyn* (London: Labour Leader, 1898).

M. Wandor (ed.), *The Body Politic: Writings from the Women's Liberation Movement, 1969–72* (London: stage 1, 1972).

B. Webb, *My Apprenticeship*, 2 vols. (Harmondsworth: Penguin, 1938).

B. Webb: N. MacKenzie & J. MacKenzie (eds), *The Diary of Beatrice Webb*, 4 vols. (London: Virago, 1982–1985).

J. Weeks, *Sex, Politics and Society: the Regulation of Sexuality since 1800*, second edition (Harlow: Longman, 1989).

E. Wilkinson, *The Town that was Murdered* (London, Victor Gollancz, Left Book Club edition, 1939).

R. Williams, *Problems in Materialism and Culture* (London: Verso, 1980).

E. Wilson, *Only Halfway to Paradise Women in Postwar Britain: 1945–68* (London: Tavistock, 1980).

A. Wiltsher, *Most Dangerous Women: Feminist Peace Campaigners of the Great War* (London: Pandora, 1985).

L. Woolf, *Beginning Again An Autobiography of the Years 1911–18* (London: Hogarth Press, 1972).

V. Woolf, *Three Guineas* (London: Hogarth Press, 1938).

The Diary of Virginia Woolf, A.O. Bell (ed.) 5 vols. (London: Hogarth Press, 1977, 1978, 1980, 1982, 1984).

The Letters of Virginia Woolf, N. Nicolson & J. Trautmann (eds) 6 vols. (London: Hogarth Press, 1975–1980).

E.M. Janes Yeo, *Contest for Social Science in Britain: relations and representations of gender and class in the nineteenth and twentieth centuries* (London: Rivers Oram, 1996).

S. Yeo, 'A New Life: The Religion of Socialism in Britain, 1883–1896', *History Workshop Journal*, 1977, no. 4.

S. Yeo, 'Notes on Three Socialisms – Collectivism, Statism and Associationism', in C. Levy (ed.), *Socialism and the Intelligentsia 1880–1914* (London: Routledge & Kegan Paul, 1987).

S. Yeo, *New Views of Co-operation* (London: Routledge, London, 1988).

S. Yeo, *Who was J.T.W. Mitchell?* (Manchester: CWS Membership Services, Co-operative Press, 1995).

Index

INDEX

p. 12 →
p. 83 : →